JOURNAL FOR THE STUDY OF THE NEW TESTAMENT
SUPPLEMENT SERIES
279

Letter Hermeneutics in 2 Corinthians

Studies in *Literarkritik* and Communication Theory

Eve-Marie Becker

Translated by Helen S. Heron

T&T CLARK INTERNATIONAL
A Continuum imprint
LONDON • NEW YORK

Published by T&T Clark International
The Tower Building, 11 York Road, London SE1 7NX
15 East 26th Street, Suite 1703, New York, NY 10010

www.tandtclark.com

British Library Cataloguing-in-Publication Data
A catalogue record for this book is available from the British Library

Typeset by Data Standards Ltd, Frome, Somerset, BA11 1RE
Printed on acid-free paper in Great Britain by Antony Rowe Ltd

ISBN 0567083276

CONTENTS

PREFACE

The present book is a modified version of my German dissertation, *Schreiben und Verstehen. Paulinische Briefhermeneutik im Zweiten Korintherbrief*, Tübingen/Basel 2002 (Neutestamentliche Entwürfe zur Theologie 4).

For the English translation the entire work has been expanded to include the most recent literature. The footnotes have been kept to the minimum necessary.

In comparison with the German version Chapter 3 has been shortened and the excursus of Chapter 4 is now to be found in context (4.4).

The fifth chapter is entirely new. It seeks to apply epistolary hermeneutic and meta-communicative text analysis to 1 Corinthians (5.1) and enquires in terms of the history of reception into the influence and interpretation of 2 Corinthians in the first four centuries (5.2).

The English version of the book owes most to the Revd Helen Heron, who prepared the translation with great linguistic and expert competence as well as reliability and friendliness. The next place belongs to her husband, Prof. Alasdair Heron, who also energetically assisted the translation.

I wish to thank Prof. Oda Wischmeyer for all her long-standing ideal and material support of this publication project. Our student assistants *stud. theol.* Margaretha Brons, *stud. theol. et phil.* Sebastian Gagel and *stud. theol.* Johanna Schmidt helped in many ways with the preparation of the manuscript. *stud. theol. et phil.* Susanne Luther is to be thanked for compiling the indexes and for her proof-reading. Prof. Stanley E. Porter and Prof. Philip Davies are to be thanked for including the book in JSNT.S.

Finally I would express the hope that this translation will make it easier for English-language exegesis to approach the questions discussed in this book of the *Literarkritik* and epistolary hermeneutics of the Second Letter to the Corinthians.

Eve-Marie Becker,
Erlangen, 7.2.2004

Bauer/Aland	W. Bauer and K. and B. Aland, *Griechisch-deutsches Wörterbuch zu den Schriften des Neuen Testaments und der frühchristlichen Literatur* (Berlin/New York[6]: 1988)
BDR	F. Blass, A. Debrunner and F. Rehkopf, *Grammatik des neutestamentlichen Griechisch* (Göttingen[17]: 1990)
CPG	M. Geerard, *Clavis Patrum Graecorum I–V. Corpus Christianorum* (Turnhout: 1983–1987)
CPL	E. Dekkers, *Clavis Patrum Latinorum. Corpus Christianorum. Series latina* (Steenbrugis[3]: 1995)
FGrHist	*Die Fragmente der Griechischen Historiker. Dritter Teil*, ed. F. Jacoby (Leiden: 1958)
HS	E.G. Hoffmann and H. v. Siebenthal, *Griechische Grammatik zum Neuen Testament* (Rieher[2]: 1990)
Lindemann/ Paulsen, *Väter*	A. Lindemann and H. Paulsen (eds), *Die Apostolischen Väter* (Tübingen: 1992)
LS	H.G. Liddell, R. Scott and H.S. Jones, *A Greek-English Lexicon. With a Revised Supplement* (Oxford: 1996)

Other abbreviations used in this book follow S. Schwertner, *Theologische Realenzyklopaedie, Abkürzungsverzeichnis* (Berlin/New York[2]: 1994).

Chapter 1

CURRENT APPROACHES TO THE UNDERSTANDING OF 2 CORINTHIANS

As always in the field of the Arts or Cultural Studies there are various possible approaches to the interpretation of texts, each of which may lead to different conclusions although they also stand in relation to each other. So too there are also various methods of approach to the interpretation of 2 Corinthians. These individual approaches reflect the variety of methods used in NT exegesis and applying to the whole area of research on the NT Epistles over and above 2 Corinthians.

The following discussion selects from the various options four important methods which dominate the investigation of 2 Cor. and constitute the research background for this study: analysis by *Literarkritik* (1.1), types of rhetorical analysis (1.2), epistolographic analysis (1.3) and epistolary hermeneutic approaches (1.4).

1.1. Literarkritik *as an approach to understanding 2 Corinthians*

1.1.1. *The method of* Literarkritik

For more than two hundred years the interpretation of 2 Cor. has been decisively shaped by the question of the epistle's literary unity. This still holds true even if *Literarkritik* currently appears to be in a 'recession'.[1] As a method of biblical criticism NT *Literarkritik* has the task of examining the 'literary unity of a text' and 'if necessary of attempting to order the text; possible earlier drafts which have been reworked, potential oral or written traditions are to be illuminated and the literary character of the document determined'.[2] In contrast to literary criticism the task of *Literarkritik* can be defined in general terms as follows: '*Literarkritik* is concerned with the delimitation, the structure, the inner unity or sources of a text and the so-called introductory questions of the author, place and date of the respective document.'[3]

It is clear from this that *Literarkritik* has two tasks: first, a *synchronic-analytical* task where it asks about the unity or *coherence* of the existing text and thereby also the literary *text–context relationship*. At the same

---

1. Schmithals, 'Erwägungen', p. 51.
2. Dinkler, 'Bibelkritik', p. 1189.
3. Meiser, *Proseminar*, p. 51.

time *Literarkritik* has a *diachronic* task, namely to determine the *original,* i.e. the *historical context* and the *'earliest text'*. Particularly in the exegesis of the Pauline epistles *Literarkritik* in the broadest sense enquires into an editorial redaction of the letters. This may have occurred (a) in a compilation of several letters or (b) in the form of interpolations. These questions raised by *Literarkritik* are not based on textual criticism. They presuppose a deliberate editorial revision of the Pauline epistles, at the latest around 90–100CE.

(a) *Compilations of letters*

If *Literarkritik* establishes the incoherence of a letter and goes on to ask about the *divisions of the epistle,* there follows the further question as to 'whether some epistles are in fact compilations of letters originally separate'.[4]

Central *criteria* employed by *Literarkritik* are 'doublings, repetitions, tensions, discontinuities, joins, rifts, unevennesses and inconsistencies'[5] within a letter. These criteria are initially criteria of incoherence. Hence the burden of proof tends in one direction: What is to be shown is not the unity of a letter but its disunity. In the analysis of *Literarkritik* the coherence factors in the text serve – reciprocally – as the 'controlling instance'.

The *factors of coherence or incoherence* are examined at the following textual levels: on the *situational* level or with regard to discrepant statements about location, time and circumstances; on the *thematic* level or with regard to the incompatibility of the contents of different statements; on the *grammatical* and *syntactical* level or with regard to gaps in the argument; on the *semantic* and *pragmatic* level; and finally with regard to the *kind of text*.

The decisive criterion of incoherence is given when it is necessary to posit 'different situations' underlying a letter.[6] The *disunity of the letter* is only established if the incoherence factors outweigh the factors of coherence. A reconstruction using the methods of *Literarkritik* is only compellingly necessary if the incoherence of a letter cannot be explained except on the basis that different communication situations underlie the letter as it now stands.

(b) *Glosses and interpolations*

Literarkritik employs considerations of language and content to examine whether *glosses* and *editorial insertions* are contained in the existing Pauline letter.

---

4. Egger, *Methodenlehre*, p. 162.
5. Merklein, 'Einheitlichkeit', p. 349.
6. Vielhauer, *Geschichte*, p. 141.

1.1.2. *The analysis of 2 Corinthians by* Literarkritik
1.1.2.1. *The approach*

The various hypotheses about 2 Corinthians produced by the use of *Literarkritik* have been so carefully documented in recent years[7] that it will suffice to give a brief outline of the treatment of the *literarcritical* question in the newer and newest commentaries and monographs.

On the one hand it is assumed that the unity of 2 Cor. can no longer be taken for granted; it 'rather requires to be demonstrated'.[8] Thus the criterion of incoherence has in various ways turned into a criterion of coherence. On the other hand the question of *Literarkritik* is felt to be so burdensome that various means are used to hold on to the unity of the existing text (see below 1.1.2.2(b)). Yet there are at least four arguments which not only support the *literarcritical* analysis of 2 Cor. but make it necessary.

First, the considerations of *Literarkritik* are admittedly not based on textual criticism, and the – for the most part unified – textual tradition begins around 200CE at the latest with P[46]. Nevertheless we must not forget that a hundred years of the *history of transmission* of 2 Cor. are still obscure, namely the time from the writing of the letter (around 55/56) to the first definite attestation of it in *Marcion* or *Tertullian* and finally to the complete written version in P[46], i.e. by the middle or end of the second century. A reconstruction of the history of 2 Cor. in this period is relevant because only so can we deal with the question as to *how* 2 Cor. might have been adapted, handed down and possibly edited. *Second,* one must investigate whether there are indications of possible *'lost' letters* in 1 and 2 Corinthians, for there are references to a more extensive Corinthian correspondence than that which currently exists (1 Cor. 5.9; 2 Cor. 2.3f.; 10.9–11). These indications raise questions about the original extent of the Corinthian correspondence or about possible compilations of letters and demand an attempted reconstruction. *Third,* indications in the text about the *situation* of 2 Cor. allow different conclusions to be drawn about the events lying between 1 and 2 Corinthians.

Hence *fourth,* we must examine whether in 2 Cor. incoherencies in language and content permit a reconstruction of the original form of the text. Such incoherencies might be seen and described on the linguistic-syntactic, semantic and pragmatic textual levels as literary and thematic tensions and breaks or as doublets or stemming from different situations. A corresponding examination of the coherence of 2 Cor. leads to a division into at most the following elements:

---

7.   See particularly Bieringer, 'Teilungshypothesen', pp. 67ff. or: 'Einheit', pp. 107ff. Also the earlier work by Dautzenberg, 'Korintherbrief', pp. 3045ff.; particularly on 2 Cor. 8 and 9, see Betz, *Korinther,* pp. 25ff.

8.   Bieringer, 'Plädoyer', p. 137.

1.1–2.13   2.14–6.13   6.14–7.1   7.2–4   7.5–16   8   9   10–13

In particular such incoherencies are mentioned as they either touch generally chs 1–9 and 10–13, or show differences between chs 8 and 9, or particularly call into question the coherence of chs 1–7, or indicate post-Pauline interpolations.

(a) *Differences between chapters 1–9 and 10–13*

It is in particular syntactic, semantic and pragmatic differences that are seen between chs 1–9 and 10–13. Chapters 10–13 (the so-called Four Chapter Epistle) are held in many ways to be 'the sharpest that Paul ever wrote'.[9]

Then a syntactically new beginning is seen in 10.1 with Αὐτὸς δὲ ἐγὼ Παῦλος. Grammatically it is striking that in chs 10–13 Paul usually speaks in the first person singular, while in chs 1–9 he also uses the first person plural. There are semantic differences in that in chs 10–13 Paul uses καυχάομαι in the negative sense, in contrast to chs 1–9. Moreover, leading concepts in chs 1–9 such as δόξα, θλῖψις, χαρά and παράκλησις are missing in chs 10–13, where conversely we frequently find lexemes from the root ἀσθεν-. Thematic and pragmatic differences can also be recognized between chs 1–9 and 10–13. The pragmatic goal of 10–13 is the Apostle's own visit, and consequently 13.10 counts as a contradiction of chs 1–9 while 7.4–16 contradicts chs 10–13.

(b) *The function of chapters 8 and 9*

2 Cor. 8 and 9 are concerned with the same situation of the collection (compare 1 Cor. 16.1–4). Yet chs 8 and 9 can be understood as *separate* writings, with one possibly following shortly after the other.

Then chs 8 and 9 count as 'doublets in mutual competition'.[10] Both writings are complete in themselves, and after 8.24 there is an obvious break. The two letters differ in respect of the target audience, in their intention and the stage of the collection. Hence ch. 8 is considered to be a 'letter of recommendation for Titus and his companions' or a testimonial addressed to the Corinthians which also holds up the Macedonians as a shining example, and begins the collection. Chapter 9, however, is thought to be 'a circular to the congregations in Achaia',[11] where the Corinthians are held up as an example and the collection in Corinth has already been completed. There are also contradictory duplicates in individual sections of the two chapters: 8.1–5 and 9.2 are considered to have conflicting contents, and 9.1 appears essentially to contradict the previous state-

---

9.   Schenke/Fischer, 'Einleitung', p. 109.
10. Schenke/Fischer, 'Einleitung', p. 110.
11. Compare Georgi, *Kollekte*, p. 57 or Betz, *Korinther*, pp. 248f.

ments. While in ch. 8 Paul frequently writes in the first person plural, in ch. 9 he often uses the first person singular.

There are, however, also arguments put forward for the *original unity* of chs 8 and 9. Both chapters are bracketed by the theme of χάρις (8.1; 9.14) and 9.15 concludes with a χάρις-saying. Moreover, there are semantic links in both chapters. But the specific pragmatic function of the two chapters is not clearly determined.

There are various reconstructions of the original location of chs 8 and 9 within the Corinthian correspondence depending upon whether these chapters are considered as separate or as belonging together.

(c) *So-called 'breaks' in chapters 1–7*

Breaks have been noticed between 2 Cor. 2.13 and 2.14 and between 7.4 and 7.5, mainly on grounds of language and content. These breaks lead to the conclusion that in chs 1–7 there are two originally separate letters, one comprising 1.1–2.13 and 7.5–16 and the other 2.14–7.4 – provided a link between 2.13 and 7.5 is established. *Inter alia* the following linguistic, semantic and pragmatic observations are made on the three sections 1.1–2.13, 2.14–7.4 and 7.5–16:

> In *1.1–2.13* Paul composes his speech mostly in the first person singular as an autobiographical retrospective. On a semantic level the dominant concepts are παράκλησις, πεποίθησις, χαρά and ἀγάπη.
> In *2.14ff.* Paul interrupts the preceding account of his travels with a paean of praise (2.14). He changes to the first person plural and rejects any self-commendation in an apologia of his apostolate (3.1; 5.12).
> The pragmatic interpretation of the thanksgiving in 2.14 is disputed: It might be the thanksgiving of a letter which was originally independent (Findeis) or a second introductory thanksgiving to 2 Corinthians (Hauck).
> *6.11–13* contains a call to reconciliation which contradicts 2.5–11 and 7.5ff.
> *7.2–4* is considered to be an autobiographical retrospection, and also a call to reconciliation.
> *7.5–16* is thought to follow on after 2.13 – particularly because of Μακεδονία, the semantic parallelism of 2.12f. and 7.5 and the continuation of the account of Paul's travels. Moreover, here too reconciliation can be recognized.

Hence there are in principle two possible *literarcritical* solutions for the classification of the three sections of text. To justify a linking-up of 2.13 to 7.5 we have the fact that the linguistic and situational flow seems to be interrupted by 2.14 and following. This being so, the passage 2.14–7.4 would then have been linked to this context at a later date by an editor.

Against connecting 7.5 to 2.13, however, it could be argued that 7.5 would represent a 'doublet'[12] and that the change from singular (2.13) to plural (7.5) as well as from πνεῦμα in the dative to σάρξ in the nominative is difficult to explain. Furthermore a direct linkage of 7.5 to 2.13 seems hardly plausible considering the particle καὶ γάρ. Accordingly 2.14–7.4 could be a digression and 2.14–17 should then 'be understood as a transition to a fresh extended train of thought reflecting theologically on the ministry of an Apostle'.[13]

(d) *A crosscheck: the unity of 2 Corinthians 1.1–2.13*

In the end the assessment of the incoherencies detected in chs 1–7 can be radically challenged by a crosscheck. Our modern so-called criteria of coherence could equally well lead to the conclusion that the section 2 Cor. 1.1–2.13, which is generally taken to be uniform, is thematically, linguistically and pragmatically incoherent.

Already in the eulogy we find both doxological and paracletic elements (1.3–7, 9b–10) along with concrete descriptions of what has gone before (1.8–9a) combined with a direct application (1.11). Likewise specific travel plans (1.15ff.) are on the one hand repeatedly given a theological interpretation (1.19a, 20–23a; 2.12–13), on the other hand related to Paul's personal history (2.1–4) and to a concrete question of ethics in the church (2.5–9), leading on to general ethical instruction (2.10–11).

Hence it is debatable whether the incoherencies detected between 2.13 and 2.14 and between 7.4 and 7.5 are *sufficient* to establish the compilation of originally separate letters or whether they do not perhaps simply reflect our modern feeling for coherent textual structuring.

(e) *Editorial insertions and glosses in 2 Corinthians*

Both an *interpolation* and *glosses* have been detected in 2 Cor.

6.14–7.1 is often rated as an interpolation, that is as a later, post-Pauline insertion. 'The section 6.14–7.1 is controversial', both in its connection to 6.13 and in its relationship to 7.2, 'because of its position, its wording and its content'.[14] A more intelligible connection with 6.13 is then seen in 7.2 (Windisch, Bultmann).

There are numerous *hapax legomena* and linguistic peculiarities (6.16 and following) in 6.4–7.1. A proximity to Qumran has even been considered. The dualisms seem uncharacteristic for Paul and their content contradicts 1 Cor. 5.10. Their function in the present context can be described as follows: 'At the end of 6.14–7.1 there exists a rapport between

---

12. Trobisch, *Entstehung*, p. 124.
13. Wolff, *Zweite Brief*, p. 51.
14. Wolff, *Zweite Brief*, p. 146.

the recipients and the sender ...'.[15] In 7.2–4, on the other hand, Paul is striving for rapport with the Corinthians.

Even in some recent and very recent studies of 2 Cor., 2 Cor. 6.14–7.1 is considered to be a post-Pauline interpolation (Aejmelaeus, Klauck, Sundermann or Schnelle). But there are also mounting attempts to maintain that 6.14–7.1 originally belongs to 2 Cor. (Bieringer, Goulder, Adewuya).

It has also been discussed whether particular parts of verses in 2 Cor. (3.17, 18b; 5.16) are not perhaps *glosses* (Schmithals).

1.1.2.2. *Hypotheses on the* literarcritical *reconstruction of 2 Corinthians*
The acknowledgement of the linguistic and literary inconsistencies observed in 2 Cor. leads either to the question of the original form of the individual letters and their chronology – i.e. on the assumption that *letters have been compiled* – or to a defence of the *unity* of 2 Cor. as we have it.

Since the history of research on this has been repeatedly rehearsed, I shall restrict myself here to a brief description of the hypotheses currently represented.

(a) *The assumption of compilations of letters*
Most recently *Klauck* and *Aejmelaeus* have divided the letter into chs 10–13 and 1–9.

2 Cor. 10–13 are assigned to the 'plaintive letter', which is followed by the 'conciliatory letter' in chs 1–9. *Lang* also adopts this order but he separates ch. 9 from chs 1–8 and interprets it as a supplementary appeal in support of the collection. Hence Lang comes to the following arrangement: chs 10–13; 1–8; 9. *Dautzenberg* places ch. 9 at the beginning, and follows it with chs 10–13 and then 1–8.

[ch. 9]   chs 10–13   chs 1–9 [1–8]   [ch. 9]

Windisch, Barrett, Furnish and *Murphy-O'Connor* and, in the most recent monographs and commentaries on 2 Cor., *Wünsch, Thrall, Sumney* and *Sundermann* put the two parts of the letter, chs 1–9 and 10–13, in the reverse order: chs 1–9 precede chs 10–13 which represent the latest letter but cannot be the 'plaintive letter'.

chs 1–9 [chs 1–8]   [ch. 9]   chs 10–13

More detailed *literarcritical* hypotheses take into account the further breaks within chs 1–7.

Thus *Bultmann* – in a similar way to *Weiss* before him – attributes 2.14–7.4 along with ch. 9 and chs 10–13 to the 'plaintive letter' while the

---

15. Wünsch, *Brief*, p. 97.

'conciliatory letter' comprises 1.1–2.13; 7.5–16 as well as ch. 8. 2 Cor.
6.14–7.1 is taken to be a post-Pauline insertion.

[Letter C] 2.14–7.4 apart from 6.14–7.1; 9; 10–13
[Letter D] 1.1–2.13; 7.5–16; 8

Zeilinger adopts a division into four parts: 2 Cor. 10–13 is a 'militant
letter' which is then followed by a 'conciliatory letter' (1.1–2.13; 7.5–16).
Chapters 8 and 9 follow as a 'begging letter' and 2 Cor. 2.14–7.4 forms the
conclusion of the Corinthian correspondence as an 'apologia'.

chs 10–13   1.1–2.13; 7.5–16   chs 8–9   2.14–7.4

Fischer and *Schenke* correspondingly differentiate the events explicitly
mentioned in 2 Cor.
    Thus Letter C (2.14–6.13; 7.2–4; 9) was drafted in Ephesus and brought
to Corinth by Titus before the intervening visit and incident; Letter D (chs
10–13), the 'plaintive letter', originated after the incident and intervening
visit to Ephesus and was likewise brought by Titus to Corinth; Letter E,
the 'conciliatory letter' (1.1–2.13; 7.5–16; 8) was written in Macedonia
shortly before the continuing journey to Corinth and brought to Corinth
by Titus. Letter E supplied 'the framework for the redactor'.[16]

[C] 2.14–6.13; 7.2–4; 9   [D]chs 10–13   [E]1.1–2.13; 7.5–16; 8

Bornkamm makes an arrangement which is likewise connected explicitly
with a reconstruction of the chronology of events. 2 Cor. 2.14–6.13; 7.2–4
is the first apologia which was written in Ephesus before the intervening
visit. Chapters 10–13 contain excerpts from the 'plaintive letter' which
also originated in Ephesus after the intervening visit to Corinth. 2 Cor.
1.1–2.13; 7.5–8.24 represent the conciliatory letter which followed Titus'
return and was written in Macedonia. Finally, ch. 9 is a separate letter
about the collection, intended for the churches in Achaia. 2 Cor. 10–13
form the redactorial frame because of the warning they contain against
false doctrine.

2.14–6.13; 7.2–4   chs 10–13   1.1–2.13; 7.5–8.24   ch. 9

Georgi and *Carrez* and more recently *Crafton, Hotze* and *Mitchell* make a
reconstruction similar to that of Bornkamm.
    Schmithals presents an extensive, much-altered reconstruction of the
Corinthian correspondence. Schmithals divides the Corinthian correspondence as a whole into thirteen letters (A–N) and assigns the fragments
of 2 Cor. to the following letters:

---

16. Schenke/Fischer, 'Einleitung', pp. 108ff.

[C]	[H]	[J]	[L]	[M]	[N]
6.14–7.1	6.3–13	4.2–14	chs 10–13	8.1–24a	1.1–2.13;
	7.2–4a				7.4b and 7.5–7;
					7.8–16;
					9.1–15

Trobisch assumes a compilation of letters which goes back to Paul himself – i.e. an author's revision: he reconstructs four letters which are arranged chronologically. 2 Cor. 2.12–13 is a redactorial background inserted by Paul himself to serve as a statement of the situation.

1.3–2.11	2.14–7.3	7.4–9.15	chs 10–13

(b) *The defence of unity*

More recent commentaries and monographs on 2 Cor. frequently adhere to the unity of the canonical 2 Cor. (Bieringer, Lambrecht, Barnett and Scott). The argumentation of the opponents of division resembles that with which the advocates of the *literarcritical* separation question the unity of 2 Cor.

The criticism of the *literarcritical* divisions of 2 Cor. is formulated *inter alia* in the following objections already mentioned above: it is pointed out that 7.5, too, does not follow smoothly upon 2.13. 2.14–7.4 can be understood as a 'digression' with semantic, linguistic and contextual associations. Moreover, definite linguistic contacts can be established between chs 1–9 and 10–13. And if chs 10 and following represent an independent letter, in 10.1 there is no *initium* or preface.

But the unity of 2 Cor. is not only defended by way of criticism of *literarcritical* divisions; it is also argued for independently. Either intervening events between 1 and 2 Cor. are excluded and the 'plaintive letter' accordingly identified with 1 Cor. (Bosenius); or one employs *rhetorical analysis*, a *theological interpretation* or looks for one's own *explanation for situational discontinuities* in the story-line of 2 Cor.

Recent rhetorical analyses affirm the unity of 2 Cor. (Amador, Witherington, Young, Ford) in that they see in the existing composition of 2 Cor. as a whole an example of 'forensic or judicial rhetoric'[17] or a uniform 'apologetic letter'.[18]

The unity of 2 Cor. is also occasionally asserted from a theological perspective, for the letter is permeated by a common theme which gives the letter as a whole an 'internal unity': 'This dominating theme is the nature and legitimacy of the apostolic office which Paul's opponents

---

17. Witherington, *Conflict*, p. 333.
18. Young/Ford, *Meaning*, p. 44.

disputed just as passionately as he himself has to defend it.'[19] The unity of 2 Cor. is likewise implicitly assumed when, instead of *literarcritical* considerations, explanations for the situational discontinuities of 2 Cor. have recently been sought in the Apostle's possibly having had a sleepless night (Heckel, as formerly Lietzmann) or being in a changed congregational situation at the time the letter was written (Schnelle).

1.1.2.3. *A provisional appraisal from a critical hermeneutic viewpoint*
Before we take up the *literarcritical* question again and continue it on a literary-historical level we must make a provisional hermeneutical appraisal. In so doing we must on the one hand reflect critically on what presuppositions of understanding lie behind the *literarcritical* divisions and hypotheses. On the other hand we must mention the aspects of *Literarkritik* which will be considered in more detail in the course of the examination.

(a) *Reflection on the* literarcritical *presuppositions of understanding*
(1) If the linguistic and situational differences in 2 Cor. are considered to be inconsistencies, they must be explained. Either the original form of the letter is reconstructed with the help of *literarcritical* hypotheses, or one maintains the unity of 2 Cor. as it stands.

If the inconsistencies lead to a reconstruction of the original form of the text, the following presuppositions of understanding lie behind this *construction of 'literarkritische Hypothesen'. First,* it is presupposed that Paul as a letter-writer conforms to the modern understanding of textual coherence. *Second,* a redactorial processing of the Pauline letters is presumed. The concept of 'redaction', however, remains to a large extent vague. *Third,* the process of compiling letters is accepted as self-evident in the history of the tradition of the Pauline epistles.

(2) If on the other hand the *unity* of 2 Cor. is maintained this comes about under the following assumptions:

First, it is assumed that the Pauline letters were handed down uninterruptedly. This being so, the process of editorial revision and a possible compilation of letters is virtually ruled out. *Second,* as explanation for the inconsistency of 2 Cor. Paul in particular is considered to be a letter-writer whose behaviour and thinking are discontinuous and who has a disconnected style of writing and a specific psychological constitution. *Third,* external circumstances such as the length of time taken to draft the letter or a possible pause in its dictation should help to explain the inconsistent style. *Fourth,* the inconsistencies perceived in 2 Cor. are interpreted either with the help of a pragmatic examination of the text –

---

19. Bornkamm formulates it thus in his 'Vorgeschichte', p. 165, although he himself divides 2 Cor. (see above).

where 'the author's pragmatic intention' was to make his readers 'more attentive ... through using breaks'.[20] Alternatively the lack of coherence in the letters is explained with the help of oral or rhetorical criticism in terms of the history of their oral origin, or regarded as a rhetorical strategy.

Hence when a plea is put forward for the unity of the letter, this is usually made with the support of 'supplementary aids and all sorts of psychological explanations'[21] which are intended to explain the observed inconsistencies.

(b) *Suggestions for an extension of the* literarcritical *question*
(1) As the survey has shown, the *literarcritical* discussion of 2 Cor. is not being abandoned in spite of the fact that it is often felt to be inconclusive. The leading question in this analysis is the assessment of the so-called coherence or incoherence of the letter.

(2) This discussion is not only significant because it uses the case of 2 Cor. to raise the question of the history of the tradition of Paul's epistles. *Literarkritik's* question whether the canonical 2 Cor. is unitary or a compilation of letters has far-reaching hermeneutical consequences for the understanding of the letter, its author and the relationship of text and context. For at least two further questions arise from this, namely (a) whether the letter as we have it is a *prototype* of Pauline epistles and (b) whether it can consequently be interpreted using the criteria of *epistolographic* or *rhetorical* analysis.

(3) These observations show it to be necessary to draw out in a differentiated and constructive fashion the following aspects which have not yet been discussed in detail in the general *literarcritical* debate.

First, we need to differentiate terminologically the concept of 'coherence' used in the text-linguistic evaluation of the unity of 2 Cor. This involves a linguistic differentiation that can be made between 'coherence' and 'cohesion', thus revealing the *hermeneutic* valency of the concept of 'coherence'.[22] In this sense cohesion describes the lexical, semantic and syntactic combination of sentences, while coherence asks about the inference of the text for the recipients – i.e. it expects that they can relate the content of the text to their own world of experience. It emerges from this that those who use the text may well be able to establish coherence where it is not indicated by the cohesive resources of the text. Coherence, therefore, is not a property of the text but a category of evaluation.[23] Hence the concept of coherence for its part represents a hermeneutic evaluation of the unity of a text by its recipients. Textual linguistics

20. Frankemölle, *Handlungsanweisungen*, p. 26.
21. Windisch, *Korintherbrief*, p. 14.
22. Here compare E.-M. Becker, 'Was ist "Kohärenz"?'
23. Heinemann/Viehweger, *Textlinguistik*, pp. 119f.

supplies linguistic, syntactic, semantic and pragmatic criteria with which to test the cohesion of a text. Whether the recipients too judge the text to be coherent depends substantially on their ability to understand and is a hermeneutical judgement. Hence modern factors of cohesion can scarcely decide upon the coherence of an ancient text such as 2 Cor.

Hence we must ask *historically* about the conditions of writing and understanding in antiquity. This includes the question whether and in what way the cohesion and coherence of texts were assessed in the ancient world (see particularly 2.1 and 2.2).

Second, we must examine whether, against the background of ancient history of tradition, a compilation of letters such as 2 Cor. is conceivable, in what manner of textual reworking this was performed and at what stage in the textual transmission it took place (see 2.3). These reflections will lead to a distinctive literary historical model for the origin and tradition of 2 Cor. (see 2.4).

Third, it will be seen that 2 Cor. contains epistolary-hermeneutic or meta-communicative statements (see Chapter 3) which enable us to draw conclusions about the various phases of the Corinthian correspondence. These statements will be interpreted in the exegetical part of this examination (see particularly Chapter 4) with a view to a reconstruction of Paul's communication with the Corinthians.

1.2. *Research on orality and rhetoric as an approach to the understanding of 2 Corinthians*

1.2.1. *Rhetorical criticism*
(a) *The purpose of rhetorical analysis*
Rhetorical analysis or rhetorical criticism interprets Pauline letters using the criteria of ancient rhetoric. This is done with appeal to the fact that the ancient theory of letters fell within the framework of rhetoric. Rhetorical analysis proceeds from the present form of the text and consequently does not seek historically for textual sources and origins. It can be defined – in contrast to *narrative criticism* – as follows: rhetorical criticism 'is concerned with the rhetoric of persuasion, that is, how the textual components work together to persuade the reader to adopt particular theses presented within the text for their assent'.[24] 'Both methods are particularly useful in the exegetical task in seeing how a text works as a whole to present a coherent (or incoherent) argument or story.'[25]

Rhetorical analysis pursues in detail the following questions: *First,* texts

---

24. Stamps, 'Criticism', p. 220. Narrative criticism on the other hand 'is concerned with the rhetoric of narrative, that is, how the components of story-telling work together to create narrative coherence', p. 220.

25. Stamps, 'Criticism', p. 236.

put into literary form should be examined under the aspect of their *verbal communication* or the spoken word, as this was predominant in antiquity. Oral criticism is oriented to similar questions (see 1.2.2). However, its concern is with a form of 'one-sided' verbal communication – i.e. simply as it proceeds from the speaker and to that extent is already formed.

Second, rhetorical analysis puts *historical* questions in so far as it attempts to ascertain the original conditions of speaking and understanding (Watson) and in this connection also asks about Paul's rhetorical training (Porter).

Rhetorical analysis of the Pauline epistles aims to ascertain the influences of general ancient rhetoric on Paul's method of speaking and writing. In so doing it reaches various assessments: in the Corinthian correspondence rhetoric is considered as playing a predominant role, both with regard to the addressees' conditions for reception and in view of Paul as a letter-writer (Bullmore). This is demonstrated in specific textual exegesis. But now we must critically reflect on this historical aspect of rhetorical analysis because it is possible to assume too quickly that the results of the rhetorical analysis correspond to the supposed intention of the author of the text. Still, in each case the historical perspective of rhetorical criticism can indicate the general aspects of ancient rhetoric relevant to the theory of communication (Cornelius).

Recent so-called socio-rhetorical criticism also includes in its analysis of a text the sociological conditions through which the historical addressees influence the rhetorical situation: 'It is my assumption that a given rhetorical unit brings different interpretative responses depending upon a whole set of historical and sociological, as well as literary factors.'[26]

Third, the unity of a letter can be ascertained and described with the help of rhetorical analysis. If the method of rhetorical analysis is applied to the exegesis of 2 Cor., it can – deliberately avoiding considerations of *Literarkritik* – discern a coherent rhetorical structure even in the thematic and linguistic incohesion of 2 Cor.: 'A rhetorical approach which focuses not upon history, but upon *inventio*, takes seriously the complexity of argumentative and persuasive dynamics and situations before considering the developmental "logic" of causalist historical reconstruction.'[27] Admittedly textual analysis cannot escape the questions of *Literarkritik* if it merely makes a rhetorical analysis of *sections* of the letter instead of seeing a whole letter as a unit. Moreover rhetorical analysis must face up to the questions of redaction history and test whether the rhetorical strategy of the text discerned by the exegete was created by the author himself or only later by a possible final redactor.

---

26. Amador, 'Socio-Rhetorical Criticism', p. 221. On socio-rhetorical criticism see also Bloomquist, 'Direction'.

27. Thus Amador, 'Corinthians', p. 94.

Fourth, rhetorical exegesis examines individual sections of a letter or complete letters to find their rhetorical forms and rhetorical plan and asks about the rhetorical stylistic devices employed. Here, certainly, it is striking not only that Paul uses rhetorical stylistic devices but that his writing also frequently shows 'stylistic features of the spoken language'[28] and consequently diverges somewhat from a specifically rhetorical formation.

(b) *A general critique of rhetorical analysis*

The criticism aimed by researchers at the rhetorical analysis of the Pauline epistles is based either on considerations internal to the text or on the question of principle whether the criteria of ancient rhetoric can adequately grasp the essence of the Pauline letters.

Consequently the orientation of *Pauline theology* itself is brought into play as a critique of the rhetorical practice current in the ancient world. To this is added the thesis that Paul, for theological reasons, used a simple and 'unaffected style' 'which drew no attention to itself ... It was in sharp and purposed contrast to a tradition swept up in the aesthetics of style and the impressive demonstration of stylistic brilliance that Paul preached the simple gospel of Jesus Christ'.[29]

It is correspondingly observed that the New Testament literature – including the Pauline epistles – is to be assigned to the field of the *genus subtile* (Reiser).

However, alongside all the methodical criteria for the rhetorical analysis of the Pauline letters which have been taken from general ancient rhetoric, the specific relevance of rhetorical criticism for research on the Pauline letters has also been acknowledged (Stamps).

Beyond all this is the fundamental debate whether rhetorical criteria can be employed in the analysis of the Pauline letters. For if we pull the scholarly theory of letters and letter-writing itself into the sphere of oral speech we must simultaneously take account of the fact that epistolo-graphic conditions are different from those of ancient rhetoric (Demetrius, *De Elocutione* §230). 'In contrast to the oral, face-to-face context of most ancient rhetoric, the epistolary genre was occasioned by situations where one or more individuals, spatially separated, wished to communicate.'[30]

Besides, letter-theorists make no specific statements on the rhetorical

---

28. Reiser, *Sprache*, pp. 72 and 74.

29. Bullmore, *Theology*, p. 225.

30. Reed, 'Epistle', p. 172. 'A fundamental distinction between the epistolary and rhetorical *genera* is that the former were relegated to spatially-separated communication, limiting the extent to which they could parallel the typical oral, face-to-face context of judicial, deliberative and epideictic speech', p. 176.

form of a letter even if the writing of letters – indeed practising writing diverse types of letters – was part of rhetorical training. Hence the deficiency of rhetorical analysis lies in the fact that rhetoric 'is used as an analytical instrument to understand texts without questioning whether the author, in producing the text, *consciously* allowed himself to be led by the rules of communication methodically recorded by the rhetorical system ...'.[31]

Finally, the *examination of style* can be seen as an alternative to rhetorical analysis (Zmijewski). For in contrast to the comparative criticism of style applied in the field of rhetorical analysis, the general, more descriptive criticism of style takes its analytical criteria from the text itself: then the examination of the style 'serves the interpretation of the text'.[32]

Hence, whereas rhetorical analysis attempts to define the intention of the text by looking for devices and *genera* of rhetorical style, examination of the style leads to a *description* of the text.

Since examination of the style in principle conducts no historical analysis it is to be preferred to rhetorical analysis in its concern to describe the existing epistolary text stylistically. For rhetorical analysis in the end remains tied to at least three contradictions which can only with difficulty be resolved: it analyses the literary structure of the letter using the criteria of the spoken word; it infers the author's intention on the basis of rhetorical criteria external to the text; and it makes an uncritical examination of the final literary form of the text – and that using historically qualified categories of ancient rhetoric.

(c) *Five examples of rhetorical analysis of 2 Corinthians*

(1) In his examination of 2 Cor. 8 and 9 *Betz* concludes that the two writings were originally independent. On the one hand Betz makes a rhetorical analysis of the structure of the argumentation of both letters. But on the other hand he acknowledges their 'literary quality'[33] against the background of ancient epistolography. Betz sees the literary character of both letters in the fact that Paul does not simply coalesce various types of epistle but employs a 'professional rhetoric'.[34] Literary epistles, according to Betz, are first of all professionally worked-out rhetorical letters. He establishes the specific literary function of both writings – in spite of the many differences in detail – in the sphere of the language of administration.

---

31. Sundermann, *Apostel*, p. 13.
32. Zmijewski, *Stil*, p. 40.
33. Betz, *Korinther*, p. 234.
34. Betz, *Korinther*, pp. 234f.

(2) *Wünsch* programmatically locates his rhetorical analysis of 2 Cor. 1–9 in the context of literary studies. Consequently the pragmatic of an epistle is not described in terms of a rhetorical genus but as a 'communicative act': 'The epistles of the Apostle Paul ... must be seen as communicative acts with which the author wished to achieve an effect. In each particular situation he makes use of an appropriate strategy to bring about his intended result.'[35]

Here, however, Wünsch is not really moving in the sphere of literary studies, for the literary aspect of the letter is not given its own appreciation. Instead the definition given of an epistolary action is assimilated to the definition of a speech as formulated in the teaching of rhetoric: 'The "address" as such ... is a deliberate articulation of the instruments of speech (thus a sequence of sounds) or its analogous substitute (e.g. in writing) which runs in time and is concluded by the speaker in relationship to the situation with the intention ... of changing that situation.'[36]

(3) How a rhetorical analysis of the Pauline letters can prove that Paul definitely fell back on *topoi* of Aristotelian rhetoric is shown by *DiCicco* using 2 Cor. 10–13 as an example: 'In fact, Paul was doing what any ancient or even modern speaker does in a speech of persuasion: the speaker projects to an audience an image of competency, good judgement and moral integrity, pushes the right emotional buttons, and demonstrates with logical appeals.'[37]

In 2 Cor. 10–13 Paul makes use of 'the three methods of proof ... quite consciously to modify the beliefs and attitudes of the Corinthians'.[38] DiCicco regards the gap between the Aristotelian theory of an oration and the fact that Paul was writing letters as at most limited.

(4) *Sundermann* conducts a rhetorical investigation of the last four chapters of 2 Cor. in a similar fashion. He attempts to find the 'rhetorical character of Pauline texts' independently of the question whether Paul was educated or trained in rhetoric. In the course of this the question frequently remains open whether this 'is due to a conscious or unconscious, intentional or unintentional process'.[39]

(5) Recent commentaries on 2 Cor. have made out a continuous rhetorical structure in the whole letter. In this connection we must pose the critical question whether the rhetorical analysis does not also in the end depend on initial assumptions of *Literarkritik* when on the one hand it takes particular sections of 2 Cor. as the basis for a rhetorical

---

35. Wünsch, *Brief*, p. 327.
36. Lausberg, *Elemente*, p. 15.
37. DiCicco, *Use*, p. ix.
38. DiCicco, *Use*, pp. 33f.
39. Sundermann, *Apostel*, p. 13.

classification of genus but on the other it can detect a coherent structure in the whole of 2 Cor.

McCant does indeed detect in 2 Cor. predominantly the formal genus of 'judicial rhetoric', but at the same time he sets against this a theological interpretation. 'As in most rhetorical literature, we have mixed genres. The thesis of this study is that Paul's goal is not self-defense. He needs no defense because he is an "apostle of Jesus Christ ...".'[40] Hence the rhetorical genus classification slides here directly into the framework of a theological interpretation.

Witherington desires to give rhetorical criticism a socio-historical dimension with the form of the so-called 'socio-rhetorical commentary'. The texts of the letters are interpreted not only in their rhetorical structure but also against the background of their social context: 'This commentary examines, then, both the social context and the rhetorical form of Paul's Corinthian correspondence as well as giving attention to insights from classical literature and Roman history and offering some of the usual linguistic and historical data of biblical commentaries.'[41]

(d) *Rhetorical analysis of 2 Corinthians – a critical perspective*

All the positions we have named within the sphere of rhetorically oriented text-analysis of 2 Cor. presuppose that Paul was familiar with rhetorical termini (cf. 2 Cor. 2.5; 3.1). These observations are based in the main on terminological similarities between Paul's language and ancient rhetorical diction. Yet at the same time there are statements in 2 Cor. in which Paul sees his linguistic ability or eloquence – and that could mean his rhetorical competence as well – called into question (2 Cor. 11.6; 10.10).

The exegetical relevance of rhetorical analysis can certainly consist in the heuristic method of observing and describing specific stylistic characteristics in the text and proceeding in a similar way to an examination of style – namely descriptively, not prescriptively. But rhetorical analysis cannot distinguish comprehensively the literary dimension of a *letter* as such, because it presumes that a letter such as 2 Cor. is a structured speech. Here it is necessary to stress the fundamental differences between vocal speech and the written word – although practical features may be common to the formation of a letter and rhetoric. For when we consider the history of letters it is a fact that 'the letter-writing tradition was essentially independent of rhetoric'.[42] Finally, the insights which can be gained from communication studies demonstrate the limitations of rhetorical text-analysis. While rhetorical analysis understands a letter as a speech formed one-sidedly by the speaker or

---

40. McCant, *Corinthians*, p. 13.
41. Witherington, *Conflict*, p. xii.
42. Stowers, *Letter*, p. 52.

writer, the theory of communication points out that the letter arises within the framework of a reciprocal communication.

1.2.2. *Oral criticism*

If one looks for the significance of oral criticism as an avenue to the understanding of a Pauline epistle, one must first consider the ancient oral culture to which oral criticism applies. Then one can critically assess the approach of oral criticism and draw it into the process of further investigation.

(a) *The intention of oral criticism*

Oral criticism counts as a method 'which focuses on principles of oral composition and interpretation'[43] and is substantially based on the contributions of research into oral communication. While rhetorical analysis examines the existing text using the criteria of ancient rhetoric, oral criticism asks historically about the *previous oral history* of texts and considers itself as a continuation of the search for the historical oral tradition. It must be said, however, that the determination of the relationship of oral and written tradition already presupposes an understanding of 'scribality'. When employing the method of oral criticism the following holds true: by 'which distinctive features oral communication can be discerned by text-internal examination can only be inductively inferred in all forms of fictitious oral communication'.[44]

In oral criticism – borrowing from the classical philological interpretation of Homer or research on so-called oral poetry[45] – an examination is undertaken as to how, in structural-poetic or in receptive-noetic respects, oral communication is expressed in written texts or is recognizable as such an expression. Oral criticism consequently has an oral-poetic and an oral-noetic component. The general cultural presupposition lies in the assumption that by putting words into writing one generates a 'distance from the world'.[46]

In the Pauline epistles oral criticism can use structural, syntactic and semantic analysis to query the oral character of linguistic statements. Oral criticism is related to rhetorical analysis in that it examines the rhetorical

---

43. Davis, 'Criticism', pp. 96–124 (passage quoted from p. 96).

44. Thus Blänsdorf, 'Werwolf-Geschichte', p. 195 in relation to narrative texts.

45. A miscellany of works in the field of classical philology take up research into oral poetry, e.g. Vogt-Spira, *Strukturen*, or Kullmann/Reichel, *Übergang*. The topic is also treated in the field of literary and cultural studies and in linguistics, see e.g. Ehler/Schaefer, *Verschriftung* or Halford/Pilch, *Syntax* and Thomas, *Literacy*.

46. J./A. Assmann, 'Schrift', p. 25 review this in relation to the Greek alphabet script. The script stands at a threefold 'distance from the world: concepts refer to the world, language refers to the concepts and the script refers to the language ...'.

effect of linguistic statements and also endeavours to prove the coherence of Pauline letters. But it differs from historical analysis in that it desires to raise solely the *non-literal*, i.e. the common oral expressions in a written communication. Research into oral communication views the essence of Pauline theology from its origin as oral theology so that at the same time the word-character of Pauline theology can be held fast in a systematic theological perspective.

(b) *Research into orality, rhetoric and scribality*

In a methodical approach using oral criticism it is first necessary to differentiate the modes of communication to establish what is in the end oral, rhetorical or written. Ancient culture is first of all characteristically oral. But this form of orality, so fundamental for ancient culture, already loses its specificity when it is connected to rhetoric, even though *rhetoric* for its part arises from the culture of orality: 'Rhetoric is the outgrowth of a media world rooted in and dominated by speaking.' But on the other hand it is true that 'Orality was transformed, indeed undermined, as it was brought to consciousness through rhetorical, scribal reflection.'[47]

Rhetoric therefore transforms the structures of oral speech. *Scribality* then opens up a further category of ancient forms of communication: 'In principle, writing never reproduces orality. Textuality arrests, absorbs, and to varying degrees overtakes speech as it inaugurates its own scribal codes.'[48] At the same time, all the oral forms of communication flow into the literary.

> In antiquity, dictation, writing and reading/hearing took place as interactive transfer of words in a pliable semantic environment. This is why texts unapologetically partook of other writings, and not only writings, but of allusions, faint echoes, and subliminal recollections as well. In producing manuscripts, dictators of texts also plugged into their memories, these interior storehouses, which processed words, images, textual echoes, and emotions alike.[49]

Scribality in the ancient world was, however, not restricted to particular literate groups and consequently – seen from a socio-critical standpoint – a sign of power and education. Furthermore the process of making literate was channelled by the history of particular forms or types: language was put into letters in administrative correspondence, in religious literature or philosophical or poetic texts or in personal correspondence. Consequently letters represent one elementary sphere of written culture.

From these general observations on the ancient processes of putting a

---

47. Kelber, 'Modalities', pp. 200 and 205f.
48. Kelber, 'Modalities', p. 208.
49. Kelber, 'Modalities', pp. 211f.

text into writing one can deduce the conditions under which the New
Testament came to be written down as follows: 'It is in this milieu, largely
non-literate, mostly dependent on criers and storytellers for knowledge
and communication, but with some connection to literates, that urban
Christianity took shape.'[50] The phenomenon of literality can be met in a
fourfold way in the Pauline churches, namely in 'the production of letters,
the reception of the letters, the possible use of Scripture in worship, and
the use of Scripture in debate'.[51] Hence literality can be encountered in the
Pauline churches on the one hand as a reception of the LXX and on the
other in the form of an epistolary correspondence between Paul and his
churches.

(c) *Influences on the understanding of 2 Corinthians*
The search for the oral prehistory of Pauline texts shows clearly that there
is a desire to check back *before* the letters took on literary form and to
ascertain the influence of oral language on the process of literalization. If
the oral elements in the style of the Pauline epistles can be shown thereby
we should not however undervalue the fact that Paul *writes letters* and
consequently departs from oral communication, literalizes his language
and literarizes it in the form of his letters.

Here we can already see that their very affiliation to literal communication is fundamental for letters in the ancient world. For the methodical
conception of oral criticism, however, critical consideration must be given
to the fact that if rhetoric already transforms the elements of oral speech,
the processes of putting something into writing do this to an even greater
extent and are accompanied by even greater transformations of the
language. Hence, conversely, checking back for the oral prehistory of a
text can scarcely recover the authentic style of the oral language and
communication preceding the text.

The question of the relationship between orality and literality in
antiquity must be raised again on two occasions in the course of this
investigation: in the context of a literary-historical reconstruction of 2
Cor. we shall consider the formative influence of oral language on the
creation and reception of epistolary literature, both from the view of Paul
as writer of epistles and from the view of the Corinthian church as
recipient (Chapter 2). Then in Chapter 3 possibilities will be shown for a
productive continuation of the orality–scribality debate on the interpretation of Pauline letters.

---

50.   Dewey, 'Textuality', p. 47.
51.   Dewey, 'Textuality', pp. 50–51.

1.3. *Epistolographic contributions to 2 Corinthians*

Taking up the perspectives which research on rhetoric and orality open up for the understanding of Pauline epistles, the epistle itself can be understood as a literal continuation of oral communication. Epistolographic research for its part provides its own contributions to the understanding of Pauline letters and cannot simply be subordinated to rhetorical analysis. First I should like to refer to general results of epistolographic research in so far as they are instructive for the hermeneutics of Pauline letters. Then I shall present individual epistolographic contributions especially relevant to 2 Cor.

(a) *The essence of the ancient letter*

The various contributions to the general investigation of ancient epistolography (Koskenniemi, Thraede) basically classify the function of letters in antiquity in three ways: *First,* the letter performs the function of a conversation with a person who is not present. Consequently Paul's communication with the Corinthians can be described as follows: 'Paul's dialogue is ... a dialogue that was carried on by correspondence.' [52]

Second, the presence of the distant person is brought about by the letter in spite of his physical absence. Not only does the letter-writer seem to the addressee to be present with him, but in writing the writer himself feels the presence of the addressee. To this extent the 'literary genre in which the person most clearly reveals his personality ... is, for Seneca as for Demetrius, the letter'.[53] But the letter can only 'reveal the personality of the writer' if the author writes in the *genus humile* or *genus subtile*.[54]

Third, letters succour friendship. Love, yearning and consolation are expressed in them.

Summing up, Koskenniemi and Thraede entitle the three functions of the ancient letter as *parousia, homilia* and *philophronesis*. In the end letters should safeguard 'the maintenance of contact, the communication of information, and the statement of request or command'[55] – and their most important task was to be a 'proof of goodwill as a substitute for a personal conversation'.[56] The letter differs from a conversation in that the letter is characterized 'by the scribality of the communication and the spatial and temporal distance between statement and counterstatement'.[57]

Already *Demetrius* (*De Elocutione* §224) – in contrast to *Artemon* – points to the difference between conversation and letter, since in his view

---

52. Collins, 'Corinthians', p. 44.
53. Müller, 'Spiegel', p. 141.
54. Müller, 'Spiegel', p. 142.
55. White, *Light*, p. 218.
56. Thus Zelzer, 'Brief', p. 544.
57. Müller, 'Brief', p. 61.

the letter represents a gift (δῶρον). Later epistolary theorists such as *Pseudo-Demetrius* differentiated between different types of letters. This represents a subsequent 'attempt to systematize the practice of letter-writing'[58] since, in fact, every written document which contained the name of the sender and an addressee was considered to be a letter. Yet in antiquity there already existed several characterizations of letters which have been continued in various ways up to the present day. The characterization of letters results from their pragmatic function which for its part is chiefly derived from its semantics. For example *Pseudo-Demetrius* names the letter of recommendation συστατικός which is intended, *inter alia*, to express praise of the person recommended (ἔπαινον συγκαταπλέκοντες).[59] When Paul in 2 Cor. 3.1 explicitly refers to letters of recommendation, it shows that he is familiar with the *termini technici* of ancient epistolography. Yet for all the epistolographic conventions Paul shows that he is a thoroughly independent letter-writer.

(b) *Epistolographic research on the Pauline letters*

Following the investigations on ancient epistolography mentioned above and as an exegetical application of them, works have been written investigating the NT letters, particularly the Pauline epistles.[60] One starts from the conditions and the forms of letter-writing common in antiquity and looks for possible analogous or specific epistolographic conditions which had a determining influence on the production and reception of the Pauline epistles.[61]

Taatz follows the genesis of early Christian letters and consequently the Pauline epistles against the background of early Jewish epistolography. That is why she assumes that Paul 'had not only the form of Hellenistic-oriental letters in his mind's eye but also a Jewish tradition of pastoral letters when he was writing his epistles'.[62]

Those exegetical investigations of 2 Cor. which take up specifically epistolographic questions either interpret the letter-form of 2 Cor. as a whole or take up individual epistolographic motifs in the letter. The ultimate scope of such programmatic interpretations of *letters* is however mainly theological.

When *Bosenius* poses the fundamental question 'Why does the Apostle

---

58. Klauck, *Briefliteratur*, p. 162.

59. Ps-Demetrius, τύποι ἐπιστολικοί 2 in Malherbe, *Theorists*, p. 32.

60. Thus Thraede, 'Einheit', pp. 21–23 and *Grundzüge*, pp. 95ff. establishes the relationship to the NT letters. Compare Probst, *Paulus*; Klauck, *Briefliteratur* or the corresponding sections of individual exegetical monographs – e.g. Bickmann, *Kommunikation*, pp. 85–88.

61. See Doty, *Letters*; Stirewalt, *Studies*; Stowers, *Letter*.

62. Taatz, *Briefe*, p. 7.

Paul state his theological ideas in the form of letters of all things?'[63] the question itself already anticipates a similarly theological outcome of the investigation for it sees in the epistolary form of Pauline theology the appropriate vehicle for Paul's proclamation:

> In a letter the Apostle can express his own existential perturbation through the Christ-event, clarify what it means to be a Christian by his own example and yet as a person retreat behind the content of the proclamation with which he has been entrusted. Since he appears only as an entity in a letter, the recipients of his letters are invited to identify with an example of Christian self-understanding but not with the person of Paul . . .[64]

Bosenius emphasizes that Paul chooses the letter-form for theological reasons and uses it with theological intent. She derives her theological interpretation of the letter-form of 2 Cor. substantially from the epistolographic motif, common in antiquity, of personal absence. Bosenius sees in the very motif that Paul, in writing letters, acts as an absentee, the theological strategy for expounding his theology of the office of an Apostle in 2 Cor.: 'Paul chooses the epistle as a means to solve theological conflicts so that when he visits he may act as συνεργὸς τῆς χαρᾶς. This differentiation between the various effects and functions which befit a visit or a letter from the Apostle presumes that Paul had a differentiated understanding of his office as apostle . . .'[65]

Scholtissek interprets the motif of the letter of recommendation which Paul takes up in 2 Cor. 3.3 against the background of the ancient practice of writing letters of recommendation. Consequently he takes up a *terminus* common in the ancient world, namely that of the συστατικὴ ἐπιστολή, but then interprets this in the form of the Pauline reception as a metaphor which, as such, has no parallel in antiquity. By relating this epistolary metaphor to Paul's confrontation with his opponents in Corinth Scholtissek in the end attaches an apostolic-theological and an ecclesiological function to the Pauline talk of a letter of recommendation.[66]

Both the contributions to 2 Cor. which I have taken as examples certainly examine the form of the letter and the epistolographic motifs it contains, but understand the Pauline adaptation of the literary form of the 'letter' simply as a *theological* achievement on Paul's part. They do not ask whether epistolary hermeneutics lie behind 2 Cor. or whether Paul developed in the course of his writing an epistolary hermeneutical concept which independently reflects the process of writing and understanding.

---

63. Bosenius, *Abwesenheit*, p. 2.
64. Bosenius, *Abwesenheit*, p. 6.
65. Bosenius, *Abwesenheit*, p. 43.
66. See Scholtissek, 'Brief', pp. 200–201, where he assigns a polemical and an apologetic function to the use of the metaphor.

Hence for the investigation of the epistolographic thematic of 2 Cor. we have at our disposal either the results of the general investigation of ancient epistolography (e.g. Koskenniemi, Thraede, Taatz) or else contributions to a theological interpretation of epistolographic motifs and forms in Paul (e.g. Bosenius). A focus on the epistolary *hermeneutic* valency of Paul's use of epistolographic motifs and forms – whether by adaptation or by productive individual originality – has not as yet appeared.

Yet the question of Pauline epistolary hermeneutics could – both by comparison with ancient epistolographic convention and independently of it – work out how Paul himself reflects in 2 Cor. the process of letter-writing and thereby in the performance of writing develops epistolary hermeneutics *in nuce*. The emphasis upon Pauline epistolary hermeneutics does not aim to give epistolographic motifs a theological or epistolary pragmatic interpretation as Bosenius does with the motif of 'absence' and Scholtissek with the motif of 'letter of recommendation'. Rather Paul's own personal statements in 2 Cor. should be interpreted with an eye to a possible epistolary hermeneutic conception.

1.4. *So-called hermeneutical contributions to 2 Corinthians*

If we wish in this study to look for the epistolary hermeneutics of 2 Cor. (see Chapter 4), we must also mention in this introduction those approaches to understanding which explicitly ask about Pauline 'hermeneutics' in 2 Cor. These – as they see themselves – 'hermeneutical' approaches are, however, either concerned with the question of *how* Paul uses the scriptures, i.e. the LXX, and *what* his way of using scripture yields for his theological understanding of christology or soteriology. Or alternatively they ask anthropologically about the suitable hermeneutical level upon which Paul's theological statements might be understood.

Hence in these exegetical contributions 'hermeneutics' means a reflection on Paul as an *interpreter of scripture*: they ask how and with what intention Paul used 'scripture' – as e.g. Exodus 34 in 2 Cor. 3. Such a way of questioning is in the end traditionally and specifically oriented towards working out what *normative* significance Paul attaches to scripture.

Hanson calls 2 Cor. 3 into play for a christological interpretation of scripture: 'I intend to defend and expound the theory that in his midrash on Exodus 34 in 2 Cor. 3.7–18 Paul understood Moses to have seen the pre-existing Christ in the tabernacle.'[67] This pre-existing Christ appears in the form of a person. *Schröter* sees in 2 Cor. 3 a soteriological interpretation of scripture by Paul:

---

67. Hanson, 'Midrash', p. 98.

> The aim of Paul's exposition is to describe the new approach to God made possible by the Christian communion. It surely cannot be denied that this includes a new understanding of scripture – and thereby also of the law. And yet to see in this the focal point of 2 Cor. 3 would mean circumscribing the potential of this text unnecessarily. What is far more important for Paul is to establish the fact that God's spirit does not reveal itself in what is written but in the transformation of the heart to a new communion.

Hence in Schröter's view the comprehensive significance of Paul's interpretation of scripture in 2 Cor. 3 lies in the fact that 'it can be related to the Christ-event and the Christian communion'.[68]

Sloan answers the question about the intention of Paul's epistolary hermeneutics for its recipients thus: in 2 Cor. 3 Paul is not primarily concerned with a new understanding of his service as an apostle: 'My reading of 2 Corinthians 2:14–4:6 maintains that our passage does not deal primarily with the question of rightly reading scripture, but of people rightly reading *Paul*.'[69]

But the explicitly hermeneutical interpretation of a text can aim to reflect the adequate anthropological-hermeneutical key to Paul's theological statements in 2 Cor.

With regard to 2 Cor. 4, *Grässer* asks about the hermeneutical plane upon which Paul formulates his theological statements. For Grässer it is clear that Paul explicates his christological remarks with the help of existential hermeneutics, for in 2 Cor. 4 we can see how Paul 'endeavours to unveil the christological event, the death and raising of Jesus, "anthropologically" i.e. as relevant to human existence'.[70]

Both hermeneutical approaches consequently pursue the interest of general theological hermeneutics in so far as they are concerned with the adequate understanding of Paul's theology following its traditional derivation or its anthropological implications.

The hermeneutical interest of the present investigation is by contrast *epistolary* hermeneutics. Hence the aim of the questioning is to ascertain from his statements in 2 Cor. how Paul reflects and shapes in his words the processes of letter-writing and letter-reception and thereby stamps in a lasting way not only the literary form of the letter but in the end also the propositional content of 2 Cor.

---

68. Schröter, 'Schriftauslegung', pp. 274–75.
69. Sloan, 'Corinthians', p. 150.
70. Grässer, *Schatz*, p. 314.

1.5. *Appreciation and critique: rhetoric, epistolography and hermeneutics as approaches to 2 Corinthians*

The approaches to the interpretation of 2 Cor. mentioned in 1.2 to 1.4 each take up individual aspects of what determines the leading question of the present investigation: *Does Paul himself formulate in 2 Cor. approaches to epistolary hermeneutics? How can we find in the text indications which might enable us to reconstruct the processes of Pauline letter-writing and reception?*

The contributions from the field of research into *rhetoric* (rhetorical and oral criticism) assume the orality of ancient communication and include epistolary communication in the ancient culture of orality. We have seen, however, that the detailed rules of ancient rhetoric already transform the nature and function of oral communication and consequently an even greater transformation of language is to be expected in the transition from orality to scribality. Hence rhetorical research can only inadequately bring the factors of oral communication into the interpretation of epistolary texts since it can only grasp them theoretically from the post-oral perspectives of the rhetorical text-books and since it does not begin from the conditions of a reciprocal communication but understands speech as a one-sidedly formed oration. From this perspective, however – in a similar manner to the examination of style – it can descriptively analyse the perceptible linguistic form and intent of the author in a text before it.

Along with these critical questions with regard to rhetorical research we must in the course of further examination pose the question of *Paul as author* which is not allowed for in the orally-centred approach of orality-research and rhetorical analysis but which can be treated philologically (linguistically) and by the field of literary studies: What significance has the circumstance that Paul is a productive literary author who transcends the conditions of oral communication and who also explicitly thinks about his literality and gives it a literary form of high quality?

The works from the area of research into ancient epistolography and the interpretation of Pauline correspondence sharpen our awareness of the contextuality of the letter, of the primarily communicative intention of the sender in his relationship to the addressees and of the conventionality of epistolographic thematic. NT studies interpreting the epistological dimension of the Pauline epistles do place the Pauline letters in the general context of ancient epistolography, but they then assess *theologically* the circumstance that Paul writes *letters* and writes *about* letters and likewise interpret the epistolographic forms in terms of theological propositions.

In order to avoid this theological imbalance in the present examination the epistolographic interpretational horizon for a Pauline epistle such as

2 Cor. will be extended *hermeneutically:* the focus will not be simply on epistological motifs in 2 Cor. or the epistolary character of Pauline theology as such. Rather Paul's reflections on the production and reception of letters will be explicated with regard to whether Paul develops the beginnings of an independent epistolographic exegesis. In this way we wish to draw out an *epistolary hermeneutics* underlying 2 Cor. itself (see Chapter 4).

When all is said and done, those exegetical approaches to 2 Cor. which claim to be *hermeneutical approaches* increase our awareness of the fact that Paul the letter-writer himself acts as an exegete when he interprets 'scripture' or presents particular anthropological categories for the understanding of his theological or christological statements.

Yet it seems appropriate that we should not only examine how Paul interprets scripture or makes his theology applicable but that we should also ask how he reflects the process of his own *writing* and how in the end he *understands* his own writing. Accordingly the epistolary hermeneutics applied under Chapter 4 to 2 Cor. will interpret Paul's statements on letter-writing and on the understanding of epistles by asking: How far is Paul an interpreter of his own letters, i.e. an interpreter of writing and understanding?

1.6. *A preview: further steps*

How will the impulses which open up the central methodical approaches to 2 Cor. cited in 1.1–1.4 now be taken up in the further course of this investigation of epistolary hermeneutics?

First the questions raised by *Literarkritik* in regard to 2 Cor. 2 will be taken up and continued as *literarhistorical* questions. At the same time I shall set Paul's letter-writing along with the post-Pauline transmission of his epistles in the context of the common ancient conditions for writing and reception (2.1 and 2.2). This will reveal whether, under what conditions, and how compilations of letters may have arisen (especially 2.3.2). More precise terminology serves to make the letter-compilation explicable on technical grounds and also conceptually comprehensible.

In Chapter 3 I shall continue in a modified way the questions raised in the epistological, rhetorical and hermeneutical approaches to the text: We must first consider which aspects of communication theory have to be taken into account in the interpretation of the written texts of letters (3.1). Second, we must name the implications which the process of letter-writing contains from the standpoint of the study of literature. Here we must also show to what extent the classification of the author as a creator of literary texts is constitutive for the exegesis of the text (3.2). Third, I introduce the theoretical model with which one can ascertain Pauline epistolary hermeneutics from 2 Cor.: in the manner in which communication constantly creates meta-communication there is also in 2 Cor. a meta-communicative level of language in which Paul reflects on his communication with the Corinthian church and thereby makes epistolary hermeneutical statements (3.3). Thus 3.2 and 3.3 develop in different ways the stimuli given by the epistolographic and hermeneutic research on 2 Cor. (1.3 and 1.4).

Finally the observations developed in Chapters 2–3 will be examined in the exegetical section and formulated as *Pauline* epistolary hermeneutics. The *literarhistorical* reconstruction is the prerequisite for determining the sequence of the individual letters contained in 2 Cor. which, for its part, must be shown to be tenable by the exegesis of the text. We must then reveal, using selected passages from 2 Cor., how Paul himself in 2 Cor. sees the relationship between orality and scribality and the process of letter-writing, to what extent in his letter-writing Paul creates a specific form of communication with the Corinthians and what are the signs that Paul, in the course of his writing, functions as a productive author in a literary sense. These exegetical observations on essentially meta-communicative statements in 2 Cor. reveal glimpses of Pauline epistolary hermeneutics and lead to a detailed perception of how in the course of Paul's written communication with the Corinthians there emerged markedly theological forms of speech. Paul's epistolary hermeneutics represent the link between simple communication with his churches and his epistolary theology.

Chapter 2

A *LITERARHISTORICAL* RECONSTRUCTION OF 2 CORINTHIANS

The following reconstruction of the process of the writing and transmission of 2 Cor. will produce a distinct *literarcritical* hypothesis which grows out of a historical consideration of how letters were written and received in antiquity and consequently should be described as a *literarhistorical* reconstruction. Therefore our investigation again takes up the presentation of the *literarcritical* problem which has decisively dominated the understanding of 2 Cor. for about a hundred years. The *literarcritical* question will now, however, be treated in a *literarhistorical* rather than in a *linguistic-literary* context. In this regard I must make a few preliminary remarks.

It has been shown that the literary uniformity and consequently the original form of 2 Cor. is a matter of controversy. The assumption that our present 2 Cor. is a compilation of letters is based on the observation of a linguistic, literary and propositional 'incoherence'. Here, however, we should differentiate between 'coherence' and 'cohesion' in our textual linguistics,[1] since the judgement on the coherence of a text occurs as a hermeneutical adaptation of the text on the part of the recipients. That is to say the recipient assesses incohesions observed in a text as either coherent or incoherent; and this occurs in a cognitive or hermeneutical process which is to a large extent determined by the immediate recipients' world of language and imagination. The question as to whether the linguistic and literary incohesions in 2 Cor. force us to judge it as incoherent and consequently to make a *literarcritical* reconstruction of the original form of 2 Cor. cannot be adequately dealt with using the linguistic-literary observations of conventional literary criticism. Here we must rather enquire *historically*, first about the conditions under which ancient letters were written, transmitted and possibly compiled; second, we must test whether our modern standards of linguistic and literary cohesion of a text are comparable to those of letter-writers in antiquity.

If we now take together such historical and philological clues about the production and reception of letters, the assumption that 2 Cor. is a *compilation* seems plausible, particularly on technical grounds in respect of writing and transmission (see 2.1 and 2.2). But this assumption that 2 Cor. is a compilation is also reinforced by considerations from

___

1. See E.-M. Becker, 'Was ist "Kohärenz"?'

communication theory, for the written correspondence of Paul with
Corinth contained in 2 Cor. indicates frequent communication and even
contains meta-communicative statements which apprise us in retrospect
about the course of Paul's communication with the Corinthian congregation and comment on the development of this communication.

Consequently the meta-communicative structure of 2 Cor. uncovered
by exegetical means will provide information about the individual phases
of Paul's communication with the Corinthians and about the letters which
arose in these individual phases. First, however, the historical clues about
the writing and reception of letters should show under what conditions the
Pauline letters could have been written and transmitted and whether in the
process of this transmission compilations of these letters might have been
made.

Phases in the formation and reception of 2 Corinthians
  2.1.   The author: Paul
  2.2.   The addressees: the Corinthian congregation
  2.3.   The transmitter: the so-called editorial generation

2.1. *Paul as a 'historical' letter-writer*

With regard to the person of Paul as a letter-writer I should like to ask:
Under what epistolographic, literary and technical writing conventions
did ancient letters which counted as cohesive arise? Looking at the
incohesions observed in 2 Cor. this question can be put the other way
round: Is there an explanation for linguistic and literary incohesions in a
letter which might be grounded either in the ancient technique of writing
or in the conventions of ancient literary aesthetics? We should therefore
gather together observations on the ancient technique of writing, on the
conventions of Graeco-Roman epistolary theory, and on ancient literary
aesthetics and literary criticism, as well as on the literary character of
significant early Jewish genres.

(a) *On the technique of letter-writing*

As a letter-writer Paul acts under the conditions of the general ancient
priority of *orality*. The 'primacy of the spoken word' holds true both for
the production and for the reception of ancient literature and consequently
also for letters. This element of orality had an impact in various respects on
the technique of letter-writing, but also at the same time on its theory.

For writers in antiquity – including Paul[2] – dictated their letters, i.e. the

---

2. Rom. 16.22; 1 Cor. 14.21; Gal. 6.11 refer to this. Later reflections of this practice can
be seen in Col. 4.18 and 2 Thess. 3.17. On the duties and importance of a secretary see
Richards, *Secretary*.

letters were transcribed by *secretaries* from dictation, perhaps on wooden tablets (see below). After being checked through and corrected by the author the letters were then copied again and signed with a handwritten greeting (autograph). To what extent the secretaries contributed to the writing as co-authors is uncertain, particularly in the case of 2 Cor. When Paul writes in the first person plural this may have an intercommunicative (see under 4.4.1) or a theological function: in so doing he deliberately places himself in the supraindividual context of apostolicity and Christian community. Furthermore, the change of person speaking is, in modern terms, effective: the grammatical incohesion regarding the subject who is speaking works as a rhetorical stylistic element, as is clear in 2 Cor.[3] The variability in style added to the 'entertainment value' generally expected by the recipient of the letter.

(b) *Conventions of Graeco-Roman epistolary theory*

There was no generally mandatory theory of letters in ancient times, yet certain epistolographic conventions developed. The letter counts basically as a substitute for an oral conversation[4] which underlines the aspect of orality for the communicative function of the letter. This can also be seen in 2 Cor. (see 2 Cor. 1.23–2.11; 10.1–11) although at this point Paul is reflecting on the process of *letter-writing* and is emphatically acting as a letter-writer.

Initially an implicit letter-theory was conveyed within the frame of instruction in rhetoric, namely as *prosopopoeia* or *ethopoeia*. *Theon of Alexandria* (first to second centuries CE) dealt with letters in the context of his *progymnasmata*. Hence letter-writing was practised in the context of oral language-structuring.

An independent letter-theory[5] which is concerned with the factor of scribality only developed at a later date – out of the practice of writing. But even this theory defines potential rather than necessary criteria of letter-writing. In principle the names of sender and addressee suffice to establish a text as a letter. In ancient times there was no differentiation between a fictitious letter and one which was actually sent.[6] It was only with *Artemon of Cassandraea* (around 100 BCE), the (re-)editor of the

---

3. See Lausberg, *Handbuch*, §518f. The use of an atypical number counts either as a solecism or as schemata.

4. See for example Cicero, *Epistulae ad Quintum fratrem* I.1.45: *sed ego, quia, cum tua lego, te audire, et quia, cum ad te scribo, tecum loqui videor ...*; see also II.10.1.

5. See also on the following the sources mentioned which are printed in Malherbe, *Theorists*.

6. Everything which 'was published as a letter, with salutation and closing formula, is therefore a letter, irrespective of whether it was actually sent to the addressee named. Hence the modern expression "real letter" cannot be applied to the ancient literary form of a letter ...', Zelzer, 'Brief', p. 551.

letters of Aristotle, that a letter-theory began to be constructed.[7]
Demetrius (at the latest first century CE), who tells us of Artemon,
makes mostly stylistic demands of letters such as brevity, clarity,
comprehensible language and the expression of personal ethos.[8] In the
interests of clarity Demetrius also demands the avoidance of 'breaks'
within the letter[9] – by which he means broken, i.e. paratactical,
structuring of sentences.[10] The work of *Pseudo-Demetrius* (second century
BCE to third century CE) classifying letters under 21 different τύποι
ἐπιστολικοί counts as the first real letter-writing manual.[11]

Admittedly in practice letters were scarcely written or understood as
belonging to a particular type or according to a particular letter-theory
but at the most as an *imitatio* of letters which had become exemplary.
Their respective genus was revealed in their semantic profile, their actual
situation and the resulting pragmatic intention.

We can see, however, from an artificial letter written by *Pliny the
Younger* that ancient letter-writers also had literary ambitions. Eco points
out that Pliny, while apparently giving Tacitus a reliable account of the
death of his uncle, Pliny the Elder, in fact fabricates a fictional narrative.[12]
But Pliny drafts this literary fiction in the ostensible form of a friendly
personal letter which professes simply to be giving information about his
uncle's death.

(c) *The conventions of ancient literary aesthetics and literary criticism*
It is only with difficulty that we can ascertain either what literary aesthetic
standards were applied in antiquity to the cohesion of text-construction
or by which criteria of cohesive text-formation literary criticism judged
texts.

---

7.   Later discussions of a letter-theory can be found in Philostratus (3rd century),
Gregory of Nazianzus (around 390 CE) and Iulius Victor (fourth century). See Görgemanns,
'Epistel', p. 1163 or also Pseudo-Libanius; see Zelzer, 'Briefliteratur', pp. 327f.

8.   See Demetrius, *De Elocutione,* particularly §§ 227f and 231.

9.   Demetrius, *De Elocutione* §226 καὶ λύσεις συχναὶ–ὁποῖαι * * οὐ πρέπουσιν
ἐπιστολαῖς; in Malherbe, *Theorists*, p. 16.

10.   On the concept of λύσις see LS, 1067: '*looseness* of structure in writing' with reference
to Demetrius, *De Elocutione* §192.

11.   Pseudo-Demetrius – see Görgemanns, 'Epistel', pp. 1162f. – was the first to make a
differentiation of the τύποι ἐπιστολικοί. See Thraede's description in *Grundzüge*, pp. 25ff.
and on the dating: here we have the earliest Greek letter-writing manual. The oldest stock of
writings could have been written before the Christian era but revisions were probably made
up to the second/third centuries CE. Compare Thraede (as above), p. 26.

12.   Thus Pliny the Younger, *Epistulae* VI.16 writes: *Aliud est enim epistulam, aliud
historiam, aliud amico, aliud omnibus scribere ...*, but in the end writes a fictitious report. See
Eco, 'Porträt', particularly p. 224.

In respect of *literary aesthetics,* explicitly different criteria such as *latinitas* or *perspicuitas* were applied in antiquity to prose or poetry[13] as to ancient rhetoric.[14] These criteria also apply in a limited sense to Pauline letters although these are classed as a *genus subtile.* In respect of *literary criticism* the concept of ancient textual hermeneutics can be described as 'centrifugal' – i.e. linguistic incohesions are acceptable so long as the text shows propositional uniformity.[15] We can refer to the distinguished grammarian *Dionysius Thrax* (*c.* 150–90 BCE) with his *Ars grammatica* as an early witness to the criticism of ancient literature. Dionysius however treated 'no questions of syntax, style or textual criticism'.[16] The *grammatica*, in the manner of a semantic grammar, includes the question of 'grammatical regularity' (ἀναλογίας ἐκλογισμός) and 'literary criticism' (κρίσις ποιημάτων).[17] Pliny's letters, for example, reveal disunity – i.e. repetitions and a diffuse representation of the most varied topics, but this is regarded as intentional on the part of the author.[18]

Welborn recently tested the literary cohesion of the sections 1.1–2.13 and 7.5–16 of 2 Cor. according to the criteria of ancient literary criticism.[19] He comes to the following conclusion: '2 Cor. 1.1–2.13; 7.5–16

13. See for example Horace, *Ars poetica* 408: *natura fieret carmen laudabile an arte* (the relationship between φύσις/τέχνη) or 333f.: *aut prodesse volunt aut delectare poetae aut simul et iucunda et idonea dicere vitae.*

14. See Lausberg, *Handbuch*, §1056/345 with reference to Quintilian, *Institutiones* IV.3.1– 5: a digression within a speech must be connected to the context: *ego autem confiteor ... atque eo vel maxime inlustrari ornarique orationem, sed si cohaeret et sequitur, non si per vim cuneatur et quae natura iuncta erant, distrahit*, IV.3.4. On the connection in the rhythm of the sentence see Lausberg, *Handbuch*, §1004. Quintilian, *Institutiones* IX.4.63: the beginning of the speech stands in no connection with what has gone before (*non enim cohaerent aliis nec procedentibus seruiunt*). On the connection in the middle of a speech see Lausberg, *Handbuch*, §1054a and Quintilian, *Institutiones* IX.4.66: *Mediis quoque non ea modo cura sit, ut inter se cohaereant ...*

15. This is the terminology of Heath, *Unity*, p. 150, who desires to see in ancient literary criticism a more centrifugal model of textual hermeneutics: 'We read on the assumption that these texts will be well-formed according to our – broadly "centripetal" – notion of coherence; but there is reason to suspect that a more "centrifugal" conception of literary unity would be more appropriate to them.' This interpretation of ancient textual hermeneutics is, however, not undisputed, see the critical revue of this work by Schenkeveld, 'Unity', pp. 1ff.

16. Wilson, 'Philologie', p. 95.

17. Wilson's translation, 'Philologie', p. 95.

18. See Peter, *Brief*, p. 119 or Krasser, 'Plinius', p. 1142 or Pliny, *Epistulae* I.2 and II.5 and Sherwin-White, *Letters*, pp. 88f. and 151: '*Pliny* does not write regular sentences and prefers the so-called "mixed" style', p. 151.

19. See Welborn, 'Pieces': Weiss' (see 1.1) literary critical hypothesis that 2 Cor. 1.1–2.13 and 7.5–16 are part of one letter is put to the test here. Criteria of the ancient literature-theory which examine the 'coherence' of this part of the letter in respect of 'continuity (συνέχεια), completeness (τὸ ὅλον) and connection (συνάψις) etc.', p. 561. See also Heath, *Unity*, p. 153.

has been shown to be a coherent work in accordance with Greek and Roman assumptions about literary unity: it possesses the characteristics of continuity (συνέχεια), completeness (τὸ ὅλον) and connection (συνάψις) in such a degree that ancient literary critics would have judged the work to be a unity.'[20]

But ancient literary criticism as well as asking questions about grammar and style also judged texts on their inherent emotiveness (pathos) or ethics (ethos) which of course left the way open for an incohesive structuring of the text. Paul's letters are manifestly emotive (2 Cor. 10.10) and he himself is aware of the emotiveness of his writing (2 Cor. 2.4). Paul's emotiveness is seen in his epistles as personal commitment, the expression of his personal love for the congregation and for Christ. Consequently this personal element should not be interpreted as purely psychological, as a personal attitude, but should have some influence on the literary critical reflection.

From the preceding observations on the technique of letter-writing and on the conventions of the ancient epistolary theory, literary aesthetics and criticism we can say: the ancient theory of letters arose within the schools of rhetoric but served primarily the acquisition of eloquence. The actual practice of letter-writing was not subject to linguistic, formal or binding rules of an epistolary theory but was completely variable. The names of sender and addressee sufficed to make the writing a letter. Hence linguistic and literary cohesion as we understand it is not an essential criterion for the uniform structure of an ancient letter. Furthermore, the ancient letter-writer did not give much thought to the uniformity of his writing, nor did the addressee expect literary uniformity. In the end Paul dictated his epistle as a written conversation, possibly with pauses, and the Corinthian congregation would not have noticed possible linguistic breaks (see also 2.2) or would have interpreted them as Paul's emotiveness.

(d) *The linguistic literary characteristics of early Jewish writings*
It is obvious that, in addition to 2 Cor., other Pauline epistles which are considered uniform from a literary point of view are in no way cohesively structured.[21] Consequently we must ask why it is that some Pauline epistles are held to be uniform in their literary form in spite of linguistic literary incohesions while others are considered to be inconsistent. Here, too, the question can be reversed: Can Paul's literary approach, which has roots in early Jewish writing as well as in the Graeco-Roman literature

---

20.   Welborn, 'Pieces', p. 583.

21.   Even in Romans, which is generally considered a model of the cohesion of Pauline letters, the transition from ch. 8 to ch. 9, for example, could appear to be incohesive; but essentially there is hardly a case for *literarcritical* hypotheses. (See however the hypotheses of division in Schmithals, *Briefe*, pp. 125ff.).

mentioned above, give us clues as to a Pauline style of writing which was possibly incohesive in general? We must look to see if Paul's style as a letter-writer was influenced by early Jewish literature. This question cannot, however, be restricted to epistolary literature. To be precise, we must make a critical examination of the linguistic literary character of early Jewish works and their continuing effect on Paul's style of writing.

As a Hellenistic Jew Paul stands linguistically and thematically in the tradition of early Jewish literature. In his epistles he takes up motifs from wisdom and apocalyptic writings where literary incohesions are typical – they are in fact a component part of the literary character of these writings as will now be shown.

We can take Jesus ben Sira as an example from the field of *wisdom literature*. This early Jewish work (*c*.190 BCE) is considered to be substantially uniform although in no way does it have a constant cohesive structure. Individual sections appear incohesive in the context, but can be interpreted as literary miniatures conforming to the structural principles of wisdom literature,[22] i.e. they correspond to the character of wisdom aphorisms. Repetitions and duplications are quite usual in the field of wisdom literature.[23] Consequently such incohesions are part of the author's literary structuring of the text. Here incohesions clearly do not lead to the writing being inconsistent but serve in a manner typical of the genre to construct coherence. In the final form in which it is available to us *apocalyptic literature* reflects a clear conflict with the constantly changing conditions of time and life. Yet even when one extracts the sections which are considered uniform, there are conspicuous incohesions. Thus in the Ethiopian Enoch,[24] which is not so much derived from sources but 'can be seen as a collection of different writings which have grown together in a long process of tradition and editing',[25] there are definite incohesions even within uniform sections of the text: in places prayers of adoration are interwoven in the sequence of autobiographical accounts and reports of visions. Something similar can be found in 2 Cor. where the transition from remarks about Paul's travels (2.12–13) to the following thanksgiving (2.14) gives grounds for *literarcritical* hypotheses of division.

Hence incohesions in statements within a writing and their generic literary form are typical of and constitutive for early Jewish writings. That is to say, they play a decisive part in creating coherence in the area of

22. On the variety of literary forms in Ben Sira see also Di Lella, *Wisdom*, pp. 21ff.

23. 'Smaller units of thematically related sayings are separated off as is customary in every collection of aphorisms. The fact that repetitions and resumptions of the same theme are thereby possible is part of the character of wisdom literature.' Sauer, *Sirach*, p. 494.

24. On the date of its origin see Uhlig, *Henochbuch*, p. 494. The Book of Dream-Visions from which I shall draw in the following, is dated in the second century BCE. See also Oegema, *Apokalypsen*, p. 134, who dates chs 83–90 to 165–161 BCE.

25. Oegema, *Apokalypsen*, p. 135.

wisdom and apocalyptic writings. With regard to his literary ability and
intention to structure, Paul as an author must be understood without
question as belonging to this tradition.

Summing up we can say that the criteria for assessing the uniformity of
Pauline letters with regard to the person of the letter-writer must to a large
extent be evaluated according to three factors: ancient letters are written
without any epistolographic guidelines, but their syntax is influenced by
oral communication. The preconceptions of ancient literary aesthetics and
literary criticism demand from the author – although not in the field of
epistolography – grammatical and stylistic competence and the mastery of
pathos and ethos. Paul's linguistic and literary achievement as a letter-
writer must in the end be evaluated against the background of the
incohesive literary structure of early Jewish literature. Hence the question
of the literary uniformity of Pauline letters can be dealt with adequately
only if it is clear that the cohesion of ancient letters is measured within the
framework of *these* conditions which till now have not been taken into
consideration – or given too little consideration – in our modern
literarcritical analysis.

2.2. *The Corinthian congregation as recipients of 2 Corinthians*

We now enquire about the further history of a letter once Paul had written
it and sent it as a finished epistle to the Corinthian congregation and then,
in a third step (2.3) will consider how the so-called editorial generation
might have handed it down, preserved and edited it.

After the epistle was dictated and written down on a wooden or wax
tablet it then reached the congregation addressed by means of couriers or
'envoys of the congregation'[26] and in this way reached Corinth. There was
in the realm of the Imperium Romanum a *cursus publicus* but only high
officials could use this for private purposes, consequently Paul could not
use an official messenger-service and therefore private couriers (*tabellarii*)
conveyed the letters.[27] The couriers for the Pauline correspondence were
Paul's collaborators who were not only couriers but simultaneously
conveyed information.[28]

---

26. See Ollrog, *Paulus*, pp. 95ff.: 'They convey letters, come with congregational
questions and reports and tell Paul the news from the congregation,' p. 96.

27. See Kolb, *Transport*, pp. 49ff. and 93ff. Only from the fourth century on could
representatives of the Church take advantage of the *cursus publicus*. See also the very full
account in Mratschek, *Briefwechsel*, pp. 279ff.

28. See the references in Rom. 16.1; 1 Cor. 16.10; see also 2 Cor. 8.16f. or later reflections
of the Pauline practice in Eph. 6.21; Col. 4.7. On couriers in general see also 1 Pet. 5.12 or 1
Clem. 65.1. See also Llewelyn, *Documents*, p. 56 with reference to 2 Cor. 7.7. This personal
transmission of information is also evident in 1 Cor.: see 1 Cor. 1.11; 16.10ff.

After they were delivered the letters were read aloud in the congregation and stored, and if they were written on wooden tablets they had to be copied. In this respect the element of orality is important not only for the process of letter-writing but also for the reception of the letter. The literalized language of the letter develops from an orally shaped verbal coherence and this – as we saw above – principally on three grounds: letters count as a written continuation of an oral conversation; letters for the most part are produced through dictation; and epistolographic forms are initially reflected upon in theory and rehearsed in practice within the framework of instruction in rhetoric. In precisely the same way the literalized speech of letters is designed for oral delivery. For letters in particular – including the Pauline epistles – were, like other texts in ancient times, orally read aloud and received.[29] Put pointedly, one could even say: 'Publication in this case occurred when Paul's letter was read aloud to the gathered community, presumably in the context of the service of worship.'[30] The themes and language of the Pauline epistles bear witness to the fact that – as in 2 Cor. (see for example 2 Cor. 1.19; 4.1ff.) – Paul understands the gospel formulated in his letters originally as an oral quantity.[31]

Accordingly the understanding of letters ensues on the level of the original reception of a letter by its addressees in hearing rather than in reading and consequently is subject to the conditions of the reception of oral speech.

There is a further connected aspect: as the addressees of the Pauline epistle the Corinthian congregation would not have been aware of possible incohesions when they received the letter – particularly if they received it aurally. In their time there was no reason to subject ancient texts to exegetical or philological reflections: 'That which is written or spoken in the present counts as problem-free, since all the hearers and readers are aware of all the attendant circumstances – here explanation or even exegesis are out

29. On the reading aloud of Pauline epistles see 1 Thess. 5.27, and Rom. 16.16 can be understood in a similar way. Dramas and lyric poetry are also composed to be read aloud, see on the so-called *recitationes* e.g. Pliny, *Epistulae* I.13.1ff.; IX.34.1ff. See also Lefèvre, 'Literatur', pp. 10ff. Furthermore orators and poets are comparable, see Horace, *Ars poetica* 43. But then the written recording of speeches led – in the case, for example, of Cicero – to their being revised, see Fuhrmann, 'Mündlichkeit', p. 55. In this way a difference between orality and a written form is recognizable, see e.g. Kröner, 'Rhetorik', pp. 63ff. The significance of scribality lies basically in that its transmission is assured. See also Dorandi, 'Tradierung', p. 10 and Barnett, 'Paul', p. 140 with n. 16.

30. Gamble, *Books*, p. 96.

31. This is the description of Paul's theological language in Kelber, *Gospel*, pp. 140ff.: 'The apostle's preference for writing letters, therefore, may point to a fundamentally oral disposition toward language.' 'The very core of Paul's gospel, the rhythmic thematization of death and resurrection, can thus be considered a product of mnemonic, oral dynamics: it is eminently memorable, repeatable, and orally usable.' (p. 148).

of place.'[32] This admittedly does not tell us whether 2 Cor. as we have it was originally uniform, but it means that at its original reception the question of its uniformity could never have been posed. The question of textual cohesion was only posed at a later date and under other assumptions. The reception of contemporaneous documents in antiquity took place in such a way that the original recipients considered as completely uniform those texts which at a later date possibly appear incohesive.

Consequently we can say: the process of reception in antiquity was also orally influenced. Modern textual reception and the exegetical criteria which developed from this reception for establishing textual cohesion are characterized on the one hand by scribality and on the other by the overcoming of the historical distance to the text. Hence the modern criteria of textual cohesion cannot be applied directly to the conditions of the formation or of the original reception of the Pauline epistles.

If then we desire to look for indicators which allow us to draw conclusions about the original form of 2 Cor. we shall hardly find them in the sphere of the original conditions for the writing and reception of ancient letters. For a letter-writer could write – as we see it – in a completely incohesive manner and yet the letter would be received by the original recipient as uniform. Consequently we shall now ask the further question relating to the transmission and editing of the Pauline epistles: What clues do the forms of ancient *textual transmission* give as to whether and how an epistle such as 2 Cor. could be edited and in the process compiled?

2.3. *Transmission and revision of the Pauline epistles*

The phase of the revision of the Pauline epistles will be examined generally under the concept 'editing'. By this, however, I mean for the most part deliberate editorial procedures on the textual form of the Pauline letters such as compilations or interpolations which are thought to have been concluded in the second or third post-Pauline generation, i.e. at the latest around 90–100 CE. With the concept of 'editing' we come methodologically into the area of editorial criticism of the Pauline letters. Related to such editorial criticism and historical editing we shall then consider quite different aspects of the history of an epistle such as 2 Cor., namely the insertion of interpolations, the possibility of compiling individual letters into an epistolary anthology, the construction of a collection of Pauline epistles or that process of editing which *Trobisch*, for example, designates as 'the author's recension'.

---

32. Dörrie, 'Methodik', pp. 122f. Dörrie further remarks: 'One would never have thought of making trivial texts such as comments in the present-day language the subject of a philological investigation. Philological effort is only expended when a gap must be surmounted, when a text poses a riddle, when the reader must perform a type of decoding.'

The critique/history of editing or 'redaction criticism'[33] of epistolary literature occurs mainly as a theological 'reappraisal of the substance of tradition'.[34] Thus redaction criticism tests whether the canonical 2 Cor. was put together by Paul himself or by a later editorial process and whether interpolations were introduced into the present text. Redaction criticism can also take up again the question of textual cohesion from a different angle: for if a letter has been found to be incohesive by literary criticism, this assessment can be re-tested by redaction criticism.

The process of the editing of Pauline letters (see below) can also be seen as a redactional process, conditioned either by the recipients or by the author: *Bornkamm* reconstructs the process of a letter-collection brought about by the recipients since he understands redaction criticism as an insight 'into the beginnings of a Pauline letter-anthology upon which it is otherwise difficult to throw light' 'and consequently into the early history of the apostolic canon'.[35] The later canonical form of the Pauline epistles is the basis for Bornkamm's hypothesis of the composition of 2 Cor. He thinks that the tendency in later years to idealize the picture of the Apostle lies, not in additions or adulterations by the 'collector and editor of the Pauline correspondence' but in 'the composition of the whole'.[36] For *Trobisch* the author himself is responsible for the editing since the collection of the Pauline letters goes back to the intention of the author, Paul. Trobisch represents the thesis of an 'author's reworking', i.e. Paul's personal editing of his letters, and thereby makes redaction criticism begin with the author himself. If this is so 2 Cor. too in its present form would have been processed by Paul himself for copying, distribution and collection.[37] This assumption is supported by the fact that ancient authors often kept copies of their letters and that the recipients made copies of valued letters which they had received. In the letters of *Cyprian* too there is evidence that he had before him copies of his own letters or copies of someone else's letters.[38] Presumably *Augustine* also had archives in which, *inter alia*, the drafts of his letters were stored.[39] Moreover in ancient times

---

33.   In the 1970s redaction criticism examined the final form of the Gospels with the following aim: 'It is concerned with studying the theological motivation of an author as this is revealed in the collection, arrangement, editing and modification of traditional material, and in the composition of new material or the creation of new forms within the traditions of early Christianity,' Perrin, *Redaction Criticism*, p. 1. In this way redaction criticism can be understood as composition criticism.

34.   Thus Merk, 'Redaktionsgeschichte', p. 381. This article is of fundamental importance for the definition of redaction criticism and the history of redaction.

35.   Bornkamm, 'Vorgeschichte', p. 190.

36.   Bornkamm, 'Vorgeschichte', p. 184. Bornkamm sees such an idealization e.g. in the insertion of the section 2 Cor. 2.14ff.

37.   Trobisch, *Endredaktion*, p. 93; *Paulusbriefe*, pp. 107f. and *Entstehung*, pp. 126ff.

38.   Cyprian, *Epistulae* 27.ii.1 and 27.iii.2.

39.   See Divjak, 'Epistulae', pp. 907f.

it was quite usual for an author to write different versions, i.e. texts were reworked by the author before publication.[40] If one assumes a revision by the author himself one comes, as far as the explanation for compilations of letters is concerned, into the realm of ancient *cento*-literature: the possible process of a letter's compilation takes place as a patchwork compilation at the stage of the author of the letter himself.

Trobisch's hypothesis is hermeneutically far-reaching for the understanding of Paul as a letter-writer and for the significance of the Pauline collection of letters. For if this is so Paul himself – like *Pliny the Younger* – initiated the collection and edition of a corpus of letters, at least in the spirit of a literary legacy. Paul in that case would already have designated his letters as literary documents. This, however, seems hardly plausible for the Pauline epistles for two reasons: on the one hand the eschatological orientation of Pauline thinking (see, for example, 1 Cor. 7.29ff.) makes a longer-term planning of the publication of a letter improbable. On the other, no signs are to be found in the Pauline letters of an editorial revision by the author himself.

As we have seen the concept of 'editing' offers too few possibilities of differentiating terminologically the various aspects and questions raised by the history of the transmission and processing of a letter such as 2 Cor. But this is methodologically necessary.[41] On the other hand the concept of 'revision' can be so subdivided that it is possible to have a differentiated perception of the transmission of the text in the form of copying, reproducing and editing up to the time the text became part of the canon. If one differentiates between these revisional processes, this does not mean that the same co-workers of Paul were not active as secretaries, copyists and collators. But the *processes* of revision should be kept separate.

In like manner one must differentiate in the so-called 'school of Paul' between the transmitters who revised the letters in the broadest sense and the theologically motivated pseudepigraphers.

The concept 'school of Paul' first appears in *H.J. Holtzmann* (1880) in connection with the critical analysis of the Pastoral epistles.[42] The assumption of a Pauline school implies on the one hand that Paul himself

---

40. See on this Heyworth, 'Autorenvarianten', p. 361, with reference to Cicero, *Epistulae ad Atticum* XII.6a.1; XIII.21a. An example of this from the time of the early church could be Cyprian's *De unitate ecclesiae* which was written in two different versions by the author himself: see W. Wischmeyer, 'Cyprian', p. 509.

41. If these processes are not distinguished, one can arrive at sweeping theological statements – as in P. Müller, *Anfänge*, p. 304 – who does not differentiate between revision, compilation and editing: 'The emphasis on the Pauline epistles as apostolic doctrine can be seen in the compilation of various letters into one longer one as a further aim of editorial work – alongside the collection and clarification of the letters. This can be seen on the example of 2 Cor'.

42. Holtzmann, *Pastoralbriefe*, pp. 110 and 117.

falls back in his letters on community traditions or on material from discussions within the school,[43] and on the other that, after the Apostle's death, the Pauline legacy was not only handed down but that Pauline theology – with Paul's authority – was continued.[44] The transmission process of the Pauline letters was therefore deliberately expedited by a generation, at the latest trito-Pauline, which 'edited'. Consequently the letters were collected, worked over and published as literature of the school.

Differentiating between those who handed the material down and theologians enables us to make the necessary distinction between on the one hand copyists or scribes who pass on, collect and disseminate the Pauline epistles and on the other the 'theologians' of the school of Paul who independently write new, pseudonymous letters.[45]

The intention behind pseudepigraphy is 'to propagate particular intentions or teachings under the guise of an established authority'.[46] In Deuteropaulinism and later in the Tritopaulines and the so-called 'catholic epistles' – right up to the time of the Apostolic Fathers – we can see that the form of the Pauline letters had authority and influenced style and that independent, even though pseudepigraphical, writings of the later generations were transmitted side by side with the genuine Pauline epistles.

Hence in the following considerations there will be a double terminological differentiation: first, the activity of the so-called redactional generation will be described generally as 'revision' (*Bearbeitung*), the individual aspects of which must then be examined more closely. Second, a distinction should be made within the so-called Pauline school between 'transmitters' and 'theologians'.

2.3.1. *Copying*

If we now differentiate in the school of Paul between transmitters and theologians, we might be able to reconstruct the individual steps in which this school dealt with the authentic Pauline letters. The first task which such a transmitter performed was that of copying.

The copying of Pauline letters must have taken place without further

---

43. Thus above all Conzelmann, 'Paulus', pp. 177ff.

44. So Ollrogg, *Paulus*, particularly pp. 203ff.

45. It cannot, however, be ruled out that the so-called pseudepigraphical Pauline letters were mistakenly attributed to Paul during the copying process although they had not originally been written under Paul's name. See Speyer, *Fälschung*, p. 41: 'If scrolls contained one or more anonymous writings alongside orthonymous ones, false attributions could easily have been made erroneously particularly when one considers that anonymous writings with a similar content to orthonymous ones were frequently added at the end of such scrolls.'

46. Fürst, 'Pseudepigraphie', p. 80, in relation to the apocryphal correspondence between Paul and Seneca.

deliberate manipulations of their content.[47] This can be seen in the early practice of quoting as contrasted with the homogeneity of the copies of the earliest existing manuscripts: while a quotation can be structured independently of the form of the text[48] the early manuscript tradition reflects how 'unexpectedly correctly and faithfully' the text of the New Testament was handed down.[49] The copyists/scribes also represent a separate group of transmitters at the time of the redactional generation.[50] Those copyists 'who take over the mistakes of the document before them' count in ancient times as 'good scribes',[51] for they could have handled the text freely, as occasionally happens, i.e. they could have corrected mistakes in it.

To clarify the interests pursued by the copyists in transmitting and copying the Pauline epistles the only helpful evidence we have in the end is that the earliest manuscripts still preserved scarcely vary. Consequently we can assume that even at an earlier date the first copyists of the Pauline letters in like manner wrote professionally and had very little theological or literary interest.[52] But glosses or interpolations could still have made their way into the text.

From the process of copying we can draw the following inference for our assessment of the present form of 2 Cor.: If 2 Cor. appears to be incohesive, this may not simply mean that it is a compilation; it can also indicate a faithful transmission of the text. This means, little can be inferred about the original form of 2 Cor. from a consideration of the process of copying.

2.3.2. *Compilation of letters*
2.3.2.1. *On the problem*

How might compilations in 2 Cor. have come into being, and how can these be explained? For if 2 Cor. as we have it is really made up of several

---

47. See here B. Aland, 'Handschriften', p. 397: 'Scribes are quite obviously a type of recipient who previously have scarcely been noticed ... Scribes are not interpreters.'

48. See already in Horace, *Ars poetica* 134f. or Quintilian, *Institutiones* x.2.5. See also B. Aland, 'Rezeption', p. 30: 'The copying of textual manuscripts and the quoting of texts in theological tracts appears to have taken place at a very early date, side by side, each uninfluenced by the other'.

49. For individual details see B. Aland, 'Rezeption', pp. 27f.

50. See also McDonnell, 'Writing', p. 490, who assesses the copying of texts in ancient Rome as having been a professional occupation.

51. Mazal, *Buchkultur*, p. 162.

52. Roberts, *Manuscript*, p. 21 characterizes the copyists as 'tradesmen, farmers, minor government officials to whom knowledge of and writing in Greek was an essential skill, but who had few or no literary interests'.

letters it represents a collection or compilation of letters – as is the relevant technical term in NT exegesis. What lies concealed behind this expression?

In general what is understood by compilation is a 'collection of excerpts from other writings'.[53] Such a compilation of documents cannot be positively proved and in classical philology is scarcely given methodical consideration. At most Pliny the Younger counts, in the sense of a self-editor, as a compiler of his own letters.[54] In NT exegesis, too, letter-compilations are taken into account but the concept 'compilation' is not defined further. What is implicitly meant is the process in which separate letters or fragments of letters were re-assembled in a redactional procedure. If this were so the letters must have been so revised that the individual prefaces and closing addresses were omitted.

But two objections can be raised to such a deliberate, *redactionally motivated* compilation of Pauline letters: first, the Pauline epistles were from the start 'public' letters which quickly became familiar through being read aloud and being exchanged. Hence it remains doubtful whether they could have been revised and compiled unchallenged at a later date. Second, it is incomprehensible that a compiler revising 2 Cor. should have made his compilation in such an incohesive form. Would it not have been more likely that this presumed editor would have polished up the letters in the course of his editorial revision?

From our observations up till now we can see that at the time of the so-called redactional generation it was possible that letter-compilations could have been made but that this is hardly conceivable during the process of copying or as a deliberate editorial intervention. Here we must consider *material* and *technical* aspects which have not been taken into account in previous hypotheses of compilation. For 2 Cor. could have been compiled for material-technical reasons. Two technical possibilities will be presented in the following.

2.3.2.2. *Two attempts to solve the problem: on the technique of compilation*
There are two possible solutions which could explain the technical requirements for the compilation of single letters into one comprehensive letter such as 2 Cor.: Paul wrote his epistles either on wooden or wax tablets or on single sheets of papyrus. In both cases the letters could have been compiled in the course of being preserved. In this connection we must reconsider the possibility that Paul as a letter-writer himself played a part in compiling the letters.

---

53. Thus the definition in *Meyers Enzyklopädisches Lexikon*, Vol. 14 (1975), p. 109.
54. On Pliny as compiler see Sherwin-White, *Letters*, pp. 50f.

(a) *Letters written on wooden or wax tablets*

Paul's epistles could have been written and dispatched on *wooden tablets*, the so-called *pinaces* (see also Lk. 1.63).[55] Wooden tablets were written upon with ink.[56] But it is also possible that wooden tablets in the form of wax tablets or *ceratae* (κῆρος) were used although wooden tablets are sometimes considered to have been generally more common: 'It is now suspected that such wooden leaves or tablets were a more common writing material throughout the Roman Empire than tablets coated with wax or papyrus.'[57]

Wax tablets were widely used in the Graeco-Roman sphere in ancient times.[58] 'The shallow depression in the folds was ... filled with wax; texts were incised into this with a stylus and could be erased with its flattened end. Cheaper than wax-tablets which were often made in workshops and sold commercially were simple little wooden tablets (perhaps the *pugillares* in the text) which were written upon with ink ...'.[59] Wax tablets, like wooden tablets, were also known and used in the Hebraic-Aramaic speaking areas.[60] They were used in different connections: for notes,

---

55. As the earliest evidence for *pinaces* see Homer, *Iliad*, 6, 168f: ... γράψας ἐν πίνακι πτυκτῶσι θυμοφθόρα πολλά. Sharpe, 'Dakleh', p. 130 also sees an indication of wooden or wax tablets in Lk. 1.63.

56. For details see Mazal, *Buchkultur*, pp. 62f. The finds in Vindolanda (England) – see Cavallo, 'Buch', p. 810 or Bowman/Thomas, *Writing-Tablets*, particularly pp. 32ff. – were wooden tablets written upon with ink but also so-called *tabulae ceratae* which were filled with wax, see also Blanck, *Buch*, p. 50 and Thomas, 'Latin', pp. 203ff. Crake, 'Annalen', p. 267 and Kornemann, 'Form', pp. 65ff.

57. Millard, *Pergament*, p. 25. See also v. Brandt, *Werkzeug*, p. 67.

58. For illustration see Turner, *Manuscripts*, p. 33. See also Roberts, *Birth*, pp. 11ff. In the ancient world wax tablets were 'probably the most common alternative for written recording and tablets with charters, letters and school exercises have come to light in many archaeological excavations of the Roman period', Bischoff, *Paläographie*, p. 29. See also Kleberg, *Buchhandel*, p. 73 and also Plutarch, *Brutus* 5.3f. or Quintilian, *Institutiones* x.3.31f.: *scribi optime ceris, in quibus facillima est ratio delendi ... ne latas quidem ultra modum esse ceras uelim ...* Moreover, papyrus was considerably more expensive as a writing-material. See also Viereck/Zucker, *Papyri*, pp. 203ff.

59. Steinmann, 'Schriftwesen', p. 85. On the differentiation between wooden and wax tablets see also White, *Light*, p. 213 and Mazal, *Buchkultur*, pp. 63ff. or Blanck, *Buch*, pp. 46ff.

60. On the use of *pinaces* in Judaism, see Haran, 'Codex', p. 219: In Israel in the Talmudic period the *pinax* was used. Its use was widespread and by force of conservatism and long use prevailed over the codex, which the Talmud does not mention at all. Among the Bar Kokhba letters (discovered in Nahal Hever) there was a wooden tablet inscribed with ink and written in Aramaic, see Sirat, 'Tablettes', p. 55 and Hezser, *Literacy*, p. 276. As earliest and only example of a *pinax* made from papyrus Haran, 'Codex', pp. 217f. cites Mishna Kelim 24.7. See also Pardee, *Handbook*, p. 163. By and large, however, Pardee determines in relation to the materials of Hebrew texts: 'all the pre-Christian Hebrew letters are written on ostraca ... while all those of the Bar Kokhba period are written on papyrus'.

inventories and contracts but also for 'taking down dictation or transcribing speeches and for drafting texts of all kinds', including letters.[61] But wax tablets do not last forever, with the result that even wax tablet findings from the eleventh century are rare.[62] If individual letters, e.g. of the Corinthian correspondence, were sent on such wax tablets, the letters contained shorter messages and a possible reply from the recipient. Then, like the parchment palimpsests later, the wax tablets could have been smoothed over and reused. Hence the letters written on wax tablets were part of a lively correspondence between Paul and the Corinthian community.[63]

But with regard to the Corinthian correspondence it is less important whether Paul used wax tablets or wooden tablets inscribed with ink. The common hermeneutical relevance of the theory of wax tablets or wooden tablets lies in the fact that it suggests a differentiated *reconstruction* of letter-production. For if one understands the letters as short, communicative correspondence letters, it is quite conceivable that they were not only written and dictated on wax or wooden tablets but that they were also sent on them and possibly sent back with a reply from the recipient. Wax tablets could also be used for longer documents. In that case several wax tablets were joined together and so arose so-called 'wax tablet books' or 'polyptycha' *(tabellae, pugillaria, codicilli)* which were an early form of codex and were used for high-quality literary texts. If we assume that Paul used such wax tablets for at least some of his correspondence with his congregations, we can establish a *continuity in the form of transmission* with the codices typical of early Christianity.

The assumption that Paul's letters were sent on wax tablets also has an important implication for the *conservation* of the letters: since wax tablets could be reused as palimpsests, copies would have to be made immediately to preserve the letters written on the wax tablets. It is conceivable that the copies which had already achieved literary value would have been made initially on wax-tablet polyptycha then later on papyrus codices or directly on papyrus or parchment in the form of scrolls or codices. These copies of

---

61. Steinmann, 'Schriftwesen', p. 85. On wax-tablet letters see Pliny, *Epistulae* VI.16.8 and on the Vindolanda findings, Bowman/Thomas, *Writing-Tablets*, pp. 37f. and in general v. Albrecht, *Geschichte*, p. 409.

62. See a report on the finding of wax tablets in the *Neue Zürcher Zeitung, International Edition*, on Friday, 1 December 2000, p. 33.

63. As an example from Latin epistolography we can consider Cicero's *Epistulae ad Familiares* VI.18.1. The recipient 'could smooth over the writing after he had read the letter and write his reply on the tablet', Mazal, *Buchkultur*, p. 65. That is why the wax tablets were later used for shorter messages, see Schmidt, 'Epistolographie', p. 324. If the Pauline epistles were drafted on such wax tablets, the letter to the Romans could have been an exception. Here we are dealing with a letter of introduction which Paul might therefore have designed as a longer, more stylized document and written on papyrus.

the letters to be preserved were stored in archives by private individuals.[64] Hence if Paul really used wooden or wax tablets for an original letter, this meant – in so far as the recipients were interested in preserving the letter – that the letter must be copied immediately. Consequently the wax or wooden tablet theory suggests that we must conceive the preservation of the Pauline letters by the Corinthian community as a recipient-oriented process of immediate copying of the letter.

In this process of copying letters it could also have come about at a very early date – namely at the end of the 50s or beginning of the 60s[65] – that there came into being compilations of letters, i.e. when several wax tablets were made into a polyptych, collected and copied onto a papyrus codex, the so-called note-books (*membranae*). The copies on papyrus then contained several letters strung together. If letters were lost[66] the compilation created an incomplete corpus of correspondence in which these losses were not apparent.

Summing up, the 'wooden or wax tablet theory' therefore facilitates the following reconstruction of a possible compilation of letters: the Corinthian correspondence was a lively communication of Paul with the Corinthians and of the Corinthians with Paul. The individual letters of this correspondence were possibly written on wooden or wax tablets. Then, if the tablets were sent back, copies must have been made in Corinth before this occurred, onto other tablets, polyptychs or codices on papyrus or parchment. This practice of preserving copies was perhaps selective and partial. This has a twofold significance for the *process of collection* of Pauline letters: first, the letter-writer, Paul, did not originally write his congregational letters for preservation and consequently hardly with a proto-canonical claim; and second, the process of collection of the Pauline letters in Corinth began with the selective copying of the letters. Hence the editorial compilation of the letters was not motivated by their content; it arose in connection with the preservation and copying of the letters. In this case the compilation would not have taken place through a complicated interlocking of individual letters but simply when they were

---

64. The letters were probably archivized in the same way as e.g. certificates and letters on papyrus scrolls in 'residences of private individuals' – i.e. stored for the most part in earthenware pots, Vössing, 'Archiv', p. 1023. Hence these were house-archives which at a later period were of service to the community. The archive of the auctioneer Caecilius Iucundus (first century CE) was found in Pompeii. This contained several documents in the form of sealed wax tablets. There was no clear distinction in antiquity between library and archive, see Vössing, 'Bibliothek', p. 645.

65. Klauck, 'Compilation', pp. 153ff. also concludes that the Pauline letters could only have been compiled at a very early date.

66. The loss of letters in antiquity is quite conceivable, see e.g. Seneca, *De brevitate vitae* 5.2, which mentions a letter of Cicero to Atticus which has not been preserved.

gathered together. This makes the process of compilation seem much more plausible.[67]

(b) *Sheets of papyrus*

But another way of letter-writing and letter-preservation is also conceivable. If Paul wrote his letters on individual sheets of papyrus this could also have led to compilations.

Papyrus was commercially cultivated only in Egypt and from there sold above all in the area of the eastern Mediterranean. Papyrus appears to have been the preferred writing-material for letters in Roman Palestine although it is thought that wooden or wax tablets were the most used writing-materials in the entire Mediterranean area in the Roman Empire. When Paul in 2 Cor. 3.3, in connection with the metaphor of the letter of recommendation, says: ἐγγεγραμμένη οὐ μέλανι, the ink mentioned could refer either to inscribed sheets of papyrus or to writing on wooden tablets. Hence the metaphor should not be understood as evidence of Paul's preference for letters written on papyrus.

If Paul sent sheets of papyrus, the process of preservation must be conceived as follows: after the individual papyrus-sheets were folded, sealed and sent by messenger to Corinth, compilations could have occurred in the collection of these papyrus sheets when the sheets were glued together into a papyrus scroll as a so-called *volumen* in the course of being put into the archives.[68] This being so, we cannot rule out the possibility that leaves were transposed in the course of collecting the letters and when they were later copied into codices.[69]

(c) *The author as compiler?*

When considering such scenarios of compilation we must also take into account the role of the author. Paul as author could have played an active part as compiler of his letter in two ways: he could have sent the addressee a letter which contained the copy of an earlier letter; or a collection and compilation of letters could have been made within the circle of his collaborators from a notebook which contained copies of earlier letters.

---

67. The Ciceronian correspondence (see below) is a restricted analogy for the compilation of a letter-corpus – not, however, as an intertwining but rather as a sequence of several letters; see Trobisch, *Entstehung*, p. 120 or Klauck, 'Compilation', p. 154: 'Partition theories are not a priori implausible, but they should be kept rather simple, serial addition being more probable than interpolation of fragments.'

68. See as example the papyrus collection *P. Vindob. Lt. 1* in the Austrian National Library: this is a textbook put together from single sheets of letters which probably reaches back to the time of Augustus (the third letter is dated 17–14 BC), see Ballaira, *Esempi*, pp. 59ff.

69. Maehler, 'Books', p. 252 refers to how the codices were produced: 'The text was written before the sheets were stitched together ... Pagination is frequent; sometimes quires are also numbered on their first pages'.

Since ancient letter-writers frequently kept a copy of their letters, a copy could be sent to the addressee if the letter was incomplete or damaged upon receipt or if he had lost it.[70] Letters were often lost through the 'unreliability of the messengers'. Consequently the author could have sent a new letter which opened with a copy of the earlier letter followed by the new script which made explicit reference to the earlier. Hence a letter itself could already be a 'compilation' of letters constructed by the author.

But another possibility is sometimes taken into consideration: Paul himself might have kept copies of his letters 'in a small codex notebook'.[71] For – as we saw above – wax tablets, for example, which were used for drafts, outlines or sketches and served the author as note-pads for the actual letter, were preserved as later copies of the letter. Cicero, too, had copies of his own letters.[72] It remains, however, an open question whether Paul kept copies of his letters for the archives or whether he intended a later publication of the letters. Moreover it is questionable whether the technical conditions under which Paul could write his letters and possibly preserve them are comparable to those under which Cicero wrote.

If Paul himself initiated the collection and compilation of his letters, the first phase of collecting the letters would not have been carried out by the congregations but by the author in the course of producing the letters. Independently of whether Paul intended this or whether this process occurred unintentionally the compilation would then have to be seen as *production-oriented*, i.e. as an act of transmitting the texts initiated by the circle involved in producing the letter. This, however, does not fit with the normal use of the term 'compilation' and belongs more in the realm of *cento*-literature. On the other hand the technical material conditions mentioned above in (a) and (b) make it possible to envisage the process of compilation as a receptive form of preserving the letters without having to suppose programmatic redactional measures on the part of the author or in the circle of his co-workers: such a 'redactional' procedure would be thinkable in the event that the possibility of making copies of the letter was used or at least existed on the part of those who produced the letter – i.e. Paul or his colleagues. Consequently I should prefer to consider the compiling of letters as a *reception-oriented act* of preserving a text.

2.3.2.3. *Analogies – (Letter-)compilations in antiquity*
The search for ancient analogies to the compilation of Pauline letters helps to make the process of compilation clearer and more plausible. The

---

70. See e.g. Cicero, *Epistulae ad Quintum fratrem* II.12.5 or *Epistulae ad Familiares* VII.25.1.

71. Thus Richards, 'Codex', p. 142 with reference to 2 Tim. 4.13.

72. See Cicero, *Epistulae ad Atticum* II.12; II.13 – in the second letter Cicero laments that the first had been lost.

three areas of ancient literature which stand in a temporal and spatial vicinity to the possible compilation-process of Pauline letters are Graeco-Roman, early Christian and early Jewish literature. In dealing with these three areas I shall not only ask in principle about the nature of the compilation but also whether and how texts were generally edited and under what conditions and with what intention texts or letters were compiled.

(a) *Graeco-Roman (epistolary) literature*

It is quite conceivable that compilations were made as editorial revisions in the course of the transmission of Graeco-Roman literature. Employing an analysis of authenticity[73] ancient textual revisions and additions in the course of editing the writings are suspected in the reception of Virgil and Ovid. But letters could be falsified or show interpolations even during the lifetime of an author.[74]

A possible analogy for letter-compilation in general in Graeco-Roman literature are the letters of Cicero.[75] These letters, however, although initially having an impact on style, did not have an unbroken reception in later times, particularly in the Middle Ages, unlike the Pauline epistles. The processes of transmission and canonization of the two bodies of letters are not comparable. Yet the conditions of production and reception of Cicero's letters allow us to draw conclusions about possible compilations of ancient letters.

The dictation of a letter could extend over several days. Thus it was possible when one received new information to add a postscript to a letter already written but not yet sent or to write a new letter (*Epistulae ad Quintum fratrem* III.1.8ff.). Temporal or local incohesions in a letter can be understood either as postscripts or as indicating a letter-compilation: postscripts in the letter could arise because of a delay on the part of the messenger (*Epistulae ad Quintum fratrem* III.1.23). However the change of locality within the letter (see §21) and the period of time in which it originated indicate that the letter mentioned, at least from §21ff., was put together by Cicero himself. On the other hand, §§1–19 are an example of a letter written continuously in one locality replying to correspondence which has arrived while it was being written.

It is a matter of dispute when Cicero's letters were compiled. Atticus or Tiro or an editor in the first century CE could have compiled these letters

---

73. See Zwierlein, *Revisionen*, p. 80.

74. Cyprian voices this suspicion in relation to a letter which he has received and wants to send back to the addressees to check its authenticity, *Epistulae* 9.II.1: ... *ne quid ex uero uel subtractum sit uel inmutatum, eandem ad uos epistulam authenticam remisi* ...

75. See the detailed analysis in Klauck, 'Compilation' or *Briefliteratur*, p. 132.

at a later date.[76] In reconstructing the sequence of the authentic letters implicit indications of chronology or occasional dates at the end of the letter are given validity.[77] These chronological criteria could scarcely be valid for the Pauline letters. The details within the text of 2 Cor. which refer to 'historical' events are not sufficient to date the epistolary correspondence. Conversely 2 Cor. can also not be interpreted from reconstructed 'historical' events.

Furthermore, the possible compilation of Cicero's letters took place under conditions which do not appear to be analogous to the process of compilation of the Pauline epistles: the process of compilation of Cicero's letters is to a large extent connected to the process of their being edited. The assumption that Cicero's letters were compiled is, however, without doubt an important indication of the possibility in principle of letter-compilations in the Roman world even if the conditions for the compilation of Cicero's letters differ in substantial respects from a possible compilation-process of the Pauline epistles.

(b) *Early Christian (epistolary) literature*

In early Christian literature the *collection of the letters of Ignatius* represents a possible example of a compilation of letters.[78] The reconstruction of authentic individual letters of Ignatius (mid–end second century CE) is, however, made more difficult by the fact that the transmission of the text is not uniform, marked by three different recensions. Here there is a fundamental difference from the uniform manuscript tradition of 2 Cor.

The *Letter of Polycarp* represents a similar problematical analogy for a letter-compilation. It is generally considered to be inconsistent and contains interpolations which are related to those in Ignatius. But here too the uniformity cannot be finally decided since the manuscript tradition does not offer a coherent text, which has to be reconstructed by recourse to Eusebius or a Latin manuscript.[79]

Finally, a 'compilation' is postulated in respect of the *Letters of Cyprian*.[80] Cyprian's preferred literary genre is the letter: 'Even all his tracts ... are tailored on the pattern of a letter.' Cyprian's letter-corpus has grown together from sets of letters, 'put together in important

---

76. See Klauck, 'Compilation', p. 140: '... but it is not clear at which stage of this process compilations were made. They may have been produced by scribes through the centuries, they may result from mechanical accidents like the damage and loss of pages or the displacement of pages in a codex.'

77. The chronological details are particularly connected with contemporary political history. On the giving of a date see Cicero, *Epistulae ad Familiares* XI.5.1.

78. See Trobisch, *Entstehung*, pp. 120f. and Vielhauer, *Geschichte*, p. 154.

79. See Eusebius, *Hist. Eccl.* III.36.13–15.

80. See Clarke, *Letters*, 1, pp. 7ff.

formations'.[81] Cyprian himself was responsible for this in that he sent letters containing earlier letters (e.g. *Epistulae* 20 and 27). To this extent in respect of Cyprian's letter-writing we can speak of 'official epistolography' or an editing of letters initiated by the author himself. The extant correspondence consists of 82 letters of which 16 were not written by Cyprian.

Hence with regard to Cyprian's letters when we talk of 'compilation' we mean their collection into a letter-corpus, which presumably was concluded only at the end of the fourth century and was barely subjected to systematic criteria though many of the letters can be arranged chronologically. In this letter-corpus there are also indications of an interpolation: a tract by Novatian (*De trinitate*) is given without a heading among Cyprian's letters.

Consequently, because of the complicated history of their transmission, neither the letters of Cyprian nor Ignatius nor Polycarp can be usefully compared with the conditions under which a compilation of the Pauline epistles took place.

(c) *Early Jewish (epistolary) literature*

When one occasionally suspects compilations in Jewish apocalypses,[82] the concept 'compilation' is used here in another sense, for the *Ethiopian Enoch* and *4 Ezra* are writings which came into being as pseudepigraphs and developed in a long process of literary growth.

4 Ezra in particular is controversial from the point of view of *Literarkritik*. The more recent assessment of this debate can be summed up as follows: 'Although such a question cannot, perhaps, be regarded as permanently settled, many scholars today tend to regard chapters 3–14 as representing the author's own conception and handiwork.'[83]

In the case of apocalyptic writings such as 4 Ezra, the *literarcritical* question is source-critical. With regard to the Pauline letters, on the other hand, the *literarcritical* terminus 'compilation' denotes the circumstance that orthonymous, authentic letters were rearranged and gathered together at a later date and certainly not that the texts for their part grew in a literary sense. The *Sibyllines*, which were written from the second century BCE to the third/fourth centuries CE, partly in a Jewish and partly in a Christian context, were subjected to just such a *literarcritical* analysis in the sense of source-criticism. They are considered to be 'collected material', particularly because of their contents.[84]

If on the other hand one looks for early Jewish writings which are both

---

81. Gülzow, *Cyprianus*, pp. 541 and 542.
82. See Volz, *Eschatologie*, p. 5.
83. Metzger, *Ezra*, p. 522.
84. Merkel, *Sibyllinen*, p. 1059.

interesting from the *literarcritical* aspect and are comparable to the Pauline letters in respect of their orthonymity, one is led to the writings of Josephus or Philo of Alexandria. The *testimonium Flavianum* in Josephus's *Antiquities* (18.3.3/63–64) is a much-discussed example of a later insertion into the text, i.e. an interpolation.

In recent years it has rarely been accepted that the *testimonium* as a whole is a later, Christian interpolation: 'One called attention to the pronounced conservatism of the Christian transmission of texts.'[85] Hence there is currently a prevailing consensus that one assumes at most a Christian revision of the passage: 'The passage is at basis genuine, although it has probably been altered in some details by Christian transmitters of the text.'[86]

In the realm of early Jewish epistolary literature, compilations of letters are otherwise rarely suspected. A letter which comes close to the NT epistles is the *Epistula Baruch*, part of the Syriac *Apocalypse of Baruch* (at the latest around 130 CE).

The *Epistula Baruch* is contained in *syrBar* 78–86/87. It was written by the author of the *Apocalypse* and consequently belongs to the original fabric of the text although here there exists a partially separate letter-transmission.[87] Thematic incohesions within the letter – e.g. 85.1–5 – are not considered to break the unity of the letter and consequently are not subjected to a *literarcritical* analysis.

Hence in respect of early Jewish literature questions of *Literarkritik* must for the most part be treated by source criticism. For in the majority of these writings which *literarcriticism* finds to be controversial we are dealing with pseudonymous or anonymous writings, the literary growth-process of which is difficult to apprehend. In the case of orthonymous writings, i.e. those of well-known authors such as Josephus or Philo, later textual revisions such as interpolations are discussed, but not revisions in the form of compilations. This is based on the fact that the authors themselves were active as writers, i.e. gave their texts a literary form and thereby led to their publication.

2.3.2.4. *Compilations of letters: an appraisal*

Possible analogies to compilations in ancient literature make us more alert to look at the specific *conditions* of the compilation of the Pauline letters. Ancient corpora of letters such as the letters of Cicero could be compiled. This, however, ensued with editorial intent. When dealing with the Pauline epistles on the other hand, four aspects appear to be specific: first, the Pauline letters are certainly orthonymous texts, but they are not

---

85. Mason, *Josephus*, p. 254.
86. Attridge, 'Josephus', p. 216.
87. See Taatz, *Briefe*, p. 59.

literary formed texts for such could have perhaps been edited later but not compiled. Second, the compilation of the Pauline letters must have taken place at an early date, i.e. they were not subject to the interests of an edition of the epistles. Third, the earliest extant manuscript transmission of the Pauline letters, which begins with P[46] (end of the second century CE), is unified. For its part it presupposes a longer preceding unified process of transmission. The codices preserved indicate retrospectively a continuous tradition of the Pauline letters and enable us to draw conclusions about the meticulousness with which the copyists copied the texts of the letters. And fourth, there are no explicit chronological details in 1 and 2 Cor. which refer to contemporary historical events and allow us to infer the sequence of the Corinthian correspondence.

Thus the question must finally be raised: Which criteria of *literarcriticism* for establishing compilations have till now proved meaningful? *Linguistic criteria* can only serve inadequately to assess the cohesion of 2 Cor. since incohesions could have been caused by the author himself in the literary structuring of the text.

But we can see that compilations could have been made through the technical means of writing: the letters were strung together during their transmission, i.e. in the course of being copied from wax tablets onto scrolls or codices for the purpose of their preservation. Hence in the compilation of letters we can conceive of a sequencing of individual letters rather than an interweaving of the same. This also indicates that complicated compilation-models for the reconstruction of the Corinthian correspondence are implausible.

The assumption that Paul's letters were compiled is significant for establishing the epistolographic typology of 2 Cor.: if 2 Cor. as we now have it was an authentic letter to a community, one could talk of a tract in the form of a letter. Now, however, it appears more likely that 2 Cor. is made up of separate letters and that these individual letters were compiled, one after the other, for technical reasons and in order to preserve them. If, therefore, 2 Cor. is a compilation of letters, the letter we have is an 'artificial letter' and not a genuine letter to a community.

Before these considerations on letter-compilation lead to a reconstruction of the original literary form of 2 Cor., I shall now outline the transition from the compilation of the letters to their editing and distribution.

2.3.3. *The 'copy'* (Abschrift) *as a process in the editing of the letter*
We go a step farther and, after considering the preservation of the letters, now turn to the publication of the Pauline epistles. This process of publication can be called edition and is usually defined as follows: '... an edition can be thought of as a mechanism intended to bring people texts

from out of an archive into a market'.[88] Edited texts are texts which already have a claim to be canonical or which are developing into such. Hence the editing of the Pauline letters does not only reflect their early prestige but also prepares for their being accepted into the canon. Here canonization is understood very generally in the cultural sense: 'Canonization is a special form of textualisation. The texts were not simply written down; their binding force was intensified.'[89] The following observations on the process of the so-called editing of the Pauline epistles will be carried out in four steps. First, we must question the intentionality of the publication of Pauline letters: can the publication of the Pauline letters really be explained as a deliberate editorial action or more as a process of collection? In a second step the technical aspect of this collection-process – i.e. the copying of the letters from the wax tablets onto a codex – will be explained. The third step will look for analogous ancient processes of collection and anthologies of letters. In the fourth and final step we must evaluate and apply the observations we have made on ancient writing materials and the technique of transmission to reconstruct the process of the writing and transmission of 2 Cor.

2.3.3.1. *On the term 'copy'* (Abschrift)

The concept of 'copy' can be a neutral description of the process of the publication of the Pauline epistles, whereas the concept of 'edition' – as we have seen – establishes a direct connection to canonization. The term 'copy' is defined in classical philology as follows: 'C[opy] must be understood in two senses: both as a c[opy] of a lit[erary] work from its first version through the various stages of its formation right up to the remodelling of the text into a book; and also as the particular c[opy] made for the programmed, "publishing" circulation of the same.'[90]

Consequently the concept of 'copy' for the moment leaves both options open with regard to the intentionality of a literary publication: texts or letters could be deliberately copied in order to be published or grow into a publishable book out of copies made for practical purposes. Following these observations we can envisage the process of copying the Pauline letters as follows: after the Pauline epistles were read aloud (1 Thess. 5.27; Rom. 16.16) and passed on (Gal. 1.2; 2 Cor. 1.1b; Col. 4.16; 2 Thess. 2.2; 3.17) they were copied for a wider distribution and by this means became familiar. The individual congregations on the spot preserved them in

---

88. 'An archive is like a wine-cellar for words; since what is produced far exceeds the possibilities of immediate consumption, prudence can suggest that the excess … should be stored someplace out of the way where it will not interfere with present needs but can wait patiently until it can be brought out someday to serve future ones', Most, *Texts*, v.

89. Assmann, *Stufen*, p. 14.

90. Dorandi/Sohn, 'Abschrift', p. 34; B. Aland, 'Textgeschichte', e.g. p. 157 describes the transmission of NT texts self-evidently as 'copy'.

family archives 'in copies' and handed them down farther.[91] 2 Tim. 4.13 is held to be the oldest reference to a Christian library. In the course of these processes letters might be lost. The genesis of the pseudepigraphical *Letter to the Laodicaeans* shows clearly that such a loss was already detected at the time of the early church and attempts made to compensate for this.

But how could the copies of letters kept in archives in the individual communities grow into epistolary anthologies? One may assume that 'collections stood at the beginning of the *Corpus Paulinum*'; initially the '*minor corpora*' which – conditioned by the technical means of production – grew up out of the copying one after the other of several Pauline letters written on wooden or wax tablets onto a wax-tablet polyptych or onto a papyrus scroll or a papyrus codex. During the process the letters could have been rearranged.

Thus the 'minor corpora' became '*prime corpora*', to which 1 and 2 Cor. could already have belonged,[92] and finally around the middle to the end of the second century – at the latest from the time of Marcion – were expanded to a '*total corpus*'. We cannot determine the place where this collection took place – it may have been in Corinth or Ephesus.[93] Possibly the minor corpora initially took shape in a decentralized way in the individual community archives.

It is clear that the copying and intercongregational exchange of Paul's letters in themselves can already be seen as a process of collecting the letters. Thus the process of editing might more properly be described as a process of 'copying': letters were copied for the purposes of preservation and exchange. Without there being any underlying interests in publishing or journalism these copies led to collections of letters being produced – i.e. the individual prime forms of the Pauline epistolary corpus. These assumptions can be supported by a further piece of technical evidence, namely the use and circulation of the codex in the Christian world.

2.3.3.2. *From wax tablet to codex*

In dealing with the question of the emergence of the codex – which is of the greatest interest, the 'most momentous development in the history of

91. Lindemann, 'Paulus im 2. Jahrhundert', p. 65.

92. 'According to the findings in both the manuscripts and in the Church Fathers, the letters to the Corinthians and that to the Hebrews always belonged to the "prime corpora"...', K. Aland, 'Entstehung', pp. 335f.

93. See above and compare the account in Lindemann, *Paulus im ältesten Christentum*, p. 32: 'One will ... simply have to be content with the assumption that the oldest collection of Pauline letters in all probability was made in one of the congregations within the area of Paul's missionary activity.'

the book until the invention of printing'[94] – one also inevitably retraces the history of the editing of the Pauline epistles since correlations can be discerned between the use of the codex and the editing and canonization of writings. As we shall see this applies even more to the use of the codex in the Christian world.

In ancient times book-scrolls and codices – on paper or parchment – counted as books and contained a unified work. But the form of the codex made it much easier to include all the works of an author. Consequently the use of the codex initiated a more comprehensive process of canonization. Therefore if codices were used in the early Christian era, this was a decisive factor in the process of the canonization of NT literature and the Pauline epistles. Hence in what follows we must ask how the emergence of the Christian codex affected the editorial process of Pauline letters or to what extent the use of the codex perhaps even initiated the canonization of the Pauline epistles. Paul's letters were – as we have seen – possibly originally sent on wax tablets or on separate sheets of papyrus. Wax tablets, however, in the form of *diptychs*, *triptychs* or *polyptychs* already represent an early form of codex – they were then known as *tabellae*, *pugillaria* or *codicilli*.[95] Hence it is suspected that the codex was originally the Roman form of a book. Codices existed – in Rome from the time of Augustus – but also in the form of so-called note-books or *membranae* of parchment. As such they remained in use but 'were used in a more varied way e.g. for drafts, occasional or daily notes or also in public and private records'.[96]

The earliest evidence for the use of a parchment codex is to be found in Martial (around 90 CE). Martial wanted to publish his own epigrammatic poetry in the form of a codex and make it manageable as reading-material on a journey even though he considered papyrus-scrolls to be of greater value.[97] We can also infer from Martial that parchment codices were already fashionable around the end of the first century CE (I.2).

Thus the parchment codex in general use from the fourth century developed from two different roots: 'In its formation' the codex is 'a reproduction of the diptych or polyptych made from wax tablets and has a

94. Roberts, *Birth*, p. 1. Roberts defines the codex thus: '... a collection of sheets of any material, folded double and fastened together at the back or spine, and usually protected by covers'.

95. Roberts, *Birth*, p. 1: 'There has never been any doubt about the physical origin of the codex, namely that it was developed from the wooden writing-tablet.' On *codicilli* see Tacitus, *Annales* IV.39.

96. Cavallo, 'Codex', p. 51.

97. See Martial, *Epigramme* e.g. I.2; XIV.184, 186, 188, 190.

precursor in the parchment notebook'.[98] Hence in its origins the codex is a Roman invention which then gains importance and popularity through the great Christian codices. This led in the fourth/fifth centuries to the transfer to codices of classical literature originally written on papyrus scrolls.

Initially these were papyrus codices which preserved the form of the parchment notebooks, but from the fourth century at the latest the more durable and resistant parchment codices were generally accepted in Christian literature too. Parchment codices could be reused as palimpsests, in this respect resembling the wax tablets.

Against the background of the development of the codex in early Christian literature the wax or wooden tablets can now be regarded as precursors of the parchment codex. On the one hand, a wax polyptych represents the primary form of the codex. If copies of wax tablets were made on papyrus or parchment codices for the purpose of preservation, there is continuity in the form of transmission. On the other hand Christian epistolary literature made use of the codex from a very early date. Roberts assumes that the Christians before 100 CE already made wide use of codices.[99]

At this period the use of the codex to this extent was generally still not the norm in the Graeco-Roman world – and consequently also not among the Jews: throughout the area book-scrolls were the predominant form. This is also apparent in the transmission of the LXX: one differentiated the Christian LXX from the Jewish LXX 'through the use of the *codex* instead of the Jewish *scroll*'.[100] Hence the Jewish or Christian origin of manuscripts was decided on the basis of the use of the codex.[101] Admittedly not all LXX texts on papyrus rolls are of Jewish provenance.

The far-reaching transition from scrolls to codices in the non-Christian world – 'the great revolution in the history of the book in antiquity'[102] – then took place between the third and fifth centuries CE, particularly in the realm of Roman jurisprudence.

If one perceives on the one hand a continuity in the history of books from wax-tablet polyptych to codex and on the other follows Roberts's thesis about the spreading of the codex-form in the Christian world before 100 CE, one can assume that the early Christian epistolary literature made

98.   Bischoff, *Paläographie*, p. 37.

99.   Roberts, *Birth*, p. 45: 'Indeed so universal is the Christian use of the codex in the second century that its introduction must date well before AD 100.' See also p. 61.

100.   Hengel, 'Septuaginta', p. 203.

101.   On the debate about this criterion for differentiating Jewish and Christian papyri, see Roberts, *Manuscript*, pp. 74ff. On p. 76 Roberts comes to the following conclusion: '... there is a reasonable assumption that a text of the OT in codex form is more likely to be Christian than Jewish. The converse again holds; such a text on a roll is, prima facie, to be regarded as Jewish in origin.'

102.   Kleberg, *Buchhandel*, p. 80.

use of the codex-form from its beginnings up to the numerous manuscript copies which have come down to us from the second/third centuries. De facto the earliest demonstrable manuscript record of the NT texts exists in the codex-form. The oldest preserved papyrus-codices are P^{52} (around the first third of the second century CE) and P^{90} (second century) along with P^{32}, P^{66}, P^{64+67} and P^{46} (all around 200). Thus the early Christians not only developed the use of the *nomina sacra*, which are of Jewish origin, but also introduced the codex – if one wishes to follow Roberts – on a large scale before 100 CE. There is, however, no clear explanation for this: rather there is a debate about the reasons for the extensive use of the codex in the Christian world. I shall now take up some aspects of this debate.[103]

(a)   The codex as opposed to the scroll was chosen because it was close to the rhetorical tradition and 'consequently was not adopted and circulated by the Christians accidentally'.[104] This being so, the publication of the NT writings in the codex-form was first and foremost an aid to recitation and was an attempt to capture the oral character of the NT transmission.

(b)   Various hypotheses are put forward as to which genus of NT writings the use of the codex-form could have created and at which time. Roberts's thesis is that the Christian codex was introduced by Mark's Gospel and spread in this way. Gamble on the other hand would like to see the beginnings of the Christian codex in the collection of the Pauline epistles. Skeat supposes that the Gospels were first written on scrolls. The codex was only given preference at the end of the first century with John's Gospel because it completed the emergence of Gospels and a 'Four-Gospel Codex' could be established.

(c)   The codex is more rigid and consequently more durable than a papyrus roll. At the same time the codex was more economical since both sides of the material could be inscribed. Hence the codex was less expensive and to that extent more within the means of the Christians.[105] Skeat, however, questions the argument from cost-saving and concludes that it is redundant for explaining the use of the codex in the Christian world.

(d)   The codex-form was more suitable for reading: 'The scroll had to be held in both hands when reading while the codex needed only one hand, leaving the other free to turn the pages or to write.'[106]

103.   This is based above all on the works of Roberts/Skeat, see Roberts, *Birth*, pp. 45ff. or the description in Gamble, *Books*, pp. 54ff. or Llewelyn/Kearsley, *Documents*, pp. 250ff.
104.   Camassa, 'Buch', p. 811.
105.   See Blanck, *Buch*, p. 100: Blanck conjectures that a papyrus-codex was 26% less expensive than a papyrus scroll. Parchment books were also cheaper than papyrus rolls.
106.   Camassa, 'Buch', p. 812.

This seems important both for the transmission and copying of the letters and for reading them aloud in the service of worship. At the same time the codex is more compact and more suitable for travellers and consequently also for Christian missionaries. 'The codex, then, can also be said to fit the essentially demotic character of Christianity ... Christian books were meant for practical use rather than being part of cultic activity, like the scrolls of the Torah in the synagogue cult.'[107]

(e) What is more, the codex enables one to compare passages within the writings because 'one can leaf back and forth without difficulty'.[108] This argument is frequently connected to the fact that – like legal texts – Christian texts were from an early date considered to be normative.[109] Yet this interpretation does not carry conviction, for here one suspects that hermeneutical judgements on the normativity and authority of NT texts are themselves being made the basis for the reconstruction of the transmission process.

(f) The argument that the use of the codex had sociological grounds since codices originally contained literature of an inferior quality has been contradicted in the most recent debate about the emergence of the codex. In that case the interpretation that by using the codex Christians wanted to differentiate themselves from the intellectual circles who rejected the codex has also become obsolete. The practical motives mentioned above deserve to be given priority over such an explanation for the emergence of the codex.

(g) Because it had wide margins the codex permitted comments and textual variants – this could also explain the emergence of scholia commentaries. Glosses and interpolations could have made their way into the letters in the wake of the collection of copies of Pauline letters in a codex.

(h) In the non-Christian world the change from the papyrus-scroll to the parchment-codex took place in the third, at the latest in the fourth to fifth centuries, partly for aesthetic reasons – namely the possibility of a more elaborate arrangement – but above all for reasons of durability.

(i) I gave above my own further attempted explanation for the early Christian use of the codex-form: if the Pauline epistles were originally written on wooden or wax tablets, the use of the parchment codex represented continuity in terms of the history of the book. 'It seems probable that the codex was immediately felt by Christians to be more convenient than the roll to carry their

---

107. Stroumsa, 'Christianity', p. 168.

108. Kleberg, *Buchhandel*, p. 73.

109. Thus e.g. Reynolds/Wilson, *Scribes*, p. 35: 'The importance of the codex for religion and law is obvious.'

message.'[110] This attempt at explanation can further be meaningfully combined with an observation on the editorial processes
relating to ancient writings.

(j)   Connected to the transition from the scroll to the codex in the
non-Christian world – howbeit at a later date – there is a fact
which also seems to be significant for the reception and copying of
Pauline letters. Since the codex had a greater capacity, *corpora* 'of
the letters of particular authors' could now be composed.[111] The
emergence of the different corpora of Pauline letters can be
understood in a similar fashion: several wax tablets or smaller
codices with individual letters or even smaller corpora were
collected and copied into a papyrus or parchment codex.

Therefore individual letters were copied and assembled into 'minor
corpora' in an *initial* process of collection. Here we must take into account
that Paul himself could have been familiar with *membranae* (see 2 Tim.
4.13). In a *second* process which marked the time of the 'literary'
publication of the Pauline epistles the minor corpora were joined together
and copied into more commodious codices.

It is even possible that, because of the collection of the Pauline letters,
the codex developed into the leading form of Christian book. If the
Pauline letters attained normative importance because they were gathered
together at an early date, the codex also opened up a 'random access' to
all letters.[112] Consequently the codex in the end was not only decisively
important for the history of books and thus of literary significance; it also
came to have a scriptural-theological function.[113]

2.3.3.3. *Ancient letter-collections as analogies*

To make the thesis of the early collection of the Pauline epistles clearer a
consideration of the ancient letter-collections and editions known to us is
illuminating. In the ancient world collections of letters are quite usual, yet
only some letter-collections can be compared meaningfully with the *Corpus
Paulinum*. An example from a later period for the independent emergence
of a Pauline letter-corpus is the pseudo-literary collection of the correspondence between Paul and Seneca. We can follow the emergence of an
edition of letters from the letters of Cicero and their collection.

Cicero (d. 43 BCE) as a letter-writer is familiar with the rules of rhetoric.

---

110. Stroumsa, 'Christianity', p. 169.

111. Dorandi, 'Tradierung', p. 15.

112. This is the thesis put forward by Gamble, *Books*, pp. 58ff. 'Their availability in a
codex permitted easy access to any part of the collection', p. 63.

113. 'The evidence shows only that Christians adopted the codex in preference to the roll
as a medium for literature sooner and more decisively than their contemporaries and so
promoted its popularity. That they did so says something important about the uses and
functions of early Christian writings,' Gamble, *Books*, p. 65.

This is particularly obvious in his public letters which have the character of speeches. His private letters serve primarily to communicate news (see *Epistulae ad Quintum fratrem* I.1.37) and are marked by the author's personal ethos but also by epistolary typologies such as *brevitas,* starting- and closing-formulae, etc. References to the early fame of Ciceronian letters can be found in Cornelius Nepos *(Atticus* 16.3*)* and Suetonius *(Augustus* 3.2*).* With his letters Cicero 'even if unconsciously and unintentionally constituted "epistolography" as a potential literary genus'. The letters of Cicero count as the first publication of an extensive private correspondence in antiquity: 'The motive for the publication is not difficult to find in the respect and loyalty of the devoted colleague (i.e. Tiro) who also wrote a biography of Cicero and accordingly considered the letters as biographical testimonials.'[114] The collection of Cicero's letters consists of the *Epistulae ad Atticum, Epistulae ad Familiares, Epistulae ad Quintum fratrem* and *Epistulae ad Marcum Brutum.* A pseudepigraphical letter, namely the *Epistula ad Octavianum,* has found its way into this collection.

The letters of Isocrates and the letters of Pliny also count as sizeable ancient letter-collections. These compilations contain predominantly real and authentic letters. The collection of nine partly fragmentary letters of Isocrates (d. 338 BCE) contains letters to prominent personages. The authenticity of some letters in this collection is disputed. In the case of Pliny the Younger (d. *c.*114 CE) we have a self-edited collection of private letters (*Books* 1–9). The correspondence with the Emperor Trajan (*Book* 10) would have been published after Pliny's death by Suetonius and Pliny's wife, Calpurnia Hispulla. The letters are for the most part stylized and structured for later publication. 'The most probable assumption is that Pliny made a selection from his actual correspondence and published this in a revised form. It is possible that some pieces were first written for the edition.'[115] Hence the tradition of self-editing in the Roman west first begins with Pliny the Younger: in the Greek east the oldest self-edited letter-collection is that of Gregory of Nazianzus.

In the case of comparable Christian letter-collections from the ancient world and late antiquity we are often dealing not with real letters but with apologetic or theological writings in the form of letters. This is true of the so-called letters of Athanasius (d. *c.*373 CE) or those of Ambrosius (d. 397). In addition we can name the letters of Ignatius (see above), Cyprian of Carthage (d. 258), Jerome (d. 420) and Augustine (d. 430) as important Christian letter-collections. The collected letters of Paulinus of Nola (d. 431) were produced in his lifetime but only posthumously edited.

---

114. Schmidt, 'Cicero', pp. 152 and 168.
115. M. v. Albrecht, *Geschichte*, p. 912.

The letter-corpus of Cyprian is the most famous from the period of the early Church: 'Cyprian shapes the style of Latin pastoral letters.'[116] We can discern a process of self-editing in the Cyprianic letter-collection. In *Epistulae* 20 and 27 Cyprian refers to earlier letters and includes these as copies. Cyprian at the same time makes detailed statements on his previous correspondence.[117] During his lifetime Jerome published two collections of what would subsequently amount to 150 edited letters. Augustine, too, possibly played a personal part in an edition of individual letters: at least there arose in his lifetime 'several collections of duplicated letters'.[118] Some of the letters of Paulinus of Nola were from the start intended for publication. The collection of his letters, however, was only edited after the death of Paulinus, probably according to a chronological sequence.

These letter-collections contain various references to the process of editing ancient letters: several copies of particularly important letters were often prepared or these were made by the recipients. Many families had house-archives – we can envisage similar private archives in the Pauline congregations – where 'letters received' and drafts or copies of the letters were preserved.[119] If and when the letters will be published depends upon the personality of the author but also upon the genus of the respective letter. Perhaps only the stylistically best letters of the respective author were edited. Copy-books were used and the letters were subjected to 'an examination' of their form and content for the edition.[120] But pseudepigraphical letters could also make their way into letter-collections. Just such pseudepigraphical letters were included in the corpora of the Pauline epistles – definitively at the latest around the end of the second century.

The *proprium* of the collection of Pauline epistles consists in the fact that the letters were passed on at an early date – when Paul was still alive – and collected and edited in a process of copying. That is to say, the Pauline letters were copied, collected and collated as minor or major corpora in close temporal continuity with Paul. The 'edition' of the Pauline epistles was not made following a programme. It was rather that an edited Pauline letter-corpus grew up in the process of the *copying of the individual letters* into minor or major corpora. We must not draw too quick a conclusion on their genus from the fact that the Pauline letters were published: they can be understood neither as private letters of an important personage nor as teaching by correspondence which was

---

116. M. v. Albrecht, *Geschichte*, p. 1249.
117. Cyprian refers to an earlier letter (*Epist.* 20) in which he included an even earlier one (*Epist.* 15). See Clarke, *Letters* 1, p. 359, on *Epist.* 27.II.1.
118. Divjak, 'Epistulae', p. 909.
119. Peter, *Brief*, pp. 32f., here with references from Cicero.
120. Sykutris, *Epistolographie*, pp. 198f.

published for that very reason. What is true, however, is that 'the letter becomes literature, not through its content but through its publication which can ensue because of the author or because of the content, after his death or already during his lifetime ...'[121].

Consequently the edition of the Pauline epistles goes back to the continuous use and development of the codex-form and takes place in an ongoing process of letter-copying.

2.3.3.4. *The reconstruction of the transmission of 2 Corinthians*

On the basis of all our previous deliberations it would now seem advisable to undertake a reconstruction of the formation and transmission of 2 Cor. Here, however, we can only demonstrate possibilities as they arise from the enquiry into the literary and technical conditions of writing and reception in antiquity. Thus the following table should be seen as a proposal for reconstruction which documents how the production and reception of letters might, with a certain degree of probability, have proceeded; one-sided reconstructions which wish to take e.g. the wax-tablet *or* papyrus as the assured material are not covered by the transmission.

The following reconstruction of the possible transmission of 2 Cor. is not only conceivable but it also draws the balance from our previous observations.

Writing-material	Wax tablets[122]/ papyrus sheets	Papyrus-codex/ scrolls[123]	Codex[124]	Codex (e.g. P^{46})
Range	Correspondence– Letters	'minor corpus' (1/2 Cor.)	'prime corpus' (incl. 1/2 Cor.)	'total corpus' (Pauline epistles)
Writing-process	Dictation	copying[125]	copy or edition	canoni-zation[126]
Procedure	Dictation	compilation, interpolation	glosses, interpolation	
Date	around 56	*c.*60–70	*c.*100	from *c.*150

121. Zelzer, 'Brief', p. 551.
122. Apart from Romans.
123. Either papyrus or, later, parchment, see above.
124. Or also a wax-tablet polyptych.
125. Mistakes could also be made at any time, see e.g. Zelzer, 'Umschrift', pp. 157ff., who remarks that many textual variants arose in the transfer of classical texts from scrolls to codices.
126. Here 'canonization' means the connected and prevailing collection of various NT writings.

2.4. *A* literarhistorical *model for the reconstruction of 2 Corinthians*

2.4.1. *On the concept of* 'literarhistorical *reconstruction*'

After the considerations advanced in 2.1 to 2.3 on the processes of the writing, reading, handing-down and transmitting of letters, conclusions about the reconstruction of the original literary form of 2 Cor. are now possible and instructive. Hence I shall now suggest my own model for understanding 2 Cor. – even if all previous hypotheses have again and again led to insoluble dilemmas. This model, however, is not to be seen as a *literarcritical* model but as a *literarhistorical* one, since it draws on insights gained from considering the production and reception of ancient texts, not simply on observations of incohesion and incoherence based on the text as we have it. The model is based on the following assumptions.

First, the correspondence of Paul with the Corinthians can be understood as a written form of communication. A *literarhistorical* reconstruction attempts to ascertain the process of this written *communication* – i.e. to establish the original sequence of the epistolary correspondence – and thereby pursues an interest similar to the reconstruction of the original textual form of the Pauline epistles generally undertaken in literary criticism.

Second, differentiations in respect of the assessment of the *textual coherence* have become obvious. Within the framework of synchronic text analysis a distinction must be made between the 'cohesion' and the 'coherence' of a text. This means that the decision as to whether a text felt to be incohesive is also understood as coherent or incoherent represents a hermeneutical judgement on the part of the individual recipient of the text and consequently cannot really be settled by *Literarkritik*. This becomes particularly clear in the very different evaluation of so-called *literarcritical* criteria relevant to the interpretation of 2 Cor. When we examine the criteria of coherence employed by ancient letter-writers we observe that ancient text-production permitted incohesive writing and that (at least) the (original) recipients of the text would not have judged incohesions in the text to be incoherent.

Third, our deliberations on the production and reception of a letter in antiquity have shown that *compilations* in the course of the copying of letters – to preserve and transmit them (70–90 CE) – are very well conceivable. Compilations could have taken place when letters were copied from wax tablets onto papyrus scrolls or papyrus codices. The individual letters were then strung together with the omission of their *prooemium* or conclusion, i.e. as fragments. Complex models of interweaving seem improbable because of the technical limitations determining the processes of transmission and edition.

From these considerations it follows that – in the sense of *literarcriti-*

cism – the *de*constructing detection of breaks, repetitions, etc. in the text as we have it cannot be a basis for a literary *re*construction of the original form of the text. Rather, the literary interests and technical possibilities of ancient textual transmission in the compilation of letters such as 2 Cor. must serve in a *literarhistorical* way as the basis of a reconstruction.

2.4.2. *The* literarhistorical *reconstruction of Paul's communication with Corinth*

The *literarhistorical* model which will now be presented for the reconstruction of the original Corinthian correspondence which exists in its canonical form in 2 Cor. is based on two facts. *First*, the *technical* possibilities of letter-compilations have been proved. But *second*, this model is to be seen as a suggestion for the reconstruction of Paul's *communication* with the Corinthians on the basis of the texts of 1 and 2 Cor. Since this communication proceeds on different levels and finally develops a meta-communication, we can present its individual phases.

Initially there is an original face-to-face communication during Paul's missionary activity in Corinth and during his second visit. In his absence Paul communicates with the Corinthians by means of letters. With this *epistolary communication* there arises a correspondence between Paul and the Corinthian congregation. Paul also receives additional news from Corinth brought to him personally by delegates.

In the course of this correspondence there evolves a further level of communication: Paul develops a *meta-communication* – i.e. he reflects upon the communication with the Corinthians and in this connection refers to earlier letters. We can then draw conclusions about the phases of the communication from these individual meta-communicative statements and consequently about Paul's earlier correspondence with the Corinthians and also as to whether the communication was effective each time. The epistolary meta-communication arises because Paul does not simply wish to give the Corinthians factual messages but wants the communication as such to achieve the desired result.[127]

---

127. The italics in the chart mark the individual letters of the correspondence which are preserved; * indicates that the letter is fragmentary; each letter is characterized in bold type.

EVENTS	REFERENCE
Mission of Paul in Corinth	1 Cor. 2.1
Reference to verbal communication	1 Cor. 1.11; 5.1; 11.18; 16.17
Earlier letter from Paul	1 Cor. 5.9
News from Corinth:	
Writing from the Corinthians	1 Cor. 7.1, 25; 8.1; 12.1
People of Chloe	1 Cor. 1.11
Corinthian delegation in Ephesus	1 Cor. 16.17
Letter from Paul *1 Cor.*?[128]	1 Cor. 16.8
Interim visit to Corinth/sadness (second visit?)	2 Cor. 2.1ff.
'Plaintive letter': *2 Cor. 1.1–7.4** = ***Letter A*** (Paul writes because of 2.2, 3b) [6.14–7.1: later insertion as an ending to letter]	2 Cor. 2.3f., 8f.
Fresh news brought by Titus	2 Cor. 7.6f.
Letter from Paul: *2 Cor. 7.5–16** = ***Letter B***	2 Cor. 7.8f., 12f.
Letters about offerings: *2 Cor. 8; 9* = ***Letters C and D***	
Attacks on Paul in Corinth	2 Cor. 10.10; 11.16
Letter from Paul: *2 Cor. 10–13** = ***Letter E*** (Reference to offerings, 12.14–18)	2 Cor. 10.10 (earlier letters)
Plans for a third visit	2 Cor. 12.14; 13.1

2.4.3. *On the interpretation of the meta-communicative statements*
Anticipating the detailed exegesis in Chapter 4, the meta-communicative statements in 2 Cor. which have been employed to assist the *literarhistorical* reconstruction will now be elucidated.

In *2 Cor. 2.1, 5ff.* Paul refers to a former, distressing visit to Corinth and writes to the Corinthians in tears (2.3f.)[129] because he wishes to avoid a further harrowing visit there (2.2). This 'plaintive letter' could in essence be completed in 7.4 and be intended on the one hand to make the Corinthians have a direct share in Paul's sorrow (1.4ff.). On the other

---

128.   The unity of 1 Cor. is disputed. See Sellin, 'Hauptprobleme', pp. 2964ff.
129.   The aorist forms here are interpreted as epistolographic.

hand Paul exhorts the Corinthians to forgive the one who caused the sorrow (2.5–11). 6.14–7.1 could be a concluding topical paraenesis, inserted as a post-Pauline interpolation at the end of the letter.

In *2 Cor. 7.8f., 12f.* Paul, having in the meantime received conciliatory news from Corinth brought by Titus (7.6f., 13b-16), returns to the earlier 'plaintive letter' and comments on it retrospectively.[130] It is clear that Paul's tears in his previous letter have really distressed the Corinthians and moved them to repentance (7.8f.). At the same time Paul retrospectively refers to the exhortation in his earlier letter to forgive the one who caused the sorrow (2.5ff.), whereby he wishes to test and challenge the confidence the Corinthian congregation has in the Apostle (7.12f.).

2 Cor. 8 and 9 are letters which were sent during Paul's mission to gather offerings, possibly as separate letters of recommendation to Corinth and Achaia.[131]

In *2 Cor. 10.10* Paul looks back at various letters which obviously were 'harsh' and 'critical'. Here one might see a reference to the effects of a possible plaintive letter (1.1–7.4), of which Paul himself had later become aware (7.8ff.). 2 Cor. 10–13 would then be the last letter in the extant Corinthian correspondence, one in which Paul once again sees himself compelled to give a paraclesis (10.1) and a self-portrait (11.1ff.) in the face of the criticism which was being directed against his person in Corinth. Therefore a further visit did not take place during the correspondence contained in 2 Cor., but was already planned from the time of the plaintive letter (2.1) right up to the last letter (12.14; 13.1).

2.4.4. *Clarification of the letter-sections and their so-called 'breaks'*

Since the *literarhistorical* model presented does not hold to the unity of the 2 Cor. we have before us, but for its own part reckons with 'breaks' in the text, an explanation for this must finally be given. Starting from the *literarhistorical* possibilities of letter-compilation discussed above I shall now explicate in relation to their suspected original independence the places in the letter where 'discontinuities' – and consequently also the different segments of the individual phases of the communication – are most obvious.

If *2 Cor. 8 and 9* were separate writings about offerings, these were strung together minus their introductory remarks and conclusions. In a similar manner the originally separate *2 Cor. 10–13* as the latest letter to the Corinthians was added to the writings about offerings minus its introduction. Grounds which speak for the independence of 2 Cor. 10–13

---

130. Here the aorists are interpreted as temporal.

131. Here see Betz, *Korinther*, particularly pp. 251ff. The sequence of the Corinthian correspondence developed there will not, however, be followed.

have been sufficiently discussed in the *literarcritical* debate. There we also find the thesis that 2 Cor. 10–13 represents the final letter of the Corinthian correspondence.

Then *2 Cor. 1–7* must contain the earliest writings collected in 2 Cor. The *literarhistorical* examination has revealed the technical possibility (and the exegetical examination will show) that 2 Cor. 1–7 contains two documents: an extensive writing (1.1–7.4) and a very brief note (7.5–16). The unity of 1.1–7.4 and the distinction between 1.1–7.4 and 7.5–16 can now be substantiated as follows:

(1)   While Paul in 2 Cor. 2.1–9 ponders on the process of writing the current letter, in 7.8–13a he looks back at this earlier letter. Consequently the communicative situation of ch. 2 differs from that of ch. 7. While in ch. 2 Paul writes in tears, is distressed (see also 7.4) and admonishes the addressees, in 7.13a he is consoled.

(2)   Both letters – 1.1–7.4 and 7.5–16 – clearly were written in Macedonia. While in 2.13 Paul tells only of his arrival in Macedonia, in 7.5 he does not simply continue this account of his journey but reports the arrival of Titus (7.6) during his sojourn in Macedonia. Consequently the two accounts of the situation reflect differences in respect of the events reported. Thus the two arguments hitherto mentioned support a division of 2 Cor. 1.1–7.16 into two original letters.

(3)   There is however no need to assume a literary break between 2.13 and 2.14 – contrary to multiple assertions – since both for Paul as a writer and for the Corinthian addressees linguistic, syntactic, semantic and pragmatic incohesions in the narrative style could be understood as coherent: in the middle of his account of previous events Paul turns to God in the form of a confession (see a similar construction in 1.9f.) and then leads into an apostolic *apologia* (2.15ff.).

(4)   7.2–4 therefore constitutes the end of the first letter – before the lost conclusion. The situation described corresponds to that in ch. 2: Paul is distressed (7.4). A later reviser has inserted 6.14–7.1 as an interpolation before the concluding exhortation (7.2) which semantically correlates with 6.11–13. Analogies to the giving of emphatic exhortations or advance notice 'about false prophets and teachers of false doctrine' are after all to be found in other writings apart from the Pauline epistles.[132]

The *process of compilation* did not, however, take place within an editorial revision of the letters. The model of a *literarhistorical* compilation does not postulate an editor who incorporated the remaining letters preserved in fragments into a letter lying before him. It was rather the case that the

---

132.   See Bornkamm, 'Vorgeschichte', pp. 180ff.

letters – essentially in the order in which they were received – were strung together in the process of *copying*, which began in Corinth right away when the wax-tablet letters were transferred onto scrolls or codices.

The loss of greetings at the beginning and end of the individual letters brought together in 2 Cor. could be explained as follows: when the letters were put together, prefaces had of necessity to be dropped. If the individual letters were all written within a short space of time, Paul might have done without *prooemia* and opened only letter A with a eulogy (2 Cor. 1.3ff.). In Galatians, too, the body of the letter (Gal. 1.6ff.) follows the extended preface (Gal. 1.1–5) without a *prooemium*. If 2 Cor. 8 and 9 are considered to have been separate writings (see above), a *prooemium* for these two letters also is obviously not now required.

The omission of the greeting at the *conclusion of the letter* can be explained in a like manner to that of the *prooemia*: it is apparent that in short or militant letters Paul clearly did not formulate greetings (see also Gal. 6.17f. and 1 Thess. 5.22–24). This would then likewise hold true at least for the end of letters A–D in 2 Cor. The χάρις-formula at the end of the individual letters of 2 Cor. would then however have dropped out in the course of the compilation, analogous to the prefaces.

Hence in the compilation of the five letter-parts of 2 Cor., only the prefaces were omitted in the letters B–E while only the χάρις-formula of the letter-conclusion was left out in letters A–D.

Specific *redactional* elements are always found in the letter-parts of 2 Cor. where glosses or interpolations (2 Cor. 6.14–7.1) are present. These were included in the course of the letters being transferred onto the codices.

2.4.5. *Results of the* literarhistorical *reconstruction of 2 Corinthians*

The hypotheses for the *literarhistorical* reconstruction of 2 Cor. presented in 1.1 reflect the fact that, in reading and interpreting 2 Cor., one again and again becomes aware of various literary incohesions. As a result of this there arise different models for the reconstruction of the original textual form of the Corinthian correspondence. In the process one must assume a phase of editorial revision which resulted in compilations of letters. Not much thought is generally given, however, to the question of the working method and the intention of the supposed editors.

Rhetorical analysis of the text (see 1.2) on the other hand abstains to a large extent from *literarcritical* reflection and perceives specific rhetorical strategies and conceptions in the form of 2 Cor. as we have it or at least in individual details of its parts. Thus rhetorical analysis can interpret literary incohesions as devices of rhetorical style, as is similarly suggested by the opponents of *Literarkritik* in defence of the literary unity of 2 Cor.

The detection of incohesions in respect of the situation and language in

2 Cor. entitles us to ask about the number of the individual letters and their original textual form. But at the same time we must bear in mind that the assessment of incohesions depends upon hermeneutical assumptions and consequently largely upon the individual interpreter. This is all the more true since the criteria according to which linguistic and literary textual cohesion are currently measured are not sufficient to test the cohesive potential of ancient texts or to give an insight into the expectations of textual cohesion in the minds of the ancient recipients of the text.

Hence although the starting-point for questioning the historical genesis of the Corinthian correspondence may lie in the perception of literary incohesions, this perception alone is not sufficient as a basis for the reconstruction of the original form of the text. To find grounds for possible compilations of letters, on the other hand, we must make a *literarhistorical* examination of the literary and technical possibilities for compilations of letters which may enable a plausible reconstruction of the original form of 2 Cor. These considerations of the general ancient conditions of text-production and text-reception have shown that compilations of letters could certainly have been carried out, but that in the case of the Pauline epistles this can be envisaged as most likely to have taken place during their reception, when the letters were copied from wax or wooden tablets onto more extensive codices which were intended to serve the conservation and transmission of the letters.

Only at the conclusion of these reflections could we take up again the observations of the literary incohesions of possible part-letters and use these in the course of a *literarhistorical* reconstruction to search for a linguistic and literary explanation distinguishing just such part-letters. This provisional reconstruction must finally be tested by exegetical examination of the relevant passages in the text (see Chapter 4).

But what is the benefit of such a *literarhistorical* reconstruction of 2 Cor. for the question of Paul's epistolary hermeneutics in 2 Cor.?

If 2 Cor. is not uniform but is made up of four or five separate letters (A–E) we have before us in 2 Cor. a collection of letters which presumably arose in the course of the copying and preservation of the letters. Paul wrote the four/five part-letters A–E (1.1–7.4; 7.5–16; 8; 9; 10–13) one after the other at intervals, and very soon after their arrival in Corinth they were copied and thereby compiled, strung together. Thus the letter-parts give us an insight into the various phases of Paul's communication with the Corinthians (see 2.3.2). If, then, one looks for Paul's epistolary hermeneutics in 2 Cor., individual epistolary hermeneutical comments are found not in a comprehensive letter but in at least four part-letters. Since Paul's correspondence with the Corinthians collected in 2 Cor. shows a chronological progression, we may perhaps extract epistolary hermeneutical statements from the individual letters which are correspondingly different and may possibly bear upon each other.

Before the beginnings of Pauline epistolary hermeneutic are elaborated in Chapter 4 of this investigation we must first theoretically describe the stages of the letter where such epistolary hermeneutical statements are to be found. This theoretical description will lead to the following thesis: in 2 Cor. Paul develops the beginnings of his epistolary hermeneutic in meta-communicative statements. Hence in 2 Cor. epistolary hermeneutic is developed as meta-communication.

If we now relate this theoretical reflection to the results of the *literarhistorical* reconstruction of 2 Cor., we provisionally perceive three things: first, Paul's correspondence with the Corinthians in 2 Cor. takes place in at least four phases of communication. Second, Paul thinks in a meta-communicative way in the respective individual letters of his communication with the Corinthians and in this way formulates epistolary hermeneutical statements on matters such as letter-writing or on the relationship between speaking and writing. From this ensues, third, that the individual epistles of the letter-collection in 2 Cor. contain meta-communicative or epistolary hermeneutical statements which refer to one another and reveal a developing epistolary hermeneutic. Hence in the canonical 2 Cor. we have a collection of letters containing epistolary hermeneutical statements in which Paul considers meta-communicatively and consequently in an epistolary hermeneutical way not simply the aspects of speaking and writing but, reflecting on earlier communication, the aspect of the reception of letters as well.

Chapter 3

THEORETICAL BASES OF EPISTOLARY HERMENEUTICS

3.1. *Communication by means of letters*

The relationship of Paul with the Corinthian congregation is one of continuous *communication*. When the Apostle is present in Corinth this communication is oral; in his absence Paul continues his communication with the Corinthians in a written form. Consequently when we describe the phases of Paul's communication with the Corinthians we must in principle differentiate between an oral communication and one transmitted in writing.

Yet we must initially ask whether and to what extent the concept of 'communication' can adequately define the personal and linguistic relationship of Paul to the Corinthian congregation. To do so we must consider the derivation of the term in the light of philosophy and the theory of communication.

(a) *What is 'communication'?*

The term 'communication' is used in various academic disciplines and should therefore be more precisely defined in these diverse aspects. What is meant when we talk of 'communication'?

Since the rise of Existential Philosophy in the twentieth century the concept of communication has proved fundamental in describing human relationships: communication constitutes their basis. 'If communication is not also the basis for love, there is no love which does not manifest itself in communication. Where communication conclusively breaks down, love comes to an end because it was an illusion; but where it truly existed communication cannot come to an end but must change its form. Communication is the love-imbued *movement* in temporal existence ...'[1]

Philosophy presents human existence as fundamentally based on communication. In a similar way Paul's communication with the Corinthians can be understood as an expression of existential solidarity. Alongside the existential import of the concept of 'communication' there

---

1. Jaspers, *Philosophie* 2, pp. 72f.

arises in twentieth-century philosophy an application of the concept – e.g. in the philosophy of *Habermas* – which signals a 'material paradigm shift from consciousness to c[ommunication]'.[2]

In *Sociology* the concept of 'communication' does have a technical informative element but it is used above all in the area of the theory of action.[3] In the theory of action communication stands for 'processes in which individuals relate to one another as thinking, speaking, feeling and acting persons'. To this extent social action is then 'necessarily communicative action since the coordination of the actions of individuals requires knowledge and understanding'.[4]

Hence in a manner similar to existential philosophy, sociology understands communication as a constitutive element in human relationships or social structures. *Textual Linguistics* likewise takes up this dimension of interaction but at the same time points out that a process of communication already begins 'when a "sender" forms the intention to communicate something to someone or to bring something about'.[5]

In the *Theory of Journalism* 'communication' is the 'broadest, generic concept' and is defined as follows: 'Communication in the broader sense means all the processes of transmitting information . . . By communication in the narrower sense, however, one understands a process of understanding and exchange of meaning between living beings.'[6] The process of communication is then made up of the three elements 'sender', 'news' and 'receiver' and can take three different forms: 'direct or indirect, reciprocal or unilateral, private or public'.[7] These three distinctions relate to the medium of communication, the aspect of dialogue or monologue, and the scale of publication.

While the theory of journalism defines the concept against the background of the manifold ways in which speech is used by the media, *Communication Studies* or the *Psychology of Communication* provide the fundamental theoretical observations which later lead to a differentiation between communication and meta-communication. Yet in Communication Studies – similar to Existential Philosophy – the prime factor is: 'We are enmeshed in communication; even our awareness of ourselves is dependent . . . upon communication.'[8]

To apply the concept of communication appropriately to the Corinthian correspondence we must first take up two distinctions from the description of what 'communication' signifies in communication

2. Brunkhorst, 'Kommunikation', p. 1510. See also Habermas, *Theorie*.
3. See Scherr, 'Kommunikation', p. 176.
4. Scherr, 'Kommunikation', pp. 176 and 176f.
5. Lewandowski, *Wörterbuch* 2, p. 551.
6. Pürer, *Einführung*, pp. 17 and 18.
7. Pürer, *Einführung*, p. 18 (in the original italicized and without commas).
8. Watzlawick *et al.*, *Kommunikation*, p. 37.

studies. This produces a third consideration relevant to epistolary hermeneutics.

(1) The process of communication does not simply involve the aspect of matter or content but also concerns the level of relationship between the partners in the communication: a message first of all contains information. But the message also has 'a further aspect which ... is just as important – namely an indication of how the sender would like it to be understood by the recipient. Hence it defines how the sender sees the relationship between her/himself and the recipient, and in this sense states his/her own personal attitude to the other'.[9] Consequently the relational aspect represents a communication via a communication and this is identical with the concept of meta-communication which will be defined later.

(2) In a communication transmitted through a medium – e.g. by letters – the process of communication takes place in two different forms: it occurs as a *personal* and as a written or *epistolary* mediated communication.

Personal communication is understood here as reciprocal face-to-face communication. It covers the area of verbal (linguistic) as well as non-verbal communication, namely intonation and voice (paralinguistic) along with expression and gestures (extralinguistic). Paralinguistic and extralinguistic aspects are constitutive for personal communication because they make a decisive contribution to the interpretation of the linguistic level (the aspect of content) in its bearing upon the relationship of the communicating partners.

Alongside a personal communication there may arise an epistolary communication – as in the case of the relationship of Paul to the Corinthians. Letters represent an indirect, one-sided and written form of communication which can take the place of a personal communication (e.g. 2 Cor. 2.1ff.).

This description of epistolary communication based on journalistic and communication studies in no way contradicts the ancient theory of letters, since this also understood letters between friends in particular as a continuation of a personal conversation between them.

The difference between oral and written communication is that in the written form the paralinguistic and extralinguistic elements are missing. If the letter, according to the ancient understanding, envisaged the distant person as being present, it is still true that the transmission of communication in writing creates separation and distance: 'The writer must invent a role in which the absent and frequently unknown reader can rediscover himself/herself.'[10] Hence – according to the understanding of

---

9.   Watzlawick *et al.*, *Kommunikation*, p. 53.
10.   Ong, *Oralität*, p. 103.

textual linguistics – there lie, at least in a (private) letter, elements both of linguistic distance and proximity.

(3) Personal and written communications contain – as we have seen – an aspect of content and a relational aspect and are to that extent structurally similar. There is, however, an essential difference between oral and written communication in respect of *how* the relational aspect is thematized meta-communicatively. In face-to-face communication para-linguistics and meta-linguistics give crucial indications for the proper understanding of the communication, i.e. of its aspects of content and relationship. Such indications are missing in written communication. If then a letter-writer such as Paul wants to thematize the feature of relationship in a meta-communicative way when employing the medium of written communication, he must do so explicitly in words. It is precisely on this meta-communicative level of letter-writing that Paul then comes to develop what will be presented as the epistolary-hermeneutical conception of 2 Cor. To begin with, we must emphasize:

Epistolary hermeneutics arise as a meta-communicative explication of the aspect of relationship in a medially transmitted written communication.

From the wealth of features mentioned we can now define as follows what 'communication' is and what is implied by the concept of communication: human relationships and social action are essentially communicative. This communication has an aspect related to the content and an aspect bearing on the relationship. *Letters* represent indirect, mediated – that is, written – communicative processes which lack the immediacy and reciprocity of oral communication. And yet epistolary communication is the only written form of communication 'in which a change of direction and consequently a dialogical communication is possible without impedi-ment'.[11] Hence an epistolary correspondence – such as that of Paul with the Corinthians – facilitates a reciprocal communication, even if it is temporally out of alignment.

In contrast to communication in person, in a letter the aspect of relationship must be explicated in writing in a purely meta-communicative fashion. This gradually leads to an epistolary hermeneutic. Part of this epistolary hermeneutic might be composed of references to earlier communication in person or by letters: in the Corinthian epistles there are references both to previous communicative dealings of the Corinthians with Paul (1 Cor. 7.1) and of Paul with the Corinthians (2 Cor. 7.8ff.; 10.10).

---

11. Ermert, *Briefsorten*, p. 62.

(b) *Transmission: Paul's communication with the Corinthians*
Paul's epistolary communication with the Corinthians is contained in 1
and 2 Corinthians. Both letters include references to two different kinds of
communication: *personal* and *epistolary*.

Both kinds of communication have in common the aspects of content
and of relationship. With regard to the content, Paul's communication
with the Corinthians – whether he was present in person (e.g. 1 Cor. 2.1ff.)
or mediated it in a letter (e.g. 1 Cor. 1.23) – contains the proclamation of
the gospel and the interpretation of this gospel for the situation of the
congregation (*the aspect of content*). *The aspect of relationship* or the meta-
communicative level of communication consists in the fact that – both in
the letters (e.g. 1 Cor. 9; 2 Cor. 6.1ff.) and during his personal presence in
Corinth (e.g. 2 Cor. 10.1) – questions relating to his apostolic authority
and integrity or the apostolic εἰλικρίνεια as well as questions touching
upon Paul's communication with the Corinthians are time after time
topics of discussion. In epistolary communication these relational aspects
must be explicated in writing.

Hence the communication in person is initially comparable structurally
with the communication mediated by letter. The fact that epistolary
communication additionally leads to an epistolary hermeneutic through
the meta-communicative explication of the aspect of relationship will be
theoretically presented in 3.3 and exegetically verified in Chapter 4.

Personal communication [manner of communication: direct, reciprocal, public and private]	Paul *speaks* to the Corinthians face-to-face
Content:	The gospel (1 Cor. 2.1ff.)
Relationship (meta-communicative/ linguistic, paralinguistic and extra-linguistic):	e.g. Paul and his office as apostle (2 Cor. 10.1); the communication with the Corinthians (e.g. 1 Cor. 3.1)
Epistolary communication [manner of communication: indirect, one-sided, public]	Paul *writes* to the Corinthians in the form of letters
Content:	The gospel (1 Cor. 1.23)
Relationship (meta-communicative/ epistolary hermeneutical):	e.g. Paul and his apostolic commission (1 Cor. 9; 2 Cor. 6.1ff.); his communication with the Corinthians (e.g. 2 Cor. 1.13f.)

3.2. *Letter Writing*

The lasting literary transition from orality to scribality took place in early Christianity in the works of Paul. In a very general sense 'communication' describes the linguistic interaction between individuals and/or social groups. But when looked at more closely the theory of communication supplies significant observations on the process of communication. For example, personal communication and communication transmitted in writing are on the one hand structurally related since each form of communication contains both what can be called an aspect of content and an aspect of relationship which meta-communicatively thematizes the attitude of the communicators to one another and to the communication itself. On the other hand personal and written communication must be distinguished in so far as in written communication – which takes place indirectly, separated by time and space and at the outset one-sidedly – both the aspect of content and that of relationship must be explicitly articulated in words.

These reflections show clearly that in the end Paul as letter-writer does not simply continue an oral communication in writing. Rather, when he commits the communication to paper he becomes involved in the literary potential of written language; he is also forced to explicate in writing the relational aspect of the communication once it takes place indirectly and is transmitted through a medium. In this way he formulates the beginnings of an epistolary hermeneutic conception on a meta-communicative linguistic level.

Hence Paul's letter-writing entails two elements, namely the transformation from orality to literality and to literature, and the meta-communicative explication of the aspect of relationship – which then leads us to ask to what extent Paul in the course of his letter-writing made his mark as a productive and innovative 'literary author'. In what follows I shall consider this mainly from the perspective of literary studies.

3.2.1. *The 'literary' author*

The question of Paul as a literary 'letter-author' arises since it has become clear that Paul moves beyond the heavily orally-weighted linguistic space of the ancient world and the arena of personal communication to *write* letters and communicate by means of letters. The concept of the literary author primarily requires clarification from the field of *Literary Studies*. Useful starting-points for defining Paul as a letter-writer can be derived from this discipline – even against the background of the debate on the 'death of the author'.

The debate on the so-called 'death of the author' triggered off by R. Barthes and M. Foucault starts from a post-structuralist hypothesis: it opposes the assumption 'that we can trace everything back to a *source* or a causal process and thus ... explain it'.[12] On the contrary, the reader is allowed almost unlimited liberty in interpreting texts. In this literary theory the author is not conceived as a present factor in his own right but is immovably localized in the text – which can be put down to the strict differentiation between scribality and orality: 'The writing is the vague, inconsistent, indefinable place whither our subject escapes, the black and white in which every identity begins to disintegrate, beginning with that of the body which is writing.'[13] Hence one could say that the author is withdrawn from his text by writing it. It must be said, however, that literary studies have recently rediscovered the 'author' as a literary figure.[14] The ensuing reflections on Paul as author can constructively follow on here.

The debate about the author has extended beyond the realm of literary studies into both classical philology and theology and, so far as one *opposes* the concept of authorship, has led to a reception-aesthetical hermeneutic of NT writings. *Reader Response Criticism* is a method of literary studies which interprets texts by examining the process of reading in a way similar to the author-research outlined above. In the process text interpretation takes place from the reader's perspective, so to speak, as 'reading-research'.

Here the hermeneutically relevant elements are on the one hand the *reader,* and on the other the *text.* In works of fiction it is taken for granted that the meaning of the text must 'be generated', 'although it is given structure by the linguistic signs contained in the text'. Hence the meaning of the text must be established by the *reader*: the immediate relevance of the text is established in reading 'as a process of communication'.[15] But the potential meaning of the text – as opposed to a purely subjectivist understanding – is already there in the structure of the text, namely in the form of the *implicit reader.* This implicit reader thus represents a key hermeneutic figure within the text, namely a 'role-offer in the text'.[16] Hence inherent in the text there must be guidelines as to how it should be understood, 'which were originally calculated to direct the communication with the intended readers and to ensure the desired effect. Such structures in the text also have an impact on later, non-intended readers'.[17] This model of reader-oriented text-interpretation also exists in textual linguis-

---

12.   Hawthorn, *Grundbegriffe,* p. 25.
13.   Barthes, 'Tod', p. 185.
14.   See Kleinschmidt, *Autorschaft,* and Jannidis *et al., Autorschaft.*
15.   Iser, *Akt,* p. 230 and p. 42.
16.   Iser, *Akt,* p. 64. 'The concept of the implicit reader describes ... a process of transference through which the structures of the text are transferred to the reader's empirical field through the imagination', p. 67.
17.   Frey, 'Leser', p. 281.

tics: for the reader decides on the coherence of the text – although this can be objectified by the analysis of the so-called factors of cohesion.[18] The model of reader-oriented text-interpretation is then also transferred to NT texts, whereby it must however be asked, particularly in respect of the Pauline epistles, whether and how far one can ignore the historical target-group named in the *adscriptio*.

Not only reader-response criticism but literary criticism in general poses critical questions about the *reference* of the texts. What is known as the *'theory of relevance'* attempts to ascertain the referentiality of texts by using structural semiotics but applies them pragmatically. It is in the end similar to reader-response criticism – i.e. it is oriented to a significant degree on reception (Maartens).

First the dialectics of interpretation and context of a text are ascertained. The concept of 'reference' leads on hermeneutically to the question of how the text and its interpretation are anchored in reality. Thus we can differentiate between a reference *behind, in* and *in front of* the texts:

> *Reference behind* the text would then normally include allusions, indirect and explicit referrals to the historical background of the text, its time of origin, historical figures ... This type of reference would be extra-textual by nature. *Reference in* would be referrals which function inside the world of the text, within the narrative or the argument of the text and is therefore intra-textual by nature. *Reference in front of* the text has to do with what the text suggests, opens up, makes possible, leads to, produces, achieves, and is by nature again extra-textual.[19]

If 'God' is not to supply the vacant place of the author in biblical texts,[20] it is all the more necessary to establish the identity of the author, e.g. of the Pauline epistles. NT exegesis deals with an aspect of this question when it asks about the *writer*, i.e. about the *'auctor'* of a document. With regard to the Pauline letters this means in the first place asking about the authenticity or pseudepigraphy of the individual letters. Yet in literary studies the question of Paul as author has a further aspect which goes beyond the ascertainment of the orthonymity of a letter. For while the term 'writer' is used to pose a general question about the originator of a text, the term 'author' implies a deliberate creative forming of the text. We encounter Paul as a historically recognizable individual who writes autobiographically (e.g. 2 Cor. 12) and who writes letters and the partially literary texts contained in them (e.g. 1 Cor. 13). 'This fact is of supreme

---

18.   On the differentiation of coherence and cohesion see Becker, *Kohärenz*; on linguistic research on reader-oriented textual processing in general see e.g. Schnotz, 'Lesen', pp. 972–82.

19.   Lategan, 'Text and Reality', pp. 121–35 (quotation from p. 127).

20.   This occurs occasionally in systematic theology (e.g. Bayer).

hermeneutical significance against the background of Jewish literature which was for the most part anonymous or pseudonymous or pseudepigraphical.'[21] The fact that Paul writes autobiographically and is innovative and creative in his use of language shows him to be a 'literary author'. Paul is also a 'literary author' in that he independently ponders upon the process of writing in an epistolary hermeneutical fashion. Finally, Paul became an important author with an impact on later literature through the further process of the reception of his letters – i.e. through their collection and canonization and the continuation of the genus of the Pauline letter in the Deutero- and Trito-Paulines.

3.2.2. *On the production of a (written) text*

Further to the question of the function of the 'author' in the literary construction of a letter there will now follow the depiction of the act of 'text' production and its requirements. Literary studies consider this question within the frame of what is called *Writing Research*. In contrast to text-linguistics, which can describe both oral and written linguistic products on equal terms as 'text', literary studies implicitly assume that the 'text' as subject of the description of text-production is a written commodity. In what follows I shall start from the interpretation of 'text' used in literature studies. Independently of the question of definition it is a fact that the concept of a 'text' can only be reconstructed within the poles of production *and* reception: 'Text-production and text-reception stand in a correlative communicative relationship. Composition is the process which forms a text capable of having meaning and reading is the process which makes a written text immediately relevant. Composition and reading, text-production and text-reception are both guided by the communicative intentions – i.e. by what a text' – or what an author – has to say.[22]

Here I should now like to turn to the aspect of text production in writing-research. The theory of writing developed here is understood as 'reflection on writing in its realization'.[23] Writing-research uses categories and concepts which could also be instructive in the field of NT exegesis of the Pauline epistles for the description of text formation, but is intended here in the first place to serve a general phenomenological description of text production.

Various theoretical models of writing-research have examined either the cognitive, psychological or sociological aspects of writing. The model

---

21. O. Wischmeyer, 'Thesen', p. 66.

22. Jeanrond, *Text*, p. 84.

23. Weimar, *Enzyklopädie*, p. 123.

chosen here as an example – 'writing as action' – reveals the following aspects which the process of writing may contain.

'Writing' is a socially interactive and communicative action. But it is also true that 'writing is, after all, only indirectly communicative; it takes place under the particular condition of temporal and spatial separation of text producer and text recipient, whose relationship is consequently mediated by [written] texts'. Moreover – in contrast to conversation between people – there is the 'temporal, situative and instrumental cost' of writing. This temporal investment, however, has the advantage that the producer of the text can plan and form it carefully. Furthermore one must make allowances for pauses in the process of writing.[24] 'The duration of the pauses is to a large extent determined by the position of the pauses, the type of text to be produced and the interaction between these conditions.' Personal letters count as writings which need less planning. What is more, the immediate products of planning are not initially complete texts 'but individual textual statements which only constitute the text when put together'. Furthermore the process of formulating is significant: here it is important that at the time of writing formulations are already available in the form of a pre-text.[25] To this extent formulation can often be understood as revision. Then 'context' means the 'totality of the conditions operative in the writing process for the production and reception of textual statements', 'which direct in the most varied ways the process of contextualizing the formulations'.[26] If one asks about the processes of text constitution in the process of writing, it becomes clear that the process of text production can be found again in the text itself: pauses, phenomena of delay, breaks and new beginnings are witness to this.

Hence, to sum up, we can name the following aspects of text production found in the field of writing-research which are also instructive for the reconstruction of how 2 Cor. was produced: writing is a communicative action in spite of the temporal and spatial distance between Paul and the Corinthian congregation. The time taken to write the letter made it possible to plan its text carefully. It can also hold true for the formulation of letters that individual sections of the texts are already available as pre-texts and are simply revised in the course of being written down. All the linguistic and textual statements to be found in the author's context have an influence on the process of writing.

---

24. The unity of 2 Cor. is sometimes upheld by appeal to the assumption of pauses in writing in face of the detection of an incohesive textual form.

25. 'Pre-texts are preliminary mental stages of textual statements which mediate between a writer's abstract goals, intentions and plans in writing and his manifestly produced textual statements.' Wrobel, *Schreiben*, p. 104.

26. Wrobel, *Schreiben*, pp. 25f. and 41; pp. 80f. and 115.

Letter-writing can be understood on the one hand as a written form of an oral communication. On the other hand, however, it represents temporally, contextually, linguistically and formally a process of creative literary text production initiated by an author working methodically and constructively.

3.2.3. *The 'letter' as a literary form*

In literature studies theoretical considerations determining the form and function of letters are conducted on the one hand in the context of research on ancient epistolography. We have already referred at various points to the observations made there. Here they need not be mentioned again in detail. But modern literature studies also calls for a theory of letters following the discovery of the letter as a distinct literary form.

Hence in what follows I shall briefly take up possible definitions of the textual type 'letter' from the research areas of ancient epistolography *and* modern literary studies. In conclusion I shall indicate the distinctiveness of a letter in the tension between 'historical' and 'literary' text.

(a) *The ancient definition of a letter*

According to the ancient understanding the form and function of a letter can be defined as follows: A letter 'is a written communication from a real, historical person to another real, historical person which usually demands a written reply. This forms the starting-point of an exchange of letters (correspondence).'[27] A typical example showing that such a written communication from a historical person to another real person can also be fabricated and contain fictitious literary features is e.g. the letter of Pliny the Younger to Tacitus. The pseudepigraphy or anonymity of ancient letters also shows letter-writers intentionally departing from real communication situations and shaping fictitious settings for the letter with borrowed authority or out of literary interest.

The perspective of ancient history or classical philology in research into ancient letters is primarily concerned to ascertain the orthonymity and correspondingly the value of the letter as a historical source.

(b) *The modern letter-theory*

According to the modern letter theory in literary studies, letters serve the written transmission of communications to an absent person and are understood essentially as a substitute for conversation. 'Conventional forms of textual demarcation ... indicate those who are communicating and how they are related socially ...'.[28] To this extent the letter has similar

---

27. Müller, 'Brief', p. 61.
28. Nickisch, 'Brief', p. 321 and similar *Brief*, p. 9.

functions to oral communication: a letter can relate either to the subject, the addressee or the author – i.e. a letter informs, appeals or demonstrates, and that irrespective of whether the letter is real or fictitious.[29] For literary studies the question of orthonymity or pseudepigraphy is of secondary importance. Letters are of 'significant value as a biographical source',[30] stamped as they are by the person of the writer and her/his existential situation. Hence letters increasingly count as important cultural and socio-historical sources. NT letters such as the Pauline epistles and letters from the early church – e.g. the letters of Augustine – are related, in the view of literature studies, to philosophical letters (Plato or Epicurus) and consequently have a literary character.

The perspective from which modern literary studies considers a letter-theory is on the one hand that of how letters are used; it emphasizes the communicative character of letters. On the other hand literary studies investigates the development of various conceptions of letters which are in varying degrees stamped by the author's subjectivity. In so doing it comes to the conclusion that letter-writing is more than the transmission of 'oral speech in the language of creative writing',[31] since in the course of writing a letter-writer discovers the 'literary' situation of the letter.

(c) *From 'historical' to 'literary' letter*
The historical and philological interpretation of letters presented here commences with the understanding of a letter as an historical document in which an 'historical' author communicates with a genuine addressee by letter. In this process questions arise e.g. about the orthonymity of the authorship, the socio-historical figure of the addressee, the original textual form of the letter and its biographical or general historical value as a source. The letter counts as a document of 'world history'.

---

historical author/writer → communication: letter → genuine addressee

---

If this letter is passed on and is taken over beyond the original circle of addressees it is no longer simply a historical document reflecting a particular communication situation. When literary studies investigates a letter it considers the person of the author as a creative producer of a literary text and it interprets the letter as a literary text – i.e. as a text which is consciously constructed using particular language and forms. It is primarily not the genuine, historical addressee but a 'fictitious' or 'implicit' reader located in the text itself who is identified as addressee. The letter counts as an item of 'world literature'.

29. Nickisch, *Brief*, p. 12.
30. Nickisch, 'Brief', p. 323.
31. Nickisch, *Brief*, p. 12.

literary author	→	'letter' as literary text	→	fictitious reader

3.2.4. *Writing as a literary enterprise: an appraisal*

Reflections on the production of letters show that letter-writing is not simply a case of an oral communication being put into writing. Rather, in the course of writing the letter-writer becomes a literary author who creatively and innovatively constructs the text of his letter in a literary form.

Initially Paul writes his epistles from a communication context which was originally orally stamped; he addresses genuine addressees and acts as an *historical author*. In the process the letters develop a literary dimension. The literary character is present where not only everyday language is used but where an 'elevated style' emerges; where a text does not simply serve to transmit information and where an author writes 'as himself and as another'.[32] For everything 'may be literature and everything which is considered immutably and indisputably literature – e.g. Shakespeare – may one day no longer be literature'.[33] Accordingly Paul can be described as a *literary* author to the extent to which one awards his letters – including 2 Cor. – the title of 'literature' according to the criteria mentioned.

But how does Paul *himself* consider or assess the process of writing and understanding? This question leads to the consideration of Pauline *epistolary hermeneutics* which for its part reflects the literary character of 2 Cor. We must not simply show *that* Paul makes epistolary hermeneutical statements of a thoroughly literary quality which lie on a meta-communicative linguistic level. We must also ask *which* epistolary hermeneutical reflections Paul employs in any particular case and *how* he himself possibly judged the 'literary' quality of his writing.

3.3. *Epistolary hermeneutics as meta-communication*

2 Cor. should not be understood simply as a written form of communication – a letter takes on literary form while it is being written. The literary quality of 2 Cor. can be seen *inter alia* in that this letter contains epistolary hermeneutical statements. Consequently Paul is also a 'literary author' in that he does not simply give the Corinthians material information but also acts as an epistolary interpreter and reflects upon the process of writing and the success of his communication with the Corinthians.

---

32. Eagleton, *Einführung*, p. 12 and Weimar, *Enzyklopädie*, p. 84; on 'Literatursprache' see Bußmann, *Sprachwissenschaft*, p. 461.
33. Eagleton, *Einführung*, p. 12.

But what method can we employ to ascertain the epistolary hermeneutics of 2 Cor.? This question will be considered in the following section. At the same time this working hypothesis will be formulated: in 2 Cor. there is to be found not only what communication studies have called the 'aspect of content' of a communication but also a further meta-communicative level of communication on which the communication's 'aspect of relationship' is considered. Paul himself ponders upon his communication with the Corinthians and consequently upon the processes of writing and understanding. If one can then determine the *meta-communication* in 2 Cor. one will simultaneously uncover the Pauline *epistolary hermeneutics* of 2 Cor.

The term 'communication' is first of all a very general designation of the communicative aspect of letter-writing. But this written form of communication has an aspect of relationship as well as an aspect of content – i.e. meta-communication takes place: Paul makes linguistic statements *about* his communication with the Corinthians. Within these *meta-communicative* statements in 2 Cor. Paul time and again reflects upon the aspects of content and relationship in his communication with the Corinthians and in so doing also refers to previous communication situations. That meta-communication arises in the course of communication can be explained as follows: 'When we no longer employ communication solely for communication but communicate *beyond* the communication itself ..., we use concepts which are no longer *part* of the communication but ... talk *about* it.'[34]

To these observations we now add a further: in that 2 Cor. contains meta-communicative or epistolary hermeneutical statements it includes specifically meta-communicative concepts, language and forms of speech which at the same time constitute an independent propositional and linguistic level of communication. Hence there develops out of the meta-communicative or hermeneutical language-level of the epistolary communication a further level which should be called a *meta-communicative surplus*.

oral communication	*face-to-face*:	
	- aspect of content	
	- aspect of relationship = meta-communication	
written communication	*letter:*	
	- aspect of content	
	- aspect of relationship = meta-communication	
	- meta-communicative surplus	

34. Watzlawick *et al.*, *Kommunikation*, pp. 41f.

Those linguistic forms and statements in 2 Cor. which have an independent theological propositional content and which Paul formulates in conjunction with meta-communicative reflections should be designated as the meta-communicative surplus.

3.3.1. *On the concept of 'meta-communication'*

Linguistics and communication studies provide in the concept of meta-communication a theoretical model for the description of a meta-level of the linguistic process. The common definitions are: meta-communication is 'communication beyond communication, i.e. communication between speakers over and beyond language ... and/or speech'.[35] Or: 'M[eta-communication] is an integral part of any everyday communication; its function consists in securing or re-establishing agreement and mutual understanding, in thematizing different levels of the current communication, e.g. the level of the expressions, words and phrases used, the view of the speaker and the expectations of the listener, the existence of particular aims and intentions, but also levels of which the partners need not be immediately aware.'[36]

From this selection of definitions arise the following particular implications of the concept of meta-communication:

(1)   A possibly everyday communication about speech which is simultaneously an 'explicit communication'[37] may be described as meta-communication.

(2)   The content of meta-communication can be both linguistic questions in the current communication as well as attitudes and expectations of those taking part in the conversation to one another or to the conversation.

(3)   Meta-communication requires meta-communicative knowledge in which those communicating can participate equally.

(4)   The pragmatic side of meta-communication within a communication between two partners in a conversation lies in the aspect of their relationship. At the same time the origin of the meta-communication also lies in the relational aspect.[38]

(5)   Meta-communication can also take place at other levels of conversation – e.g. in the introduction or as a conclusion of a speech.

(6)   Meta-communication is polyfunctional: meta-communication is

---

35.   Bußmann, *Sprachwissenschaft*, p. 483.

36.   Lewandowski, *Wörterbuch* 2, p. 706.

37.   Heinemann/Viehweger, *Textlinguistik*, p. 202.

38.   Here compare Watzlawick *et al.*, *Kommunikation*, pp. 53ff. 'Every communication has an aspect of content and one of relation, such that the latter determines the former and is thus a meta-communication', p. 56. See also Heinemann/Viehweger, *Textlinguistik*, p. 200.

directed towards the 'planning of linguistic statements' and in particular to the avoidance of 'breakdowns in communication'. As meta-communication reveals the contextuality of communication, intertextuality emerges.[39]

3.3.2. *Forms of 'meta-communication'*

Meta-communication takes place as an explicit communication about a current or preceding communication and is essentially grounded in the relational aspect of a communication. It then develops in detail different forms of speech which will now be distinguished in preparation for the analysis of the text.

(a) *'Meta-speech'*

The term 'meta-speech' is taken from linguistics and signifies 'speech ... used ... in statements about another speech'.[40] In the end every linguistic statement about speech can be defined as meta-speech.

(b) *'Meta-fiction', 'meta-narration' and 'meta-argumentation'*

A literary text can 'be its own meta-speech' in the form of *meta-fiction*.[41] Meta-fictional statements relate self-referentially to statements in literature or narration 'which do not aim to present the content as apparently real but ... to make the recipients aware ... of textuality and "fictionality" – in the sense of "artificiality"'.[42] Here a literary text gives inherent information 'about its own technical narrative elements such as language, narrative structure and plot'.[43] One can speak of *meta-narration* when meta-fictional elements exist in non-fictional narration, i.e. if an author speaks about the form of his (authentic) account. An example of this might be autobiographical passages. Analogous to this I should like to suggest the term *meta-argumentation* for argumentative or non-narrative texts.

(c) *'Meta-textuality' and 'intertextuality'*

The term 'meta-textuality' is not as yet a fixed concept in linguistics or literary studies. Hence *meta-textuality* can be a form of intertextuality – namely the literary relationship of texts one to another in so far as meta-textuality represents the reflection of a pre-text in another text. 'This form

---

39. Heinemann/Viehweger, *Textlinguistik*, p. 202.
40. Lewandowski, *Wörterbuch* 2, p. 709.
41. Hawthorn, *Grundbegriffe*, p. 202.
42. Wolf, 'Metafiktion', p. 429.
43. Klarer, *Einführung*, p. 17.

differs from palintextuality in that the statements are not made *with* the words of a different text but *about* them.'[44]

Quotations and allusions on the other hand can be understood as *palintextual* statements, i.e. texts are repeated verbatim whereby the illocutionary role – i.e. the pragmatic function – of the original speech-act need not be retained.[45] *Meta-texts* on the other hand may fall back upon the literal material of the pre-text but need not do so: 'Meta-textuality and palintextuality can now be differentiated by definition in that the use of expressions from the pre-text represents a necessary characteristic of palintextuality ..., for metatextuality this represents simply an accidental feature'.[46]

If we now attempt to define meta-textuality as opposed to inter-textuality, which places texts side by side and looks for their literary dependence, meta-textuality describes the higher level upon which in a text the 'textuality or constructed character of the objective text' is expressed 'thematically' and thereby already explicated in the text itself.[47]

Hence in a macro-text such as 2 Cor., wherever meta-communicative structures are discernible they can be differentiated and interpreted in particular e.g. as meta-linguistic, meta-argumentative or meta-textual statements. Correspondingly the Pauline epistolary hermeneutics revealed by such meta-communicative structures have linguistic, argumentative and text-theoretical aspects.

3.3.3. *Meta-communication in 2 Corinthians*

Meta-communicative structures can be detected in numerous places in 2 Cor. These can be more narrowly defined according to the individual forms of meta-communication named above such as meta-speech, meta-argumentation, etc. In conclusion these diverse forms of communication will now be listed and their respective (epistolary) hermeneutical function determined.

(1)　A *meta-communication* always takes place where Paul reflects in principle upon the process of communication with the Corinthians (e.g. 2 Cor. 1.13f.; 6.13; 7.8ff.).

(2)　This linguistic process, which may be described generally as 'meta-communication', contains diverse specific meta-communicative forms or types which one can further differen-tiate as follows:

(2.1)　in the meta-communicative process with the Corinthians Paul expresses himself particularly in the form of *meta-speech* when

44.　Stocker, *Theorie*, p. 55.
45.　Stocker, *Theorie*, p. 53; cf. 4.4.5.
46.　Stocker, *Theorie*, p. 58.
47.　Wolf, 'Metatext', p. 366.

he writes about the language of his speaking to the addressees (2 Cor. 8.8; 12.19);

(2.2) autobiographical passages may be described as *meta-narration*, and where Paul himself makes statements about the manner of his argumentation (2 Cor. 8.8, 10) this may be designated *meta-argumentation*;

(2.3) on the one hand Paul formulates his statements in the form of *intertextuality* to the extent in which he implicitly or explicitly refers to biblical statements (e.g. 2 Cor. 3.7ff.; 4.13; 8.15; 9.9; 10.17; 13.1; 6.16ff., here: God speaking) or to possibly written statements of his opponents (2 Cor. 10.10);

(2.4) on the other hand Paul makes *meta-textual* statements to the extent in which he retrospectively refers to earlier letters as formulated writings and to their effect (2 Cor. 2.3f., 9; 7.3; 7.8f., 12f.; 10.9, 11).

The individual types of meta-communication and their respective hermeneutical functions can thus initially be represented theoretically for 2 Cor. in the following pattern:

Meta-communicative type	Hermeneutical function
meta-communication in general	process of communication
meta-speech	language of speaking
meta-narration	autobiography
meta-argumentation	argumentation
inter-textuality	interpretation of biblical passages or reference to other texts
meta-textuality	earlier letters

In what follows I shall analyse the passages in 2 Cor. which reveal meta-communicative structures from which relevant epistolary hermeneutical reflections by Paul can consequently be discerned. In the process the exegetical presentation will not follow the order of the distinctions made here of the individual types of meta-communication which can be expected in 2 Cor. Rather the pattern of the exegesis for its part represents a distilled synopsis of those aspects which Paul reflects upon in 2 Cor. as his emerging epistolary hermeneutics.

Chapter 4

WRITING AND UNDERSTANDING

LETTER HERMENEUTICS IN 2 CORINTHIANS

In the first chapter of this investigation we observed a desideratum in the important approaches presently being undertaken to the understanding of 2 Cor. What is missing is an epistolary hermeneutical interpretation. Now we have extended *literarcriticism* to a *literarhistorical* reconstruction of the processes of letter production and letter reception, and this reconstructed correspondence sequence must now be tested by exegesis. The impulses which led to the rhetorical, epistolographical and explicitly hermeneutical textual analyses will also be taken up but at the same time they will be further developed in a distinct model of *epistolary hermeneutics internal to the text*.

By 'internal to the text' is meant the linguistic (particularly the syntactic and semantic) dimension of a text while 'external to the text' designates the reference of a text in reality. Understood in this way text-internal relations constitute the cohesion of a text.[1] Text-internal hermeneutics can pose general questions about the statements the text itself contains on the production and reception of letters. In this concentration on the text, text-internal hermeneutics borders upon what literary studies can achieve by 'text-immanent analysis'.[2]

The following exegesis searches for an epistolary hermeneutical conception internal to the text of 2 Cor. – i.e. it works out which statements 2 Cor. contains to show how Paul himself viewed and reflected upon the process of writing and understanding his letters. In the process we must take into account on the one hand the *conditions* which underlie the writing and reception of letters in antiquity as well as in the present – namely the situation of the communication, the transition from orality to scribality, the form of the letter, the processes of writing (i.e. of formulation and dictation) and the conditions of early letter reception.

On the other hand the communication and meta-communication in 2 Cor. will be investigated using the categories suggested for *describing* the various levels of epistolary communication, for the *transition* from orality

1. See Gülich/Raible, *Textmodelle*, p. 42.
2. Here compare the description in Rusterholz, 'Verfahren', pp. 365ff.

to scribality takes place in epistolary communication. Within the frame of this communication by writing Paul consequently also emerges as a 'literary' *letter-writer* when he formulates explicit meta-communicative statements. These *meta-communicative* statements on the one hand interpret the process of writing on the epistolary hermeneutical level and also create a meta-communicative surplus on the *theological-propositional* level.

Hence the *leading questions* which now need to be considered in the exegesis are the following:

- Which statements does Paul make on the process of letter-writing? Does Paul comment upon the various phases of his epistolary communication with the Corinthians?
- How does Paul 'speak' to the Corinthians? How does Paul evaluate the relationship between orality and scribality? To what extent does Paul reflect upon the form of the letter?
- What can we infer from 2 Cor. about the reception of the Pauline letters and about the success of communication through letters?
- How does the 'theological' style of 2 Cor. arise in the context of meta-communicative statements?

The text-internal epistolary hermeneutical exegesis analyses the segments of the text in which Paul writes about his current and earlier letter-writing. At the same time there is to be found in 2 Cor. a reference to the reception of the Pauline epistles in Corinth itself.

The epistolary hermeneutical aspects brought to light in the detailed exegesis will be compiled in the conclusion.

4.1. *On Letter-writing – 2 Corinthians 2.3f., 8f.; 7.8f., 12f.; 9.1; 13.10*

4.1.1. *Translation*

(A) 2 Cor. 2.3f., 8f.

2.3a And I am writing this very letter so that, when I come, I shall not be grieved by those over whom I should rejoice

2.3b since with regard to all of you, I am certain that my joy is your (joy).

2.4 I am writing to you in much doubt and anguish of heart, shedding many tears – not to cause you distress but to let you know the love which I have for you particularly.

(...)

2.8 So I warn you to affirm your love for him:

2.9 for this is why I am writing, that I may see how you are proving yourselves (and) whether you are obedient in everything.

(B) 2 Cor. 7.8f., 12f.

7.8a　If I have caused you distress in the letter, I do not regret having done so.

7.8b　And if I did regret it – for I see that that letter caused you grief for a short time –

7.9a　I now rejoice, not because you were distressed, but because your distress caused you to repent:

7.9b　for you felt such a godly grief that you were not punished by us in any way.

　　　(...)

7.12a　Consequently, if I am writing to you it is not on account of the one who did the wrong nor on account of the one who suffered the wrong

7.12b　but so that your zeal for us might become clear among you in the sight of God.

7.13a　Therefore we are comforted.

(C) 2 Cor. 9.1f.

9.1　It is unnecessary for me to write to you about the offering for the saints:

9.2a　for I am aware of your willingness which I boast about to the Macedonians ...

(D) 2 Cor. 13.10

13.10　That is the reason why I am writing this in my absence, so that when I am with you I shall not need to treat you severely using the authority which the Lord has given me for building up and not for tearing down.

4.1.2. *Exegetical observations*

The verses which are interpreted here do not make up a connected section of the text; it is rather a matter of passages in the text which originally may possibly have been parts of different letters. The same subject is common to them all: Paul comments on his writing to the Corinthians. Consequently the relevant hermeneutical question is: Why and how does Paul describe his reason for writing to the Corinthians?

(A) 2 Corinthians 2.3f., 8f.
(a) The meta-argumentative function of 2.3f.

2 Cor. 2.3f. is usually taken in the *context* as the conclusion of the unit 1.23–2.4[3] or located within 1.12–2.13.[4] The following exegetical observations suggest that, after the thematic opening of the epistolary corpus (1.12–14), we have in 1.15ff. a description of Paul's altered travelling plans which gives explicit grounds for the omitted visit to Corinth (1.15, 23; 2.1) and extends at least up to 2.11. In this section Paul gives a comprehensive explanation of why he is writing to the Corinthians instead of visiting them. From 2 Cor. 2.3f. we can draw the epistolary hermeneutical conclusion: 'In place of the visit there is a letter.'[5]

Paul reflects upon this process of letter-writing. Ἔγραψα (2.3, 4) is usually understood as a temporal aorist. If this is so, Paul is here referring to an earlier letter. This earlier letter is then assumed to be either 1 Cor.,[6] or a writing no longer existing which was sent in the period between 1 and 2 Cor.,[7] or it was the so-called 'plaintive letter'[8] which has either been lost[9] or is reconstructed from 2 Cor. as it now stands.

If Paul is referring to an earlier letter (cf. 7.8, 12) he is speaking meta-textually. But there is a second possibility, namely that we take the aorist as *epistolographic*.[10] If Paul is using the aorist epistolographically and is reflecting upon the letter in front of him, he is making *meta-argumentative* statements.[11]

The following observations speak for the second possibility. Paul decides (ἔκρινα) not to make another painful visit (μὴ πάλιν) to the Corinthians (2.1). In 2.2 and 2.3b he gives as reason for this (γάρ) the fact that, if he causes the Corinthians distress, he himself cannot have pleasure (εὐφραίνων) in anyone. For he knows (πεποιθώς) that the χαρά of the Corinthians is inseparably bound to his own (2.3b). Instead of visiting them Paul writes (καὶ ἔγραψα τοῦτο αὐτό, ἵνα μὴ ἐλθὼν λύπην σχῶ ἀφ' ὧν ἔδει με χαίρειν).

Hence the two verbs ἔκρινα and ἔγραψα are to be interpreted on the same temporal level as *epistolographic aorists*. In ἔκρινα Paul conveys his

---

3. As in the commentaries of Klauck, Wolff and Windisch. Bultmann, *Brief*, pp. 41ff. understands 1.15–2.4 as a connected section.

4. So e.g. Lambrecht, *Corinthians*, pp. 25ff. or Thrall, *Corinthians*, pp. 128ff.

5. Klauck, *Korintherbrief*, p. 28.

6. Thus Bosenius, *Abwesenheit*, pp. 29f.

7. So Wolff, *Zweite Brief*, p. 41.

8. See e.g. Windisch, *Korintherbrief*, p. 80.

9. Thus Lambrecht, *Corinthians*, p. 31.

10. Trobisch, *Entstehung*, p. 124 also interprets the aorist as epistolographic but as having the function of a 'formulistic component of the letter-ending'.

11. Bosenius, too, in *Abwesenheit*, p. 29 points out that if ἔγραψα is an epistolographic aorist it must be concerned with 'comments *about 2 Cor.*'.

'frame of mind ... at the time of writing'.[12] The decision to write to the Corinthians instead of visiting them reflects Paul's emotional state at the actual time of writing. Correspondingly ἔγραψα relates as an epistolographic aorist to the process of the current writing. The specific aorist-aspect indicates a reflexive element in respect of Paul's emotional state.

The τοῦτο αὐτό is used adverbially and relates to what has just been written. The preposition ἀπό stands for παρά. Individual Corinthians are therefore not the originators but the cause of Paul's potential grief. Analogous to 2.3, 2.4 also contains a negative final clause (ἵνα μὴ/οὐχ) which states the aim of the letter negatively: the Corinthians should not be distressed but – in the sense of a positive antithesis – realize the ἀγάπη which Paul has for them.

Hence Paul uses meta-argumentation on the one hand to the extent in which he depicts his emotional state while writing the current letter: Paul writes ἐκ γὰρ πολλῆς θλίψεως καὶ συνοχῆς καρδίας ... διὰ πολλῶν δακρύων (2.4). On the other hand he expresses himself both negatively and positively on the intention of his argumentation. Both his emotional state and the purpose of his writing are reflected in the semantic antithesis.

(b) *The semantic inventory of 2.1–4*

The various 'lines of thought in the text' can be grasped with the aid of the *semantic inventory*.[13] The semantic lines, which are functionally dominant, then permit us to draw conclusions about the pragmatic epistolary function of the text.

2.1–4 first of all contains lexemes with meanings belonging to the field of *'grief'*, such as λύπη (2.1, 3) and λυπέω (2.2, 4), and which are on each occasion defined by an object or a prepositional phrase. We also find θλίψις, συνοχὴ καρδίας, πολλὰ δάκρυα (2.4) which are not supplemented by any further expressions.

The concepts λύπη and λυπεῖν are most prominent in 2 Cor., and specifically in 2.7. In 2 Cor. 6.10 – similarly to 2 Cor. 2.3 – Paul contrasts the λυπούμενοι with the χαίροντες; it is clear from Rom. 14.15 that λυπεῖν can thwart an action done in ἀγάπη; moreover, those who have no hope grieve (1 Thess. 4.13). Λύπη and ἀνάγκη are brought together in the context of the offerings (2 Cor. 9.7). Both come from the heart just as Paul feels λύπη in his heart (Rom. 9.2). The grief can have a specific cause and can increase (Phil. 2.27). In the context of 2 Cor. 7.8ff. Paul had caused grief to the Corinthians in an earlier letter, the one mentioned in 2 Corinthians 2. Thereby he caused a λύπη κατὰ θεόν which then led to a μετάνοια εἰς σωτηρίαν (7.9f.). The λύπη τοῦ κόσμου on the other hand, leads to death (7.10b).

---

12. Koskenniemi, *Studien*, p. 194.
13. See Egger, *Methodenlehre*, pp. 96ff. (quotation from p. 97).

In the case of δάκρυον and συνοχή we are dealing with Pauline hapaxlegomena. Paul uses θλῖψις in many senses. In the Corinthian correspondence θλῖψις entails probation, a trial period (2 Cor. 4.17; 8.2); it is made felt in suffering and deprivation (2 Cor. 8.13), both in the list of difficult circumstances (2 Cor. 6.4–5) or in the eschatological horizon (1 Cor. 7.28); it denotes a Christian way of life which can be filled with παρρησία, καύχησις, παράκλησις and χαρά (2 Cor. 7.4). In terms of subjective human experience χαρά and χαίρω can be understood as the opposite of θλῖψις or λύπη (2 Cor. 6.10; 7.4, 9; 8.2).

The group of words meaning *'joy'* (εὐφραίνω, χαίρω, χαρά, ἀγάπη) which is used as the contrast to 'grief' dominates the epistolary pragmatics because it is clearly bound up with the communication of the intention of the letter: in 2.2–4 Paul expresses his attachment to the Corinthian congregation.

In Paul χαρά in principle never appears 'as a profane attitude' but is 'linked to his work as apostle':[14] συνεργοί ἐσμεν τῆς χαρᾶς ὑμῶν (2 Cor. 1.24). But 'joy', considered in the absolute, can also describe an inner state which is based on the relationship of the Apostle to the congregation (2 Cor. 7.7, 13, 16; 13.9, 11) and has a theological dimension.

Ἀγάπη counts as standing in opposition in that in 2.4 it is set over against λυπέω. It is pointedly given priority. Paul wants the Corinthians to be aware of (γινώσκω) his love. The expression περρισσοτέρως εἰς ὑμᾶς applied to the addressees is, apart from 2 Cor. 2.4, only otherwise found in 2 Cor. – namely in 7.15 and in a similar way in 1.12 (πρὸς ὑμᾶς) and 12.15 (ὑμᾶς ἀγαπῶ[ν]). In this way Paul stresses his particular attachment to the Corinthians. Thus the expression τὴν ἀγάπην ἵνα γνῶτε as contrasted with λυπηθῆτε again shows precisely why Paul is writing in distress. He is not writing to cause them grief but with the intention that they should comprehend (γινώσκω) the ἀγάπη which binds him particularly to the Corinthian congregation.

Hence in 2.1–4 Paul ponders upon the process of writing with an eye upon the attendant emotional circumstances and the purpose of his writing. This can be described with the aid of three epistolographic topoi.

(c) *Epistolographic topoi in 2.1–4*

First, in his writing Paul gives indications of his own personality. Hence one could say that his soul is reflected in the letter: σχεδὸν γὰρ εἰκόνα ἕκαστος τῆς ἑαυτοῦ ψυχῆς γράφει τὴν ἐπιστολὴν (Demetrius, *De Elocutione* §227) in so far as Paul refers to his emotional state (2 Cor. 2.3f.) while he is composing the current letter.

In ancient letters the self-portrayals of the epistolary 'I' have a meta-communicative purpose since they seek to establish a relationship with the

---

14. Conzelmann, 'χαίρω', p. 359.

recipient of the letter. In that they reflect the individuality of those participating in the communication, letters and dialogue are related so that one can 'gather from the letters the author's frame of mind'.[15]

Here however there is a difference between the epistolary theory and the actual practice of writing: it has to be recognized that 'the assertion that the innermost nature of the author comes to expression in a letter is hardly ever realized in practice, if anywhere in Seneca'.[16]

Second, the letter contributes to φιλοφρόνησις (Demetrius, *De Elocutione* §231). In antiquity the genre of the *'letter between friends'* existed as a distinct epistolary τύπος (Ps.-Demetrius, τύποι ἐπιστολικοί 1 or Ps.-Libanius, ἐπιστολιμαῖοι χαρακτῆρες 11) but in the pagan realm of the pre-Christian era it took a 'stereotyped' form in language and content.[17] The ἀγάπη-motif constitutive for 2 Cor. 2.4 is first expanded within the field of epistolary literature in Christian writings. 'Where Christian writers choose to use ἀγάπη, they do so ... out of epistolographic convention: either as a verbal adaptation to the recipient or adopting antiquity's ideas of friendship.'[18] The lexemes Paul uses from the field of meaning associated with 'joy', and in particular the definition of the reason for writing in 2.4, consequently have a philophronetic character.

Third, ancient letter-writers understood the letter as a *conversation* or as a substitute or as 'one half' of the conversation: εἶναι γὰρ τὴν ἐπιστολὴν οἷον τὸ ἕτερον μέρος τοῦ διαλόγου (Demetrius, *De Elocutione* §223). Accordingly letters are considered as conversations with people who are not present, and the letter appears 'as a presence of the friend generated by the resources of language'.[19] The scenario of a letter between friends is also represented in the apocryphal exchange of letters between Paul and Seneca: 'Pseudo-Seneca is for Pseudo-Paul present "in" the letter in such a way that he "hears" what he "says"'.[20]

In the course of this the process of writing can also be explicitly thought through: thus Seneca (*Epistulae morales* 40.1) refers to the process of writing the letter in such a way as to imagine through the letter the physical presence of the friend who is writing. One might discern such a reference in the Pauline letters in Gal. 6.11. In 2 Cor., however, Paul is not only seeking to achieve proximity to the addressees but expresses himself meta-communicatively because he is reflecting upon the process of writing – i.e. he wants to engage in epistolary hermeneutics.

Paul takes up the motif of the substitute for a conversation when he

---

15. Thraede, *Grundzüge*, p. 23.
16. Müller, 'Spiegel', p. 143.
17. Koskenniemi, *Studien*, p. 126.
18. Thraede, 'Einheit', p. 39.
19. Müller, 'Spiegel', p. 141.
20. Fürst, 'Pseudepigraphie', p. 92.

explains (1.15, 23; 2.1, 3f.) that he is writing to the Corinthians although he would rather be with them in person. Yet letter and conversation are for Paul by no means equivalent forms of communication. For Paul thinks about the fact that (and the reason why) he is *writing* to the Corinthians instead of visiting them, and he informs them of this in meta-argumentation. Thus Paul uses the letter as a medium of written meta-communication, so that in the first instance meta-communication takes place as if in a face-to-face communication – although there this occurs not only in linguistic but also in para-linguistic and extra-linguistic ways. But he formulates *epistolary hermeneutic* observations in the shape of epistolary meta-communication in which he writes *about* the communi-cation with the Corinthians and consequently about letter-writing itself. Moreover what is specific about written meta-communication is that both reflexive distance is created *and* a challenge to overcome this distance is formulated. Thus in 2 Cor. Paul expresses himself meta-communicatively and does not merely choose the letter-form in the first instance 'to solve theological conflicts'.[21]

Compared with the normal practice of epistolographic communication in antiquity it can be seen that Paul has a disproportionately strong personal and philophronetic style of writing and – going beyond using the letter as a substitute for conversation – deliberates meta-communicatively about it.

(d) *Similarities and differences between 2.3f. and 2.8f.*

Between 2 Cor. 2.8f. and 2.3f. there are various *similarities*. Both in 2.3f. and in 2.8f. Paul reflects in a meta-argumentative fashion on the letter he is writing.

Hence 2.8f. together with 2.1ff. should be linked to the *context* of the explanation for the changed plans for his journey (1.15ff.) (see above). It is also connected *semantically* to 2.1ff. by the lexemes with the root λυπ-. Moreover the *temporal aspect* in 2.9 is equivalent to 2.3f. for here, too, Paul uses the aorist ἔγραψα epistolographically, i.e. he relates it to the current process of letter-writing.

The *difference* between 2.1–4 and 2.8f. exists in respect of their *pragmatic purpose*. In 2.1–4 ἔκρινα and ἔγραψα, as transitive verbs in the main clauses, indicate the pragmatic function: Paul expresses himself meta-communicatively when he reflects upon the letter as a medium of communication in place of a visit. He describes his current emotional state while drafting the letter and mentions the objective of his writing: the Corinthians should be aware of his love.

By comparison in 2.5–9 the transitive verbs in the main clause are παρακαλῶ and ἔγραψα. Correspondingly 2.8f. contains a further

---

21. Thus Bosenius, *Abwesenheit*, p. 43.

statement on the purpose of the letter: Paul is writing to the Corinthians to find out (γινώσκειν) their δοκιμή and to see whether they are obedient in all things (εἰς πάντα ὑπήκοοί ἐστε).

Paul starts from an exemplary but possibly real case (2.5ff.) which, however, in the meantime belongs to the past: the perfect λελύπηκεν expresses a completed action but one which still has an effect in the present. The wrongdoer has already received his punishment (2.6). Paul *now* – i.e. at the time of writing – desires that he should be forgiven (2.8).

Hence starting from a specific case, but now stylizing and generalizing, Paul gives instructions on how the Corinthian congregation should deal with a presumed (τις) wrongdoer. This person does not distress Paul but in the end causes distress to the whole community (2.5); since he receives punishment (ἐπιτιμία) for this (2.6), Paul exhorts (παρακαλῶ) the congregation to forgive him (χαρίσασθαι) and show him love (2.7f., 10), for this is in accordance with Christ and liberates from the influence of Satan (2.11). In 2.10f. Paul concludes with a general Christian observation which represents the *meta-communicative surplus*.

In 2.8f. Paul conceives the writing as an act of 'admonition'. The introductory εἰς τοῦτο in 2.9 is to be understood as both anaphoric *and* cataphoric. Looking back to 2.8, 2.9 includes the *reason* why Paul is writing. At the same time εἰς τοῦτο points forward cataphorically to the final purpose of the letter in 2.9. If εἰς τοῦτο refers to the preceding v. 8 it is connected either to παρακαλῶ or to the content of the 'admonition' (κυρῶσαι εἰς αὐτὸν ἀγάπην). Hence Paul justifies his 'writing' either on the ground *that* he admonishes the Corinthians or on that of the *purpose* for which he admonishes them. There is a difference between 2.3f. and 2.8f. in the *final purpose* of the letter. In 2.4 the Corinthians should not be distressed but apprehend Paul's love for them; in 2.9 Paul wants to discern their δοκιμή.

In 2.9 we again have a final clause (ἵνα) with a subjunctive aorist (γνῶ) which, however, in contrast to the final clauses in 2.3, 4, is not negated. In 2.3, 4 Paul is therefore reflecting upon his writing defensively and consequently explains the *cause* of his writing: he wishes primarily to avoid the mutual distress that might be occasioned by a possible visit to Corinth. In 2.9 on the other hand Paul is taking the offensive in describing the *purpose* of his letter. In 2.4 γινώσκειν implies a compassionate perception and understanding, whereas in 2.9 it has the sense of a conducive anticipation – namely to test the obedience of the Corinthians (εἰ εἰς πάντα ὑπήκοοί ἐστε cf. also 13.6). Δοκιμή is very rare in the whole of Greek and in the NT is used by Paul alone; it should be translated as 'proved character'. Hence with δοκιμή Paul is describing the character of Christian existence to be found in proving oneself and being put to the test. The following εἰ-clause can be taken as a clarification of this δοκιμή. The Corinthians are to be tested to see if they are obedient.

2.3f. and 2.8f. are therefore *meta-argumentative* statements to the extent to which in the course of the argument they reflect upon and explain the act of writing. In 2.3f. Paul considers the medium of 'letter-writing' as alternative to a visit (ἔκρινα – ἔγραψα) and the line of thought which is connected with 'joy' is effectively dominant. In 2.8f. on the other hand Paul mentions a specific *pragmatic aim* of his writing, namely that of paraclesis: in view of a presumably real incident in Corinth Paul writes to the Corinthians to admonish them and put them to the test.

(B) 2 Corinthians 7.8f., 12f.

In various *literarcritical* hypotheses 2 Cor. 7.8f., 12f. are assigned to the same letter as 2.3f., 8f. We must critically question this general *literarcritical* verdict in what follows because, in contrast to 2.3f., 8f., a temporal interpretation of the aorist forms in 7.8f., 12f. seems plausible. In that case, the section 7.8–12.13a will belong to a letter other than 2 Cor. 2 since it contains remarks about a *previous letter*.

(a) *Meta-textuality and meta-communicative surplus in 7.8–10*

In the analysis of 2 Cor. 7.8f. two details support the interpretation of the aorist forms as temporal: first, with the expression ἐν τῇ ἐπιστολῇ in 7.8 Paul is definitely referring to a writing described as a 'letter' (cf. 1 Cor. 5.9). This is an instrumental dative. Second, in 7.8f. the verbs in the past tense are usually placed in semantic opposition to verbs cast in the present form.

7.8 ἐλύπησα – μεταμέλομαι
     μετεμελόμην – βλέπων[22] – ἐλύπησεν
7.9 χαίρω – ἐλυπήθητε – ἐλυπήθητε
     ἐλυπήθητε – ζημιωθῆτε

While the present forms indicate his emotional state while the current letter is being written, the verbs in the past tense, particularly those in the aorist, point to an earlier situation: Paul is thinking about the effect of an *earlier letter* to the Corinthians. Hence he is expressing himself *meta-textually*.

2 Cor. 7.8, 9 is constructed in the narrower context around the verbs λυπέω and μεταμέλομαι[23] which are taken up in the sense of key-words and are semantically opposed to the expression ὥστε με μᾶλλον χαρῆναι (7.7).

In 7.8a Paul declares that he does not regret the grief which his earlier letter occasioned. It is admittedly not clear from this whether Paul intended to cause such distress by his letter or not. Paul simply comments

---

22. Cf. P[46].
23. Paul uses μεταμέλομαι only in 2 Cor. 7.8.

on the fact *that* the plaintive letter had distressed the Corinthians in such a way that he now does not regret it. Verse 8b connects with the motif of repentance by means of a key-word (μεταμέλομαι), again in the form of a conditional clause. Verse 8b sounds like a moderation of 7.8a and syntactically is simply continued in 7.9a (νῦν χαίρω). In a parenthesis inserted into the conditional clause (βλέπω) Paul stresses that he is aware of the distress caused to the Corinthians.

At this point many exegetes see a lack of logical syntax.[24] This also coincides with the difficulties uncovered by textual criticism.[25]

I would suggest the following syntactical structure for 7.8–9a:

7.8a Protasis:	ὅτι εἰ καὶ ἐλύπησα ὑμᾶς ἐν τῇ ἐπιστολῇ
Apodosis:	οὐ μεταμέλομαι
7.8b Protasis:	εἰ καὶ μετεμελόμην
Parenthesis	βλέπων ὅτι ἡ ἐπιστολὴ ἐκείνη εἰ καὶ πρὸς ὥραν ἐλύπησεν ὑμᾶς
7.9a Apodosis:	νῦν χαίρω, οὐχ ὅτι ...
7.9b Explanation:	ἐλυπήθητε γὰρ κατὰ θεόν
Final/consecutive clause:	ἵνα ἐν μηδενὶ ζημιωθῆτε ἐξ ὑμῶν

7.10a Generalizing definition of the λύπη κατὰ θεόν
7.10b Generalizing definition of the λύπη τοῦ κόσμου

The present participle βλέπων in 7.8b permits a syntactical coordination or a modal or causal subordination of the parenthesis to the main verb of the protasis ('if I have caused you distress – whereby I see that'). This parenthetical insertion scarcely seems necessary in the logical progression which is heading for the νῦν χαίρω in 7.9a but it shows clearly that here Paul – as generally in 7.8, 9 (cf. the use of key-words and conditional constructions already mentioned) – is regarding the effect of his earlier letter upon the Corinthians with increasing circumspection (εἰ καὶ πρὸς ὥραν).[26] This being so, the parenthesis might certainly have been occasioned by an 'anacoluthon in dictation'.[27] Because the letter is the subject of the ὅτι-clause, it is clear by implication that Paul is here exercising caution. He does not make himself the subject but transfers the distressing effect – which Paul himself explicitly did not intend – to the letter.

---

24. Here see e.g. Thrall, *Corinthians*, p. 491.
25. Windisch, *Korintherbrief*, p. 230.
26. This can be understood to mean 'relatively speaking', Barnett, *Epistle*, p. 374.
27. Thus Windisch, *Korintherbrief*, p. 230. He interprets this as follows: '... P[aul] wrestles with the words. This is caused by the fact that he wishes to make a definite statement but with reservations ... P[aul] wishes to show just cause for three things – his letter, his temporary regret and his current unrepentant joy'.

Hence in 7.8 Paul leaves open the extent to which he regrets the distress caused to the Corinthians and makes the letter rather than himself responsible for this distress. Notwithstanding all possible regret he emphasizes: νῦν χαίρω. In 7.9a he gives the reason for this joy, saying that he rejoices not over the distress as such but because the distress of the Corinthians led to their μετάνοια. This μετάνοια conforms to a distress κατὰ θεόν. In 7.9b Paul points out that the Corinthian congregation – ἵνα here must be taken as both consecutive *and* final – have thereby escaped punishment at the hands of the Apostle.

Finally in 2 Cor. 7.10 Paul differentiates between a λύπη κατὰ θεόν and a λύπη τοῦ κόσμου. Here Paul is using general theological terms and in this way creates a *meta-communicative surplus*.

After Paul has actively expressed his present joy in 7.9a, he bases it passively from the point of view of the Corinthians: ἐλυπήθητε, and that εἰς μετάνοιαν. Apart from 2 Cor. 9.7f. there is only one other instance of the use of μετάνοια in Paul, in Rom. 2.4: if we hold on to the basic meaning of μετάνοια as 'a change of heart', in Rom. 2.4 the χρηστὸν τοῦ θεοῦ leads (ἄγειν) man to μετάνοια. In 2 Cor. 7.9a it is for the moment the 'grief' – qualified in 7.9b by the expression κατὰ θεόν – which produces such a repentance or conversion. The news of this conversion of the Corinthians was brought to Paul by Titus and the comfort he experienced among the Corinthians (7.6f.). In 7.10 Paul further qualifies the connection between λύπη κατὰ θεόν and μετάνοια (εἰς σωτηρίαν). This he does in the shape of an antithetical parallelism, the theological evaluation of which is controversial. Is it a general statement 'in the form of a maxim'[28] or a 'concrete statement which fits the effect of the Pauline letter to Corinth into the antithesis between God and the world'?[29]

In 7.10 Paul formulates a theological statement which develops out of his meta-communicative reflection and thereby creates a meta-communicative surplus. Paul expresses himself meta-textually and in this connection retrospectively interprets the distress occurring in Corinth theologically, i.e. he inserts the contrast between θεός and κόσμος.

While the λύπη κατὰ θεόν achieves a σωτηρία ἀμεταμέλητος[30] the λύπη τοῦ κόσμου brings death. But the idea that Paul in this antithetical differentiation assigns the 'worldly grief' 'to his own person' and the grief κατὰ θεόν 'to his letter'[31] and in so doing gives prominence to the salutary character of his letter in contrast to a disastrous visit to Corinth can only with difficulty be read into 7.10. Rather calling 7.10 a meta-communicative surplus signifies that a statement which Paul makes in the context of a

28. Thus Windisch, *Korintherbrief*, p. 231.
29. Lietzmann, *Korinther*, appendix, p. 206.
30. Cf. also Rom. 11.29. For Paul the non-regrettable – in Rom. 11.29 related to God – is linked to concepts of salvation.
31. So Bosenius, *Abwesenheit*, p. 40.

meta-communication develops a propositional theological dynamic of its own over and above such a meta-communicative function.

Hence in the retrospective we find the *distress* of the Corinthians (ἐλυπήθητε), its *consequence* (μετάνοια) perceptible to Paul, and Paul's *theological interpretation* of this (7.9b: κατὰ θεόν, 7.10a: εἰς σωτηρίαν ἀμεταμέλητον) as well as an action actually intended by Paul.

On balance we can establish: Paul reflects meta-textually on his earlier letter and its effect upon the Corinthians. This earlier letter distressed them but did not cause them any actual damage. Since the Corinthian distress was κατὰ θεόν and led to μετάνοια, it brought about a σωτηρία ἀμεταμέλητος (7.10a). It remains open whether Paul originally intended to cause this distress with his letter. It is more likely that Paul retrospectively and meta-textually interprets the effect of the letter and its consequences theologically, assesses them soteriologically and thereby creates a meta-communicative surplus.

Because Paul interprets the whole process of distress and conversion in retrospect κατὰ θεόν, he does not declare that his letter-writing is salutary but qualifies the *effect* of the letter, namely that the Corinthians *were made* (passive!) to be distressed, as a theological possibility in a soteriological dimension. Paul does not portray himself as a letter-writer who deliberately pursues a particular theological purpose in his writing but reflects *retrospectively* in a meta-textual fashion upon the effect of his earlier letter and interprets this theologically. In the process he releases a meta-communicative surplus.

Hence we must stress a fundamental epistolary-hermeneutical difference between 2 Cor. 2 and 2 Cor. 7: in 2 Cor. 2 Paul interprets his present writing and, using meta-argumentation, names the pragmatics of the current letter; in 2 Cor. 7, commencing with the effect of the letter, Paul interprets his earlier writing in a meta-textual way and thereby creates a meta-communicative surplus. Consequently in the context of meta-communicative reflection on letter-writing, the meta-communicative surplus does not arise as meta-argumentation with a specific pragmatic intention concerning the current letter but as meta-textuality, as a reflection on the effect of an earlier letter.

(b) *Meta-textuality and meta-communicative surplus in 7.12f.*
Paul mentions retrospectively – i.e. after he has become aware of the reactions in Corinth to his earlier writing – the reason for and the purpose of the earlier letter and expresses himself in a meta-textual fashion: here too ἔγραψα functions as a temporal aorist and the meta-textual expression is causal (ἕνεκεν).

This ἕνεκεν with the genitive expresses a reason, whereas Paul constructs the epistolary-hermeneutical statements in 2 Cor. 2.4, 9 as final clauses with ἵνα and consequently as a declaration of intent.

Although 7.12 must therefore represent a consequence (ἄρα) of what has gone before, Paul is formulating it *ex eventu*. 'We have to suppose that he is retrospectively attributing to himself an intention which was not present at the time of writing, but which, in the light of the letter's effects, might appear to have been its real purpose.'[32]

Accordingly in 7.12a Paul was, it is true, induced to write to the Corinthians because of certain events in Corinth (ἕνεκεν τοῦ ἀδικήσαντος οὐδὲ ἕνεκεν τοῦ ἀδικηθέντος). But he maintains that he wrote, not because of these events but – seen retrospectively – with an evocative intent which was of a sociative, communicative and theological character: ἕνεκεν τοῦ φανερωθῆναι τὴν σπουδὴν ὑμῶν[33] τὴν ὑπὲρ ἡμῶν πρὸς ὑμᾶς ἐνώπιον τοῦ θεοῦ.

The *sociative* element is to be seen on the one hand in the accumulation of personal and possessive pronouns; on the other, Paul uses σπουδή for his participatory enthusiasm for the tasks of the congregation.[34] Paul expresses the *communicative* element by means of the motif of 'being revealed', i.e. through the outwardly visible proof of their zeal for Paul. The ὑπὲρ ἡμῶν is not only personal but is to be understood *pars pro toto* for Paul and his co-workers and their work for the gospel. This enthusiasm should be visible to the Corinthians themselves (πρὸς ὑμᾶς). The *theological* element, namely the Corinthians' responsibility ἐνώπιον τοῦ θεοῦ, is added. This is a general theological *topos* of Paul's.[35] With these sociative, communicative and theological perspectives Paul creates a meta-communicative surplus.

In 7.13a there follows διὰ τοῦτο παρακεκλήμεθα: Paul is currently comforted – the perfect has the sense of the present, yet the events reported still continue to have an effect on the subject. Here the meta-textual observations on the earlier letter, its motive and effect, and the ensuing events in Corinth reach their conclusion. The comfort only appears with the revelation of the Corinthians' zeal for Paul (διὰ τοῦτο). In this respect Paul retrospectively sees a 'main purpose' of the earlier letter[36] as being to rouse this enthusiasm. From this perspective the earlier letter takes on a cybernetic function. But it is a retrospective in which Paul expresses himself meta-textually, not about a current letter but about the effect of an earlier writing.

---

32.   Thrall, *Corinthians*, p. 495. Windisch, *Korintherbrief*, p. 236, again thinks differently: the ἄρα shows 'that nothing other came to pass than what P[aul] expected'.

33.   On the originality of this version see Thrall, *Corinthians*, p. 496 n. 73.

34.   See the other instances in Rom. 12.8, 11 and in 2 Cor. 8.7, 8, and 8.16 – the enthusiasm for a person is here, too, to be taken ecclesiologically.

35.   Compare further instances in Rom. 14.12; 1 Cor. 1.29; 2 Cor. 4.2; Gal. 1.20; compare also Rom. 3.20 and 2 Cor. 8.21.

36.   Windisch, *Korintherbrief*, p. 239.

(c) *The differences between chapters 2 and 7*

Between the meta-communicative statements in 2 Cor. 2.3f., 8f. and 7.12f. there exist not only those differences which are caused by the different interpretations of the aorist as epistolographic or temporal. The past history, Paul's current state while writing the letter – which is reflected in the semantics – as well as the purpose of the letter all make it clear that in 2 Cor. 2 Paul is referring to the letter he is currently writing while in 2 Cor. 7 he is referring to an earlier letter. These differences can be summarized yet again in the following table:[37]

The *past history* described	the current *state of mind*	*the purpose of the letter*
2 Cor. 2.3f., 8f. λύπη through τις (2.5ff.) ἡ ἐπιτιμία (2.6)	πεποιθώς (2.3b) ἐκ γὰρ πολλῆς θλίψεως ... (2.4a) παρακαλῶ (2.8)	τὴν ἀγαπὴν ἵνα γνῶτε (2.4) κυρῶσαι εἰς αὐτὸν ἀγάπην (2.8) ἵνα γνῶ τὴν δοκιμὴν ὑμῶν (2.9)
2 Cor. 7.8f., 12f. Titus' report (7.6f.): ἐπιπόθησις, ὀδυρμός, σπουδή ἐλύπησα ὑμᾶς ἐν τῇ ἐπιστολῇ and ἐλυπήθητε and μετάνοια (7.8, 9a)	οὐ μεταμέλομαι (7.8a) χαίρω (7.9a) παρακεκλήμεθα (7.13a)	theological interpretation of the λύπη (7.9b,10) = *meta-communicative surplus* ἕνεκεν ... τὴν σπουδὴν ὑμῶν (7.12b)

Hence while in 2 Cor. 2 Paul is reflecting upon the letter he is currently writing, in 7.8ff. he returns to an earlier letter. Accordingly the epistolary hermeneutics in ch. 2 develop from meta-argumentative statements which relate to the current process of letter-writing. In 7.8ff. on the other hand Paul formulates epistolary hermeneutical statements in the context of a meta-textual reflection and creates a meta-communicative surplus.

(C) 2 Corinthians 9.1f.

From 2 Cor. 3.1 and chs 8 and 9 it is clear that Paul also knew and could write practical letters. 2 Cor. 9.1f. is the beginning of the second so-called 'offertory letter' which, like ch. 8, might be the 'fragment of an administrative document'.[38] The literary relationship between 2 Cor. 8

---

37. For their part these differences are the basis for the verdict that the aorist in 2 Cor. 2 is epistolographic while that in 2 Cor. 7 is temporal.

38. Betz, *Korinther*, p. 256.

and 9 is disputed.[39] Within the extant Corinthian correspondence Paul broaches the subject of the collection of offerings in 1 Cor. 16.1–4: περὶ δὲ τῆς λογείας τῆς εἰς τοὺς ἁγίους ... In 1 Cor. 16.1–2 Paul introduces λογεία as a fixed term for these collections.[40]

2 Cor. 8 and 9 are fragments in that they lack the opening and closing formulae. In 8.1ff. support is requested among the Corinthian congregation for the collection for the early Christian community in Jerusalem; 8.16–24 can be understood particularly as a letter of recommendation for Titus and his companions.[41] On the other hand, 9.1ff. is often taken as a letter about offerings in the form of a circular letter to the congregations in Achaia.[42] 'Achaia', however, as addressee, does not necessarily mean a number of individual congregations: the *adscriptio* in 2 Cor. 1.1 (in contrast to 1 Cor. 1.2) shows that 'Achaia' denotes the countryside surrounding Corinth and the Christians living there who count themselves as belonging to the Corinthian community. Consequently 2 Cor. 8 and 9 might be separate writings addressed to Corinth *and* Achaia, which Paul wrote consecutively during his mission to gather offerings in Macedonia (8.1; 9.2, 4).

(a) *On the form and structure of 9.1f.*

In 9.1 Paul does not use a finite form but constructs his statement on the current letter with a non-finite verb: περὶ μὲν γὰρ ... περισσόν μοί ἐστιν τὸ γράφειν ὑμῖν. Thereby he explicitly moderates the necessity of his writing but chooses the form of a letter to prepare them for the sending of the 'brethren' (see 9.3, 5). He begins the actual recommendation of the collection with the περί-phrase.

With περὶ δέ Paul answers specific questions from Corinth (1 Cor. 7.1) or himself takes up a specific topic (1 Cor. 7.25; 8.1, 4; 12.1; 16.1, 12). Thereby 1 Cor. receives a formally structured thematic profile. The set phrase is a 'topic marker, a shorthand way of introducing the next subject of discussion ... By the formula περὶ δέ an author introduces a new topic *the only requirement of which is that it is readily known to both author and reader.*'[43] When Paul uses this formula in his letters it is an indication that the topic under discussion has already been the subject of an earlier communication.

---

39. Compare Thrall, *Corinthians*, pp. 36–43 and recently also Mitchell, 'Korintherbriefe', pp. 1691ff.

40. See LS, p. 1055, which translates λογεία as 'collection for charity'. This term is also used in secular Greek for a collection of money, cf. Bauer/Aland, p. 965; on the term see also Beckheuer, *Paulus*, pp. 110ff. or Classen, 'Sprache', p. 334 n. 83. He subsumes λογεία as a *terminus technicus* under the terms from 'business life' or 'legal life'.

41. See Beckheuer, *Paulus*, pp. 142ff.

42. See e.g. Georgi, *Kollekte*, pp. 56ff.

43. So Mitchell, 'Concerning', p. 234.

In 2 Cor. 9.1, however, the phrase used is περὶ μέν and this is supplemented by ἔπεμψα δὲ τοὺς ἀδελφούς (9.3). Consequently this μέν-δέ expresses: 'It is *in fact* unnecessary to write to you about the offering for the saints' – 9.2 contains the reason (γάρ) – '*but* I am sending the brethren'. The question whether περὶ μὲν γάρ in 9.1 necessarily begins a new letter[44] or can also have a connecting function to the preceding context[45] is not important since 2 Cor. 9 – if it is an independent writing about offerings – has been preserved without an epistolary opening. In 9.1ff. περὶ μὲν – δέ means particularly 'in fact – but': hence in his writing Paul is aiming for the real message that he is sending brethren to Achaia/Corinth to finalize the collection (9.3–5).[46] But the epistolographic expression περί so typical of Paul is also one which is basically used for the beginning of a new topic. That a new theme is mentioned in 9.1 is clear from the explicit definition of διακονία: περὶ ... τῆς διακονίας τῆς εἰς τοὺς ἁγίους. What is meant here is the collection of money for the original Christian community in Jerusalem (Rom. 15.25).

In 2 Cor. διακονία predominantly means the apostolic ministry (2 Cor. 3.7ff.; 4.1; 5.18; 6.3f.) ultimately in regard to the Corinthian congregation (2 Cor. 11.8). In 2 Cor. 8 and 9 διακονία and διακονεῖν are applied to the collection of offerings – i.e. to support 'through alms and assistance'[47] (2 Cor. 8.19f.; 9.13; 8.4; 9.1, 12; see also Rom. 15.31).[48] Hence εἰς τοὺς ἁγίους – εἰς should be understood as an 'expression of modification'[49] – means the company of the Christian community in Jerusalem. The collection of offerings is, after all, important for Paul himself as a missionary programme.[50]

Paul indicates why he does not have any further need to make the collection a central theme in his letter to the Corinthians: because (γάρ in

---

44.   This is the thesis in Betz, *Korinther*, p. 166: 'The particle μέν signifies that γάρ ... does not have to relate to something that has preceded.'

45.   Stowers, 'Integrity', pp. 347f. propounds this thesis.

46.   It is therefore natural to take the aorist form ἔπεμψα in 9.3 as an epistolographic aorist: Paul sends the brethren while he is writing but formulates this from the perspective of the reception of the letter.

47.   Bauer/Aland, p. 369.

48.   Explicitly named as διακονία εἰς τοὺς ἁγίους in 2 Cor. 8.4; 9.1 and as διακονία τῆς λειτουργίας ταύτης in 9.12.

49.   See BDR §207.3, particularly n. 4.

50.   Compare Collins, *Diakonia*, p. 219: 'The concept of the gift to the needy church of Jerusalem as a delegation from the churches of Asia is vital to Paul because in Jerusalem he hopes to receive the acknowledgement of an act of fellowship that has been demonstrably public on the part of the churches founded by him.'

9.2a) he is aware of their προθυμία[51], i.e. the eagerness of the congregations in Achaia (9.2b) to contribute to the collection.

(b) *The meta-argumentative function of 9.1f.*

Does 9.1f. contain an independent statement or is it simply a rhetorical topos?

Stylistically 9.1 could be a topical *paraleipsis*[52] or a *praeteritio*.[53] A *praeteritio* is 'the announcement of the intention to omit certain things. In most cases the speaker immediately after such an announcement passes on to treat other things. The announcement of the intention to omit certain things includes the naming of these things.'[54] Both aspects – the omission and the naming – can be found in the context of 9.1–5, 6ff.: Paul indicates that he is not intending to promote the collection but does so in 9.6ff., 12f. In 9.2–5, however, he does in fact refer to past events and talks about the dispatch of co-workers.

9.1f. is a meta-argumentative statement of a rhetorical nature *and* at the same time leads up to a statement with content: 9.1f. is rhetorical in that – contrary to the content of the proposition – it introduces the following writing about the offering (9.6ff.). 9.1f. preserves its own internal significance in that in 9.1 the topic of the offering is certainly broached in a pointed if rhetorical way, but this is then followed in 9.3–5 simply by a clear message to Achaia/Corinth. Hence initially in 9.1f. Paul in fact does not begin a discussion about the offerings but leads up to a practical message before he then takes up the theme of the offerings in 9.6ff. The *meta-argumentative* function of 9.1f. consists in the fact that Paul explicitly wants to be sure that the following letter is not understood as a 'literary' writing but as a 'technical' one on the subject of the collection of offerings with a specific message. When Paul then does make fundamental deliberations on the giving of offerings (9.6ff., 12f.) these appear as a *meta-communicative surplus*. The meta-argumentative statement in 9.1f., however, identifies what then follows (9.3–5) as an 'administrative writing'.

(D) *2 Corinthians 13.10*

2 Cor. 13.10 forms the conclusion of the corpus of what was presumably the last letter in the Corinthian correspondence; in 13.11–13 there follows the epistolary ending. The section 12.14–13.10 can be called an 'apostolic

---

51. Paul uses προθυμία only in the writings about offerings in 2 Cor. 8.11, 12, 19; 9.2; in the NT it only appears elsewhere in Acts 17.11 where it is used in connection with the reception of the apostolic proclamation of the gospel.

52. Thus Wolff, *Zweite Brief*, p. 180, with reference to BDR §495.3.

53. Paul professes 'at most to touch upon the theme but in so doing he in fact creates the basis for a more extended treatment', Klauck, *Korintherbrief*, p. 72.

54. Lausberg, *Handbuch*, §882.

parousia' with individual paraenetic elements; 13.11 functions as a brief 'letter-ending paraenesis'.[55] The account of the preparations for the third visit begins in 12.14. In 12.19ff. there is a change of genre from *apologia* to *paraenesis*. Seen as a whole, 12.19–13.10 contains admonition. The pragmatic assessment of 12.19–13.10 and consequently of 13.10 itself, however, is debated in regard to details. 13.10 is considered to belong either to the context of 13.1ff. or 13.5ff. so that 13.10 is assigned either a paraenetic or paracletic function or that of the conclusion of a speech.[56] There is no dispute that subsequent to the talk about foolishness (11.1–12.13) Paul begins in 12.14 to speak about his third visit. This topic contains some warnings but in the end these are cancelled out by the conclusion of the letter (13.11–13).

13.10 can be described as a reflexive comment in view of the epistolary announcement of a visit which begins with 12.14ff.

(a) *The meta-argumentative function of 13.10*

Paul reflects in *meta-argumentation* in 13.10 on his current writing in connection with his preparation for the visit (12.14ff.) which also contains admonitory sections. To which parts of the letter is Paul referring in this particular case?

For the moment 13.10 will be seen in the narrower *context* of 13.9b; διὰ τοῦτο gives a reason.

13.9a χαίρομεν. . . ὅταν. . . ὑμεῖς δὲ δυνατοὶ ἦτε
13.9b τοῦτο καὶ εὐχόμεθα
        τὴν ὑμῶν κατάρτισιν
13.10a διὰ τοῦτο ταῦτα ἀπὼν γράφω

The connection of διὰ τοῦτο ταῦτα ἀπὼν γράφω in 13.10a to the preceding 13.9b is established by τοῦτο. In 13.9b τοῦτο represents the object for which Paul prays, namely the κατάρτισις of the Corinthians. If διὰ τοῦτο in 13.10a takes up this expression again, the writing ἀπὼν functions as an intercession for the restoration of the Corinthian congregation. This can also be confirmed by 13.11: κατάρτισις is admittedly a hapaxlegomenon in the NT, but in 13.11 Paul uses the verbal form καταρτίζεσθε – not in a meta-argumentative function but in the imperative – to challenge the Corinthians to this 'being restored'. In this way 13.9b and 13.11 are connected semantically. That the purpose of Paul's writing is indeed to ask for this restoration is confirmed by the inclusion of the imperative from the root καταρ- in 13.11.

But 13.10 also extends beyond the immediate context of 13.9, 11. For in

---

55. Schnider/Stenger, *Studien*, p. 93.
56. Bultmann, *Brief*, pp. 238ff.; Klauck, *Korintherbrief*, p. 102; Sundermann, *Apostel*, pp. 214ff.; Thrall, *Corinthians*, pp. 871ff.

13.10, after the apostolic *parousia* has been time and again permeated by 'I'- and 'we'- passages,[57] Paul once more changes to the first person singular and writes about *his* writing. Paul also writes in a summarizing fashion in that with ταῦτα in 13.10 he finally looks back on the whole section of the letter (from 10.1 or 12.14).

Thus διὰ τοῦτο ταῦτα ἀπὼν γράφω can be taken as a meta-argumentative explanation of the whole section of the letter commencing with 12.14 or 10.1. After the experiences of his second visit, defending himself against the Corinthian congregation (13.3) and in view of his third visit (12.14; 13.1) Paul now makes his feelings clear in advance while he is still absent (προλέγω ... ἀπὼν νῦν ...): ὅτι ἐὰν ἔλθω πάλιν οὐ φείσομαι (13.2).

Hence in 13.10 Paul is writing as an absentee *about* his current missive (first person singular, present) and names his *goal* in a final clause (ἵνα): he wishes, παρών, that he will not have to 'deal severely' (ἀποτόμως χρήσωμαι) as he could in accordance with the ἐξουσία given to him by the Lord. There is no object in the form of a personal or possessive pronoun (e.g. ὑμῖν, ὑμῶν) which would indicate the addressees of the letter or the recipients of possible severe action at the hands of the Apostle 'present' in the congregation. Hence in 13.10 Paul does not direct his remarks specifically to the Corinthians.

The adverb ἀποτόμως is a hapaxlegomenon in Paul. With ἐξουσία in relation to his office as Apostle Paul usually means his apostolic rights (see 1 Cor. 9.4–6, 12, 18). Only in 2 Cor. 10.8 and 13.10 is the apostolic ἐξουσία qualified as one given by the Lord.[58] Here, then, we are talking about a specific ἐξουσία which Paul characterizes more closely with regard to its function: εἰς οἰκοδομὴν καὶ οὐκ εἰς καθαίρεσιν (10.8; 13.10). In this way the preposition εἰς with the accusative can be taken as a statement of purpose. While καθαίρεσις is to be found in the whole of the NT only here and in 2 Cor. 10.4, Paul uses οἰκοδομή particularly in the Corinthian epistles and usually in an ecclesiological connection: for the 'edification' of the congregation (1 Cor. 14.3, 5, 12, 26; 2 Cor. 10.8; 12.19; compare also Rom. 14.19; 15.2) or the congregation as a 'building' (1 Cor. 3.9) or as an eschatological topos (2 Cor. 5.1).

Hence in 13.10 Paul names an aim of his writing which at least refers back to 12.14ff. and consists in the fact that Paul, as an absent Apostle, also writes with a paraenetic intention so as not to have to let his apostolic

---

57. In the context of 12.14–13.10 the 'I'-passages are to be found in: 12.14–18a, 20–21; 13.1–3, 6, 10; and the 'we'-passages in: 12.18b-19; 13.4, 7–9.

58. In a similar fashion in Rom. 13.1ff. Paul qualifies the ἐξουσία of the state – as a political and legal or technical administrative entity – as one given by God. Here see O. Wischmeyer, 'Staat', pp. 156ff.

authority have an ecclesiological effect in Corinth when he is there in person.

(b) *The* parousia-*motif*

Finally, the participles ἀπών and παρών appear together frequently in Paul's writings (1 Cor. 5.3; 2 Cor. 10.1f., 11; 13.2, 10). This comparison of the 'absent' and 'present' Apostle is to be found in meta-communicative contexts. This *parousia-motif* is an established epistolographic topos in the context of philophronetic letters.[59] But does this topos now give expression to *more* than the awareness of the distance between those communicating or to the attempt to establish closeness by means of the letter?

Possible interpretations of the *parousia*-motif are as follows: 'It is ... no longer simply a matter of the closeness attested to in the letter but a total identity of the letter with the Apostle's "sentence". This makes the letter a binding judgment in the hands of the congregation.'[60] Or Paul modifies this epistolographic topos: he is not primarily concerned with the φιλοφρόνησις but with the 'fulfilment of several other goals: encouragement ... claim to authority ... intensification of the threat'.[61]

The *parousia*-motif in 2 Cor. 13.10 can be interpreted as follows: Paul reflects meta-argumentatively upon the process of writing from 10.1ff. or 12.14ff. (ταῦτα ... γράφω) and does so in connection with the advance notice of his visit. But this implies that Paul is aware of the difference between presence and absence. The fact that Paul is writing about his writing is also evident when he contrasts his writing as ἀπών with his acting in ἐξουσία as a present Apostle. Furthermore, Paul names the intention of his missive. It consists in the fact that Paul wishes to avoid acting as soon as he arrives in Corinth in the harsh manner corresponding to his specific apostolic ἐξουσία. This has been given to him by the Lord for building up and not for tearing down the congregation (13.10). Paul is implicitly taking pains to restore the congregation by intercessory prayers (13.9b) and admonition (13.11).

Hence with the *parousia*-motif Paul on the one hand makes clear the difference between his presence and his absence; his function as an absent letter-writer does *not* correspond to that as a present Apostle.[62] But on the other hand he does not attribute to his writing any specific function which goes beyond the function of a personal visit.[63] Hence Paul writes equally

---

59. See Koskenniemi, *Studien*, pp. 38ff. or Thraede, *Grundzüge*, pp. 97ff.
60. Thraede, *Grundzüge*, pp. 99f. on 1 Cor. 5.3.
61. Bosenius, *Abwesenheit*, pp. 110ff.
62. Contrary to Thraede, *Grundzüge* (see above).
63. Against the determination of the function of the writing in Bosenius, *Abwesenheit* (see above).

in place of as well as *in view of* a visit. He reflects upon the process of his writing in the current argumentation and this explicitly with the parousia-motif in 13.10 – i.e. in meta-argumentation.

4.1.3. *Epistolary hermeneutic aspects*

What does Paul tell us about his letter-writing in the various parts of the text (A)–(D)?

In *2 Cor. 2.3f., 8f.* Paul reflects upon his current missive in a meta-argumentative way. He tells of his emotional state and names a two-fold intention of his writing: he is writing to the Corinthians instead of visiting them (2.3f.), he is writing out of love for the Corinthians (2.4) and his purpose is paracletic (2.8).

In *2 Cor. 7.8f., 12f.* on the other hand Paul uses the meta-textual method to describe the effect of his previous letter. Thus he retrospectively describes the effect of the letter on the Corinthians as soteriological (7.9f.). Furthermore, Paul gives reasons for the consolation he personally experiences (7.12). Consequently he formulates retrospectively such a pragmatic function for his earlier epistle, which had a paracletic and cybernetic aim (7.9). With his soteriological style Paul creates a meta-communicative surplus (7.10). While the epistolary hermeneutic factors in ch. 2 consequently derive from meta-argumentative statements with concrete pragmatic epistolary aims they do so in 7.9ff. within a meta-communicative framework which here is founded in the 'perceived effect' and is expressed meta-textually.

In *2 Cor. 9.1f.* Paul takes up a theme already known to the Corinthians (περὶ μέν), namely that of offerings. Paul reveals his missive to be 'technical' to the extent in which he points to a specific message, namely the sending of 'brethren' to Corinth/Achaia. The letters about offerings consequently have a more administrative than literary or theologically normative character (cf. 8.7–11).

2 Cor. 13.10 should be read as a meta-argumentative discussion on letter-writing which relates back to 10.1 or 12.14. Paul differentiates the process of writing as an act of the absent Apostle from the action of the Apostle present among them, which takes place in ἐξουσία.

The statements on letter-writing consequently develop the following epistolary hermeneutic aspects: Paul formulates his epistolary hermeneutics retrospectively. In place of a visit he writes to the Corinthians in a meta-communicative way. He considers in meta-argumentation *or* meta-textuality the process and purpose of letter-writing and in so doing formulates *epistolary hermeneutic statements*. In the process he interprets the events in and his relationship to Corinth theologically and thereby creates a *meta-communicative surplus* (7.10; 9.6ff., 12f.). The various meta-communicative statements on γράφειν show that Paul is consciously deliberating upon the process of inscription and upon the scribality of his letters. In deliberately reflecting upon the process and purpose of his writing and the form of the letter Paul develops elements of his epistolary hermeneutics.

4.2. *On the reception of the letters – 2 Corinthians 10.9–11*

4.2.1. *Translation*

10.9   I do not wish to raise the impression that I want to frighten you with my letters.

10.10a One says 'the letters are weighty and strong

10.10b but the bodily presence is weak and the speech is contemptible'.

10.11a Such a person should consider this:

10.11b as we are with our words in our letters when we are absent

10.11c we are the same when present in our deeds.

4.2.2. *Exegetical observations*

The verses 9–11 which are taken together here from the last extant letter of the Corinthian correspondence are connected semantically by the motif of 'letter'.

Paul speaks of letters in the plural, i.e. he is talking about several letters the effect of which is under discussion here. Although it is clear that these were letters from Paul and his fellow-workers, the 'letters' in 10.9–11 are not supplemented by a genitive pronoun of authorship such as ἡμῶν: hence it is not the authorship but the *effect* of these letters which is under discussion. In this respect Paul makes the reception – in the sense of the effect – of his letters the central theme in 10.9–11. In 10.10 he talks about letters in the nominative plural, and they function as the subject of the clause to which the predicates βαρεῖαι and ἰσχυραί are related. In 10.9 and 10.11 the 'letters' are in the genitive plural and joined to the preposition διά, i.e. they are thematized from their modal function.

Hence in 10.10 Paul discusses the effect of his letters from the viewpoint of his opponents and in 10.9, 11 in view of their modal function. In that Paul not only picks up inter-textually possible remarks of his opponents but himself writes *about his own* letters he here formulates *meta-textual* statements.

(a) *On the effect of Pauline letters according to 10.9–11*

In 10.9 Paul expresses negatively the effect *he* intended his letters to have: Paul states in the *negative* expression of will that he does not wish to frighten the Corinthians (ἐκφοβεῖν). Earlier in 10.8 Paul had used a *positive* formulation to say that he uses the ἐξουσία given to him by the

Lord to build up and not to destroy the congregation. In view of the connotation of the verb ἐκφοβεῖν in the Judaeo-Hellenistic provinces[64] Paul's meaning in 10.9 can be understood in the sense that he wishes to clear away from his letters the possible impression of terror and consequently counteract possible hostility. Nevertheless the infinitive ἐκφοβεῖν is structured as a comparison (ὡς). 2 Cor. 10.10, 11 are connected over and above the motif of the letter by the comparison of the present and absent Apostle (see also 10.1, 2; 13.2, 10). When in 10.10 Paul takes up a quotation of possible opponents in Corinth he takes up a pre-text inter-textually (to speak in terms of text-theory). That 10.10 is a quotation is on the one hand clear from the ὅτι-recitativum and on the other because between 10.10a and b an explicit speaker is mentioned in the third person singular (φησίν).[65] In so far as one sees in 10.1ff. a clash between Paul and opponents in Corinth one will take 10.10 as a climax, namely as an explicit report of antagonistic criticism.

With this quotation Paul takes up what he himself knows about the effect of his letters. To this we can add further structural, semantic and form-historical observations.

In 10.10ab there is both a parallel *and* a chiastic structure:

10.10a αἱ ἐπιστολαί μέν,	φησίν	βαρεῖαι καὶ ἰσχυραί,
10.10b ἡ δὲ παρουσία ...		ἀσθενὴς ...
ὁ λόγος		ἐξουθενημένος

There is an obvious parallelism in the arrangement of nouns and predicative pronouns; 10.10ab are connected one to the other adversatively by the particles μέν ... δέ, and semantically the strength of the letters (10.10a) is contrasted in a chiasmus with the weakness of the Apostle when he is present speaking (10.10b).

In a *semantic* respect it is striking that 10.10ab contains vocabulary which is in part unusual for Paul. Here the question arises whether Paul is quoting a statement formulated in these words by opponents or accusers or whether he is transforming them into his own way of speaking (on this see the form-historical observations below).

The letters are first described as βαρεῖαι καὶ ἰσχυραί. There are many instances of the lexeme βαρύς – for Paul a hapaxlegomenon – in its general sense: the examples in the NT relate either to the observance of

---

64. ἐκφοβεῖν is a hapaxlegomenon in the whole of the NT. There are however several occurrences in the LXX where, apart from those in the Wisdom Literature (Job 7.14; 33.16; Sap. Sal. 11.19; 17.6, 9, 19) they are mostly found with the negative as in Paul – particularly in the prophetic literature (Mic. 4.4; Nah. 2.11(12); Zeph. 3.13; Ezek. 34.28; 39.26).

65. The singular form φησίν is to be preferred to the variant reading φασίν – see e.g. Lambrecht, *Corinthians*, p. 157 – not least because of the congruence with the number in 10.11a (τοιοῦτος).

commandments and statutes (1 Jn 5.3; with the negative in Mt. 23.4, 23) or to αἰτιώματα (Acts 25.7). In the LXX there are examples which use βαρύς in connection with ῥῆμα (Exod. 18.18; Num. 11.14) or λόγος (Dan. 2.11). The conjuncture of βαρύς and speech is evident in ancient rhetoric: in Aristotle[66] βαρύς denotes the 'deep' in contrast to a high (ὀξεῖος) or middle (μέσος) vocal register (τόνος) in which an orator should declaim. By contrast Aristotle names the 'loud', 'quiet' and 'middle' voice (φωνή) as μεγάλη, μίκρα and μέση.[67] As a rule in rhetoric in general βαρύς describes 'the quality of the tone or accent or the kind of style'.[68] From 10.10a we could possibly surmise that the 'thorn in the flesh' which Paul mentions (12.7) was caused by a vocal abnormality.[69] For if his letters are βαρεῖαι and βαρύς also stands for vocal strength, but the presence of the Apostle by contrast is marked by weakness (10.10b), the παρουσία ...ἀσθενὴς καὶ ὁ λόγος ἐξουθενημένος could point to a malady which impedes his power of vocal expression.

Two semantic lines can be made out for the connection of βαρύς with speech: first, βαρύς denotes a 'claim' in the content (e.g. 1 Jn 5.3; Dan. 2.11); second, the aesthetic 'shaping' (e.g. Aristotle), the vocal expression or the rhetorical pathos of spoken utterances. Thus we can envisage two possible views of the effect of the Pauline letters in 2 Cor. 10.10: either Paul's letters were considered to be demanding, or they achieved a rhetorical effect. Evidence can be cited for both views.

Since in 10.1–8 Paul appeals to the apostolic ἐξουσία with expressions relating to struggle (e.g. 10.3), it is possible that ἐπιστολαὶ βαρεῖαι refers to the *demands contained in* the letters which Paul writes to the Corinthians. Alternatively the letters reveal a *power of phonetic expression* which fails to function when Paul is there in person, possibly because of a physical weakness. At the same time – assuming 2 Cor. as we have it is a compilation – we can excerpt from it indications of the *pathos aroused* by Paul's letters: for in 2.3ff. Paul is weeping while writing and in 7.8ff. he summarizes the soteriological effect of this letter. Hence it is clear that the so-called 'plaintive letter' could provoke the Corinthians to feelings of remorse and cause them to change their ways. Thus 10.10 might be a

---

66. See Aristotle, *Rhetorik* 1403[b] 30.

67. Compare Lausberg, *Handbuch*, §1079.3, who refers to the rhetoric of Iulius Victor in connection with the *genus grande*. Iulius Victor, *Ars rhetorica* 438.12 describes the *genus grande* in Greek as βαρύ.

68. Classen, 'Sprache', p. 333 with reference to sources.

69. See Jegher-Bucher, 'Pfahl', particularly p. 39. She sees Paul's 'defect' in the fact 'that when he is speaking he is as stiff and awkward "as if he had swallowed a ruler"'. This meant that his speeches were quiet and unimpressive.

repetition of the effect of the plaintive letter (1.1–7.4) which Paul himself interprets retrospectively in the following letter (7.8f.).

Paul also picks up the accusation of possible opponents who describe the ἐπιστολαί as ἰσχυραί. Paul uses the adjective ἰσχυρός[70] frequently with a theological (1 Cor. 1.25, 27) or ecclesiological (1 Cor. 4.10; 10.22) connotation. Except for 1 Cor. 10.22 ἀσθεν- forms the semantic opposition to ἰσχυρός in the verses mentioned.

Now, however, Paul paradoxically says weakness is strength (1 Cor. 1.27). In 2 Cor. 10–13 Paul frequently speaks of ἀσθένεια in relation to his own person (11.30; 12.5, 9, 10; 13.4): he boasts about his weakness (2 Cor. 11.30) and creates a *meta-communicative surplus* in talking about his personal weakness. For Paul refers to a dominical word to legitimize his weakness (2 Cor. 12.9f.) and makes 'weakness' a constitutive part of his theology of the cross (2 Cor. 13.4).

When in 2 Cor. 10.10a Paul makes the point that his letters are thought to be 'strong' and 'weighty' (ἰσχυρός and βαρύς), this is an indication of their effect in Corinth as was clear in the case of the 'plaintive letter'. The verdict on the personal presence of the Apostle is contrary to that on the powerful impact of the letters. Paul adds this in the adversative in 10.10b: Paul's appearance is characterized as ἀσθενής and his speech or λόγος as ἐξουθενημένος. But against the background of Paul's 'weakness'-theology this judgement by the opponents is shown to be invalid, for Paul wants to boast about his weakness, not his strength (see above).

With the phrase παρουσία τοῦ σώματος Paul is speaking about his own 'personal presence'[71] (in a similar manner to e.g. 1 Cor. 5.3). There is a conjunction of 'presence' and ἀσθενής in Josephus.[72] Paul makes frequent use of the participle ἐξουθενημένος or forms of the verb ἐξουθενέω[73] for which there are many examples in Judaeo-Hellenistic writings.

(b) *The question of the pre-text in 10.10*

If Paul in 10.10ab is picking up a quotation or a possible pre-text – i.e. is quoting hostile accusations – he is writing *inter-textually*. Form-historical considerations might bring us closer to answering whether Paul is

---

70.   The only NT instances which describe the 'strength' of vocal utterances are Heb. 6.18 (παράκλησις) and Rev. 18.2 (φωνή). In profane Greek literature *Dionysius of Halicarnassus* uses ἰσχυρός in connection with discussions on precise literary structuring with a provocative effect (*De compositione verborum* 22). Here it is related to the 'literary style': see LS, pp. 843f.

71.   Bultmann, *Brief*, p. 192. It is understood in a more comprehensive way in Thrall, *Corinthians*, p. 631: 'This expression is to be understood in a comprehensive sense, of the apostle's whole outward character and personality, not only his personal appearance in the narrower sense.'

72.   See Josephus, *Antiquitates* 1.273.2.

73.   See 1 Cor. 1.28; 6.4; 16.11; Gal. 4.14; 1 Thess. 5.20; Rom. 14.3, 10.

referring to such a pre-text or whether he is linguistically transforming possible accusations into a statement of his own and is consequently writing *meta-textually*. Some suspect that Paul is here quoting from an indictment[74] or that he is arguing in the style of the diatribe.[75] But what references to sources does Paul give in the Corinthian correspondence?

Paul frequently takes up the arguments of others, including his opponents (e.g. 1 Cor. 1.12; 15.12). Occasionally he explicitly names the sources which keep him informed about the situation in Corinth: either he has before him written enquiries (1 Cor. 7.1, 25; 8.1; 12.1) or has received verbal reports (1 Cor. 1.11; 16.17; 2 Cor. 7.7). In a similar manner Paul might in 2 Cor. 10.10 be referring to a 'letter of complaint' or be taking up a 'catchword' which 'was verbally mentioned to him by Titus or other visitors to Corinth'.[76] In 2 Cor. 10.10, however, Paul makes no mention of a source. Moreover, I preferred to use an impersonal translation of φησίν above because it seems unlikely that the third person singular – like the τοιοῦτος in 10.11a – indicates a specific opponent as in 11.4.

Hence the tradition-historical origin of the expression in 2 Cor. 10.10 cannot be determined with certainty. We can, however, assume that when Paul takes up these putative hostile accusations he is taking up a stance against a criticism of his person generally known in Corinth. Moreover it is clear that in 2 Cor. 10.10 we have the only statement Paul gives in the form of a quote about the effect of his letters.[77]

We are equally unable to make a definite decision about the tradition-historical background of the semantic assessment of the letters as 'weighty' and 'strong'; semantically, a judgement on either the rhetoric or the content of the Pauline epistles may be implied.

(c) *Paul's self-quotation in 10.11*

Paul has not only heard about the effect of his letters in Corinth – in written form or by word of mouth – but communicates *his* answer to the Corinthians in a letter. In 10.11 Paul answers, in the *appellative* (λογιζέσθω) and in a *self-quotation*, the opponents' criticism which he acknowledged in 10.10ab. He *describes* himself in his 'presence' and 'absence'.

At the same time Paul *differentiates* his effectiveness in his work as an absent and as a present Apostle: as an absent Apostle Paul writes epistles; when he is present he shows himself to be an Apostle through what he

---

74.   Thus Betz, *Apostel*, e.g. p. 119.
75.   See Bultmann, *Brief*, p. 192 and *Stil*, pp. 10 and 66f.
76.   Windisch, *Korintherbrief*, p. 305.
77.   This is at the same time the oldest statement about the effect of the Pauline epistles. Then come 2 Pet. 3.15f. and Polycarp, *Phil.* 3.2 among the Apostolic Fathers; see Windisch, *Korintherbrief*, p. 305.

does. Alongside the differentiation of absence and presence there emerges an *equivalence of value*: for Paul considers the word which comes by letter in his absence (ἀπών) as having the same value as the work of the Apostle when he is present.

Paul's differentiation on the one hand and statement of equivalence on the other can be observed in the grammar of 10.11.

The two participles ἀπόντες – παρόντες stand together in a chiasmus:

10.11b	τῷ λόγῳ δι' ἐπιστολῶν	ἀπόντες ...
10.11c	παρόντες	τῷ ἔργῳ

In the first place λόγος and ἔργον appear as semantically opposed in the chiastic structure of 10.11bc. This counter-positioning of λόγος and ἔργον in the dative, which here is a *dativus modi*, is only to be found elsewhere in Paul in Rom. 15.18. Initially, then, the letter of the absent Apostle and the action of the Apostle present stand in semantic opposition.

Paul then, however, transcends this discontinuity between the Apostle's writing and personal presence by setting absence and presence pronominally on the same level in their modal effect (dativus modi): οἷοί ... τοιοῦτοι. Hence Paul sees a continuity between writing letters and a personal appearance in respect of their effect.

In the end one can conclude a specific *pragmatic intention* from this continuity, namely that of the *paraenesis*: if Paul's epistles are already felt to be weighty and effective and Paul claims the same identity as an absent letter-writer and an Apostle present in person, this could be demonstrated on his next visit in Corinth (see e.g. 10.2 or 13.10). For then Paul, being there in person, would be as 'strong' and 'weighty' as his letters have previously been found to be.

4.2.3. *Epistolary hermeneutic aspects*
(a) *The significance of the Pauline epistles*

If letters (as in 2 Cor. 10.9–11) are thematized *meta-textually* in a culture which is predominantly oral, this has two implications: Paul had a lively correspondence with Corinth so that his letters have a special significance. What is more, they were clearly found to be weighty and important because of the claims they contained and the effect achieved by their emotiveness (see 2 Cor. 7.8ff. in connection with the 'plaintive letter').

(b) *Orality and scribality*

According to 2 Cor. 10.10f. Paul does see a difference between his effectiveness as a present or absent Apostle; but none at all between the spoken and the written λόγος. The effectiveness of his spoken λόγος by comparison with that of his letters is disparaged by some of the Corinthians in 10.10; but in 10.11 the same λόγος is connected to the written form of the letter and Paul equates the effect of this written λόγος with the impact of his presence as an Apostle. 'The contradiction between written and oral statements is abolished in the correspondence between word of authority and vigour of action.'[78]

Hence Paul assumes a uniform concept of λόγος and does not differentiate between oral and written λόγος as the Corinthians apparently do. This being so, Paul himself does not claim any special status for his epistles even if this might have been ascribed to their first reception – in contrast to the perception of the Apostle's personal presence.

(c) *Meta-textuality*

2 Cor. 10.9–11 is as a whole a meta-textual statement *about* the effect of the Pauline epistles in Corinth. First, the circumstance that Paul's opponents, in their criticism of his personal presence, clearly also make public statements about his letters, is meta-textual. This meta-textuality, however, lies in the area of reconstruction and can only be accessed hypothetically from the existing text. Second, Paul takes up these statements about the effect of his letters inter-textually (10.10), if he is quoting them, or he transforms them meta-textually in his own words. Third, Paul attaches his own meta-textual statements in which he simultaneously qualifies the significance attributed to the impact of textuality: Paul does not wish his letters to raise the impression of terrifying (10.9). In 10.11b Paul makes it clear that the λόγος transmitted by the letters is the same oral λόγος which is considered to be ἐξουθενημένος by his opponents (10.10b). And in 10.11c he sets the λόγος transmitted in writing on a par with his apostolic ἔργον which finally develops and will develop an effect equivalent to that of the letters when the Apostle is present in person. With this paraenetic implication Paul finally leaves his meta-textual statement and returns to the current epistolary situation.

Meta-textuality in 2 Cor. 10.9–11

Possible opponents make meta-textual statements in Corinth about Paul's epistles (hypothetical reconstruction from 10.10)

Paul cites oral (or written?) accusations or pre-texts inter-textually (10.10) or transforms them meta-textually

Paul formulates meta-textual statements (10.9, 11):
- Paul does not wish to frighten them with his letters (10.9)
- the written λόγος corresponds to the spoken (10.11b)
- the written λόγος and personal ἔργον are commensurate in their effectiveness (10.11c).

---

78. Heckel, *Kraft*, p. 17.

4.3. *Writing and understanding: the meta-communication of 2 Corinthians and its epistolary hermeneutical yield*

In his absence Paul writes letters to the Corinthians. Thus the letter serves initially as a substitute for an oral communication, i.e. for a conversation, and makes no claim for apostolic authority but has primarily a communicative/intercommunicative function. The letter, however, has specific elements which permit letter-writing to become an independent form of communication. Paul takes these specific elements into consideration and thereby develops elements of an epistolary hermeneutic.

(1) *Paul writes as ἀπών*

Paul is spatially and temporally separated from the Corinthians when he is writing. In what he writes he is responding to written enquiries or orally transmitted accusations or criticism. He understands his letter as a substitute for a visit, makes practically no difference between the oral and the written λόγος but at the same time differentiates between the functions of visit and letter (13.10). Paul does not remain in the defensive position of one who is reacting but becomes a productive and literarily effective *epistolary author*.

(2) *Paul becomes a literary author of letters*

Paul is in many respects an epistolary author. He is, first, in the sense of an originator together with his co-senders, the author of his letters (1.1). Second, in the history of the early reception of the epistles he becomes identified with them as author because the authorship of and the responsibility for his letters were assigned to him at a very early date (10.10f.). Third, he is an author because he independently takes up topics and is productive in the literary field. He makes himself the subject of his writing in autobiographical passages – which although this may have been caused by the need for apologetics (chs 10–13) is in the first place oriented autobiographically and confessionally (see 11.6; 12.19). He productively tackles conventional epistolographic forms (see 3.1ff.). He also formulates important theological statements linguistically and propositionally. Paul's literary productivity as a letter-writer grows especially out of the *meta-communicative perspectives* of his writing.

(3) *Paul writes using meta-communication*

In the course of his letter-writing Paul reflects upon and comments on his communication with the Corinthians. This meta-communication has aspects of content, relational focus and communication-theory. Paul reflects upon the content of the communication, the relationship to the Corinthians aimed at by the communication and the form of the communication itself – as e.g. his oral speech and letter-writing. Thus he develops elementary epistolary hermeneutical reflections and creates a meta-communicative surplus.

Hence in this meta-communication contained in 2 Cor. we can detect the beginning of Pauline epistolary hermeneutics.

(4) *Paul transforms orality*

Pauline epistolary hermeneutics begin with an implicit classification of the relationship between orality and scribality. Paul considers himself first as a *speaker*: he does not differentiate – in contrast to the Corinthians – between the spoken and the written λόγος (10.11). In the letter he communicates with the Corinthians as speaker and in so doing moves on different *levels of speech* (see 6.11–13; 7.2–4): he introduces his linguistic statements *performatively* and in the process makes use of the action-oriented aspect of language; he speaks to confirm (6.12; 7.4b) or to convince (8.7ff.), or he turns to the Corinthians appellatively (6.13). The differentiation of these levels of speech shows clearly that Paul can depart from the framework of meta-communication and cross over into a level of speech immediately directed at the Corinthians.

But Paul *transforms* his affinity to oral speech in two ways: first, he relates his speaking to the current execution of his letter-writing as is clear e.g. from the meta-linguistic statement in 6.13. Second, he reflects explicitly upon the process of letter-writing.

(5) *Paul formulates epistolary hermeneutics*

As a *letter-writer* Paul reflects and comments upon the process of writing. With these meta-argumentative, meta-textual or meta-linguistic statements Paul develops elements of epistolary hermeneutics which explain how he wishes his writing to be understood:

(5.1)   Paul writes using *meta-communication* when he is thinking about his speaking, his competence in communicating or his writing in general. He writes explicitly in relation to the reading of the Corinthians, whereby their understanding is under an eschatological reservation (1.12–14).

(5.2)   Paul uses *meta-argumentation* in his writing when he reflects upon the current writing-process or comments on the current level of argumentation (e.g. 2.3ff.).

(5.3)   Paul writes *meta-textually* when he refers to statements in earlier letters (7.8ff.) or makes comments of principle about his letters (10.11). In so doing he also gives a theological interpretation to his writing and to the impact of his letter as a kind of meta-communicative surplus (e.g. 7.10).

(5.4)   Paul writes *meta-linguistically* when he reflects particularly upon the mode of his language in the letter to the Corinthians (e.g. 6.13).

(5.5) Out of the meta-communication there evolves a *meta-communicative surplus* and consequently also epistolary theology. For in the course of the meta-communication Paul creates a linguistic and propositional surplus (e.g. 8.9) and thereby opens up various theological perspectives.

(6) *Paul's definition of the letter in 2 Corinthians*

Summarizing these observations on Pauline epistolary hermeneutics in 2 Cor. we may present the following definition of a 'letter' as obtained from the exegesis of the text:

> Paul writes as a productive literary author and intends to communicate. In carrying out his writing he formulates epistolary hermeneutical statements on a meta-communicative level. The epistolary hermeneutics represent the reflexive level of the writing upon which Paul on the one hand considers the writing and understanding of his letters and on the other formulates theological language and sense – which, as a meta-communicative surplus, finally lead from Pauline epistolary hermeneutics to a Pauline epistolary theology.

4.4. *Special analyses*

4.4.1. *On the function of co-senders in the Pauline epistles*

Why are co-senders – such as Timothy in 2 Cor. – mentioned in the Pauline epistles?

The question of a co-sender or co-author of the Pauline letters is controversial. It is sparked off by two observations in particular: first, (apart from Romans) Paul time after time mentions co-senders in the *praescriptio* to his letters; and second, the letters always contain alternately so-called 'I' and 'we' passages. This raises a further question – without for the moment treating these observations separately – i.e. the question of co-authorship: Did Paul draft his letters in 'teamwork'[79] or does the mention of a co-sender simply make it clear that Paul is 'surrounded by a team of fellow-workers'?[80]

These questions are relevant to the epistolary hermeneutics in that, if Timothy was the co-author of 2 Cor., this might explain the possible incohesions in the text *and* the letter must then be considered as having an official character in regard to its epistolographic pragmatic intention.

79. Müller, 'Plural', p. 200.
80. Schnider/Stenger, *Studien*, p. 4.

(1) *On the function of the co-sender*

In the superscriptions to his prescripts (apart from Romans) Paul names co-senders. The significance of multiple senders in antiquity should not be too highly estimated. But looking at the ancient examples we can say: 'When we study Paul's literary activity within the socio-cultural situation of ancient letter-writing, it is the inclusion of named co-senders that is remarkable.'[81] The naming of co-senders can, then, be seen as an unusual epistolographic feature.

The question is why Paul names co-*senders* and to what extent these also functioned as co-*authors*. The reason for naming co-senders is sometimes seen in the fact that the co-senders served as bearers of the letter, or in establishing 'good relations between the correspondents'.[82] It is more difficult to establish to what extent the co-senders were also co-authors: 'It would require that we find extensive sections where "we" unequivocally includes only co-senders.'[83] Timothy at least has been ascribed such a role as co-author of 2 Cor. and at least 2 Cor. 1.1–14 can be considered as a collectively written section.

If we look at the structure of the Pauline *praescriptiones* the following is immediately obvious: they are constructed *communicatively* with reference to the addressees and, in so far as they mention co-senders, *inter-communicatively* with reference to the senders. For on the one hand *superscriptio* and *adscriptio* establish a communication between sender and addressee; on the other hand in 2 Cor. (cf. also 1 Cor. and Phil.) both sender and addressee stand in a wider nexus of communication: alongside Paul as sender stands Timothy as co-sender, and alongside the Corinthian congregation the Christians in Achaia are named as co-addressees. Hence in *superscriptio* and *adscriptio* sender and addressee are related communicatively to each other but they are also connected inter-communicatively to a co-sender or co-addressee.

This observation can be extended to the other Pauline *praescriptiones*, for in Romans the *adscriptio* contains merely a non-specific indication of the addressees which again corresponds to the singular authorship in the *superscriptio*. In Galatians the ἐκκλησίαι are mentioned as the recipients – i.e. the plural senders correspond to addressees in the plural. The mention of 'brethren' as co-senders in Gal. 1.2 shows that here we can scarcely envisage a co-authorship but that Paul in drafting his letters is referring to a larger circle of co-senders.

81. Byrskog, 'Co-senders', p. 235.
82. Byrskog, 'Co-senders', p. 248.
83. This is the criterion named by Byrskog, 'Co-senders', p. 249.

Letter		*superscriptio*	*adscriptio*	
1 Cor. 1.1f.	Paul	Sosthenes	ἐκκλησία	ἐπικαλούμενοι
2 Cor. 1.1	Paul	Timothy	ἐκκλησία	ἅγιοι
Gal. 1.1f.	Paul		ἐκκλησίαι (plural)	
Phil. 1.1	Paul	Timothy	ἅγιοι	ἐπίσκοποι ... διάκονοι
Phlm. 1f.	Paul	Timothy	Philemon	Aphia Archippus, κατ' οἶκόν σου ἐκκλησία
Rom. 1.1,7	Paul		πάντες οἱ ὄντες ἐν Ῥώμῃ	
1 Thess. 1.1	Paul Timothy	Silvanus	ἐκκλησία Θεσσαλονικέων	

Only in 1 Thessalonians are three senders – who are, moreover, mentioned as equals – set against a singular addressee. This is in keeping with the linguistic structure which predominantly uses the first person plural. Hence it may be suspected that we can consider co-authorship only in the case of 1 Thessalonians. These observations on a plurality of senders are consistent with examples from ancient epistolography. In the *Epistulae ad Familiares* Cicero names his son, Marcus, as co-sender of letters to his wife and daughter (XIV.14; XIV.18); but when he is writing simply to his wife he does not make a specific mention of his son (e.g. 14.15). Here, too, a plurality of addressees could have led to a plurality of senders.

We can therefore observe that in the same way as communication between sender and addressee is established by *superscriptio* and *adscriptio*, intercommunication between sender and co-sender and between addressee and co-addressee is achieved by the naming of co-senders or co-addressees.

superscriptio:	sender	↔	co-sender
↓↑	↑↓		
adscriptio:	addressee	↔	co-addressee

Paul does not simply establish communication with the Corinthian congregation by means of the letter. When he writes to plural recipients and simultaneously mentions a co-sender he frees himself from the 'loneliness of the composing "I"' usual in a letter and presents himself to the addressees as a letter-writer who is himself in a dialogue. Yet Paul also writes personally when he writes autobiographically: 'In the space between monologue and dialogue lie the possibilities and limitations of epistolary communication.'[84]

---

84. Müller, 'Brief', p. 61.

Now we must pose the further question: Does this permit us to draw conclusions for understanding the change between the singular and plural person in 2 Cor.?

(2) *On the significance of the so-called 'we'-passages*

In contrast to the prooemium in 1 Cor. 1.4ff. the eulogy in 2 Cor. 1.3ff. is already written in the first person plural. If the 'we' passages predominate in 2 Cor. 1–9, the 'I' passages are predominant in 2 Cor. 10–13.[85] What significance then can we attribute to the change of person in 2 Cor.?

Changes of person are typical of almost all the Pauline epistles. In the main the following four functions are differentiated for the significance of the 'we'. *First*, there is the literary plural, the *pluralis sociativus* – i.e. the association of the addressees with the writer. *Second,* the association of a particular section of the addressees with the writer. *Third,* a general Christian or human 'we'. *Fourth,* the association of co-senders or co-workers. The last-mentioned function can be stated more precisely in a similar manner to the function of the *praescriptio* which was described above as inter-communicative. For the 'we' is *inter-communicative* in that it establishes the association of the senders: on the one hand the *biographical* 'we' allows the sender to give news about joint experiences (of the circle of co-workers or co-senders). On the other hand the *equalizing* 'we' conveys that over against the plural 'you' of the addressees to whom Paul in the letter frequently speaks there stands a 'we', i.e. a company of senders.

Hence the change of person creates an inter-communication within the group of senders. The significance of the 'I'-passages then emerges all the more clearly: for, particularly in 2 Cor., Paul is compelled to make personal statements and take personal responsibility.

(3) *Conclusion*

It has become clear that both the naming of co-senders and the change of person in 2 Cor. have a *communicative* or *inter-communicative function*. The sender and co-sender named in the *praescriptio* have a communicative function to the extent that they establish a communication with the addressees. The fact that sender and co-sender are named parallel to the addressees and co-addressees has then an inter-communicative function: for not only the addressees as a larger community but the senders too, for their part, are likewise in a communicative situation, namely with the co-senders. Correspondingly the function of the 'we'-passages within the body of the letter is to register in the course of the epistolary communication that such an inter-communicative situation exists within the circle of senders.

---

85.   Here see the percentage breakdown in Carrez, 'Nous', p. 475.

4.4.2. Γράφειν *in Paul*

In his letters Paul writes *about* his letter-writing and in so doing uses various forms and tenses of the verb γράφειν.[86] The aorist form ἔγραψα in 1 Cor. 5.9 and 2 Cor. 2.3f., 9; 7.12 is controversial in respect of its temporal aspect (see above).

In the Pauline letters forms of the verb γράφειν appear in the following connections:[87]

(1) Paul introduces *scriptural references* (e.g. Rom. 1.17; 2.24, etc.) with the perfect passive γέγραπται, stylized to a standard formula. As an alternative a paraphrased reference to scripture can also be formulated in the active (e.g. Rom. 10.5: Μωϋσῆς γὰρ γράφει ...). Consequently Paul also says δι' ἡμᾶς γὰρ ἐγράφη ... (1 Cor. 9.10).

(2) Paul uses aorist forms of the root γραφ- when he is making *formal statements on his written correspondence*:

(2.1) In Rom. 16.22 Tertius describes himself using an aorist participle (γράψας) as a letter-writer. In a similar fashion Paul in Phlm. 19 and Gal. 6.11 refers in the first person singular aorist (ἔγραψα) with the phrase τῇ ἐμῇ χειρί to the letter as being in his own handwriting. These aorist forms relate selectively to a greeting or a signature at the end of a letter. They are epistolographic aorists – i.e. Paul puts himself in the time-frame 'in which the recipient is reading the missive'.[88] 'Although the writer is still engaged in its implementation, he can speak of it as something completed.'[89] This epistolographic aorist also has an autobiographical function. This is presupposed in 2 Thess. 3.17 and here is generalized by a present form: Ὁ ἀσπασμὸς τῇ ἐμῇ χειρὶ Παύλου, ὅ ἐστιν σημεῖον ἐν πάσῃ ἐπιστολῇ οὕτως γράφω. This gives the stamp of authenticity to what has been written.

The epistolographic aorist is also found in verbs such as πέμπω (e.g. 2

---

86. The article γράφω by Schrenk, pp. 742ff. contains no further differentiation on the use of the tenses, but compare on Paul's stylistic use of tenses in his letters Koskenniemi, *Studien*, pp. 189ff. More recent research papers may also be consulted: Stagg, 'Aorist', pp. 222–31; McKay, 'Perfect', pp. 289ff.; Thorley, 'Aktionsart', pp. 290ff. See also the monographs of Porter, *Aspect* or Fanning, *Aspect*, particularly pp. 198–240 and the reference to this in Voelz, 'Present', pp. 156ff. The differentiation between *Aktionsart* – an objective description of the action suggested in the verb – and *aspect* – the grammatical concept which the author pursues when writing – is important. See also the various contributions to the discussion in Porter/Carson, *Language*, particularly pp. 18–82.

87. Here I shall consider only verbs with the root γραφ-, not further possible prefix forms.

88. Thus the classical definition of the aorist 'of the epistolary style' in BDR §334. Apart from the verb γράφειν there are examples of the epistolographic aorist e.g. in 2 Cor. 8.17; 9.3, on which see also the discussion in McKay, 'Observations', pp. 154ff. In general see also Fanning, *Aspect*, p. 281; Porter, *Aspect*.

89. Koskenniemi, *Studien*, p. 192.

Cor. 9.3) which make an event taking place during the writing of the letter appear to be in the past and consequently describe it from the viewpoint of the recipients of the letter.

(2.2) In 1 Cor. 7.1 the second person plural aorist (ἐγράψατε) shows that Paul is referring to an earlier letter from the Corinthian community. The aorist is temporal – i.e. Paul is talking about a document lying before him which was written at an earlier date by the Corinthians.

(3) Paul reflects on his letter-writing to the congregation using various present or aorist forms:

(3.1) With constructions using the present infinitive active (γράφειν) or passive (γράφεσθαι) Paul is not speaking in the absolute about his letter-writing but understands it as specifically determined. For he either connects the statements to a particular necessity which is negated and which is then followed by an explanation introduced by γάρ: Περὶ δὲ ... οὐ χρείαν ἔχετε γράφειν ὑμῖν / ὑμῖν γράφεσθαι, αὐτοὶ γάρ ... (1 Thess. 4.9/ 5.1f.) or Περὶ μὲν ... περισσόν μοί ἐστιν τὸ γράφειν ὑμῖν οἶδα γάρ ... (2 Cor. 9.1f.); or he writes in a general way about how he personally feels about his writing: τὰ αὐτὰ γράφειν ὑμῖν ἐμοὶ μὲν οὐκ ὀκνηρόν (Phil. 3.1).

(3.2) By comparison Paul uses finite forms of the verb to write in the 'absolute' about his letter-writing. In the first person singular present the statements have either a durative or an iterative character. Paul is either reflecting upon his current writing or he is giving fundamental explanations about his letter-writing. The current writing can be intended in a final way, or again negatively (οὐκ ἐντρέπων) or antithetically (ἀλλ' ὡς τέκνα μου ἀγαπητά...) (1 Cor. 4.14). Here the present should be understood as durative (ταῦτα). It is hermeneutically very significant whether γράφω in 1 Cor. 14.37 has a durative or an iterative sense, for Paul is writing about either something currently required or something permanently valid in the claim ὅτι κυρίου ἐστὶν ἐντολή. The present is necessary here to the extent to which Paul places his writing in relation to the recipients' understanding (ἐπιγινωσκέτω ἃ γράφω ὑμῖν) and makes a permanent statement about it similar to 2 Cor. 1.13: the present (γράφομεν) marks a universally valid statement that the process of writing is interdependent with the addressees. In contrast to 2 Cor. 1.13, in 1 Cor. 14.37 their understanding is demanded. Γράφω has a durative emphasis in Gal. 1.20 and 2 Cor. 13.10. In Gal. 1.20 Paul is prepared to answer for what he writes about his biography even ἐνώπιον τοῦ θεοῦ ὅτι οὐ ψεύδομαι. In 2 Cor. 13.10 Paul names in a final clause the reason why he is writing ἀπών: he does not wish παρών to make use of the authority given to him by the Lord.

(3.3) Paul constructs some statements about his letter-writing in the first person singular aorist. With these we must differentiate between the temporal and the epistolographic aorist.

In Rom. 15.15 ἔγραψα relates to what has been written in Romans up to ch. 15, and Phlm. 21 should be understood in a similar fashion.[90] The ἔγραψα in 1 Cor. 9.15 on the other hand is logically related to the nearer context, namely to how Paul currently justifies and understands his life as an apostle. Common to all three texts is the fact that the aorist is epistolographic: Paul is either looking back at what he has written in the context of the letter-ending or he is reflecting on a section of the text he has just written.

If then in 2 Cor. 2.3f., 9; 7.12 and 1 Cor. 5.9 we have a temporal aorist, Paul is here returning to an earlier letter. This interpretation of the aorist is important hermeneutically since the hypothesis that there were letters preceding 1 and 2 Cor. is based substantially upon it.

First I would offer some observations on 1 Cor. 5.9, 11; then follows the interpretation of the aorist in 2 Cor. 2.7: in 1 Cor. 5.9, 11 Paul uses ἔγραψα twice in a short space. In 1 Cor. 5.9 he refers to a previous letter, the possibly lost so-called pre-letter. This can be inferred from the expression ἐν τῇ ἐπιστολῇ. There are linguistic indications to support this assumption of a pre-letter: there is no other instance in the extant Pauline epistles of συναναμίγνυμαι (1 Cor. 5.9, 11). 5.9 could be a summary of the Pauline *paraenesis* in the so-called pre-letter: συναναμίγνυσθαι πόρνοις. It is given in summary form because Paul had already in the pre-letter given a more detailed explanation which then follows once more in 5.10. The terms for vices in 1 Cor. 5.10 (πόρνοι, πλεονέκται, ἅρπαγες, εἰδωλολάτραι) are taken up again in their entirety in 1 Cor. 5.11 and then repeated in 1 Cor. 6.9f. and – apart from εἰδωλολάτραι in 1 Cor. 10.7 – are not found elsewhere in Paul. The number of groups designated as iniquitous increases – as if rising to a climax. Thus 1 Cor. 5.11 contains additional iniquitous concepts to 5.9f. (λοίδοροι, μέθυσοι), which for their part are only otherwise found in the Paulines in 1 Cor. 6.10. Finally in 1 Cor. 6.9f. there appear four further groups who are not mentioned in either 1 Cor. 5.9f. or in 1 Cor. 5.11 (μοιχοί, μαλακοί, ἀρσενοκοῖται, κλέπται).[91] This creates intensification in the argumentation: 1 Cor. 5.9 gives a summary warning about associating with πόρνοι who in 5.10 are classified as πόρνοι τοῦ κοσμοῦ. In 5.11 Paul introduces further groups and situates them, exemplified in a person (τις), in the actual life of the congregation: ἐάν τις ἀδελφὸς ὀνομαζόνεμος ... τῷ τοιούτῳ μηδὲ συνεσθίειν. This too effects intensification. Finally in 1 Cor. 6 the Corinthian congregation itself is addressed on the matter of how to treat ἄδικοι (6.1, 9). Thus in 1 Cor. 6.9f. in contrast to 5.11 there is an

90. Contrary to BDR §334.2.

91. Of these μοιχοί, μαλακοί and ἀρσενοκοῖται are hapaxlegomena in Paul. In the context of the list of vices this is also true of κλέπται (κλέπτης appears in Paul in 1 Thess. 5.2, 4 where, however, the context is eschatological).

intensification in the following three respects: here Paul is talking of ἄδικοι within the congregation; these are not referred to in the dative as opponents of the community (as in 5.9f. and 5.11) but in the nominative with regard to their state (οὔτε . . . βασιλείαν θεοῦ κληρονομήσουσιν); and finally the groups designated by vices are increased by four.

From these observations it seems reasonable to see in 1 Cor. 5.9f. a reference to a previous letter in which Paul had given a warning in principle about associating with the πόρνοι τοῦ κόσμου. Paul takes up this warning from his earlier letter in 1 Cor. 5.9 in a summary, in 5.10 with an explication since there is now an actual problem of πορνεία (5.1) in the Corinthian congregation. Hence in 5.11 Paul then brings the earlier general warning up to date in the current congregational situation (τις ἀδελφός). From this we may suspect that ἔγραψα in 5.9 refers to the previous letter, but in 5.11 it relates to the closer context of what has just been written. This suspicion is reinforced by the fact that 5.11 is introduced by νῦν δὲ ἔγραψα. This νῦν δέ is admittedly often interpreted as logical, but here should be understood as temporal. For the basic meaning of νῦν δέ is 'but now'; furthermore, there is no parallel for a logical interpretation in the Paulines. The aorist ἔγραψα in 1 Cor. 5 can then, in rapid succession, relate temporally to an earlier letter *and* reflect epistolographically what has just been written. What conclusions can we now justifiably draw from 1 Cor. 5 for our interpretation of the occurrences of ἔγραψα in 2 Cor. 2.3f., 9 and 7.12? Are they temporal or epistolographic uses of the aorist? Is Paul referring to an earlier letter or to part of what he has just written?

The aorist forms ἔγραψα in *2 Cor. 2.3f., 9 and 7.12* are usually interpreted as temporal as in 1 Cor. 5.9 – i.e. as references to an earlier letter. Then an intermediate letter is assumed before 2 Cor. 2.3f. etc. This, following 2 Cor. 2.4, is known as 'the plaintive letter' (διὰ πολλῶν δακρύων). This interpretation is derived from the context and justified as follows: the τοῦτο αὐτό in 2.3 can admittedly 'be related either to what precedes it or to what follows it'.[92] But the phrase διὰ πολλῶν δακρύων in 2.4 makes it clear that this letter does not correspond to the emotional state in chs 1–2 but is the so-called plaintive letter. The ἔγραψα in 2.9 is interpreted correspondingly as a past tense – i.e. with a view to 2.5–8 – 'as the reason for an instruction contained in an earlier letter from Paul to the Corinthians'.[93] 2 Cor. 7.8, like 1 Cor. 5.9, is taken as a reference to an earlier letter (ἐν τῇ ἐπιστολῇ) which, in a similar manner to 2 Cor. 2.4, was connected to λυπεῖν.

These arguments could indeed suggest that we should interpret ἔγραψα

---

92. Windisch, *Korintherbrief*, p. 80 n. 2.
93. Bosenius, *Abwesenheit*, p. 29. This argumentation however only appears to make sense if a so-called incident is presupposed.

in the places mentioned (2 Cor. 2.3, 4, 9; 7.12) as a temporal aorist.[94] But here we shall nevertheless take the instances in 2 Cor. 2.3, 4, 9 as epistolographic. This can be substantiated as follows: our observations on 1 Cor. 5.9, 11 have shown that even in a close context two aorist forms of ἔγραψα can have two different meanings. They need not necessarily be understood as analogous, particularly since with the δέ in 5.11 there is also a clear syntactical caesura. In that case it is even less possible to interpret 2 Cor. 2.3, 4, 9 and 2 Cor. 7.12 as analogous in respect of the temporal aspect.[95]

Five observations support taking ἔγραψα in 2 Cor. 2.3, 4, 9 as referring to the current letter:

> *First*, the θλῖψις mentioned in 2.4 need in no way refer to the emotional state of an earlier letter because there is already a mention of θλῖψις in the eulogy (1.4) and in the account of previous happenings which is attached to the eulogy (1.8).

> *Second*, the preceding text – namely eulogy and earlier plans for the journey – makes it reasonable to assume that ἔγραψα in 2.3f. refers to what has just been written.

> Accordingly in 2.1ff. Paul explains – because of his changed plans for the journey (1.15ff.) – the omission of a visit to Corinth. Paul has decided against a visit to Corinth (2.1) because he does not wish to be distressed again; this he last experienced in the province of Asia (1.8).

> *Third*, the case hinted at in 2.5ff., the possible author of which is mentioned as τις in 2.5 and as τοιοῦτος (or αὐτός) in 2.6–8, allows us to draw no conclusions about genuine events in Corinth; for Paul picks up this incident in stylized language and leads into a general Christian admonition (2.10f.).

> There is a suspicion that in 2.5ff. as in 7.12 Paul is returning to a specific person who had offended him. But now with the use of τις we can establish that Paul often speaks using a fictitious example, either using conditional clauses (εἴ τις)[96], negative final clauses (μή τις),[97] or indefinite address (τις ὑμῶν)[98] or in potential anticipation (ἀλλὰ ἐρεῖ τις).[99] The majority of instances of τις are to be found in the two letters to the Corinthians.[100] This being so we might be permitted to conclude that this exemplary/fictitious Pauline language arises from a lively correspondence with the Corinthian congregation

94. Porter, *Aspect*, p. 228 assigns *inter alia* 1 Cor. 5.11 and 2 Cor. 2.3; 7.12 to the 'epistolary aorist'.

95. Against Bosenius, *Abwesenheit*, pp. 29f. or Thrall, *Corinthians*, p. 168, who both assume identity between 2.9 and 7.8.

96. e.g. 2 Cor. 5.17; 10.7; 11.20, 21 or 1 Cor. 3.4, 12, 17, 18; 5.11; 7.12.

97. e.g. 2 Cor. 8.20; 11.16; 12.6 or 1 Cor. 1.15.

98. 1 Cor. 6.1; 15.35.

99. 1 Cor. 15.35.

100. Of the 50 instances of τις in the nominative 39 are in 1 and 2 Cor.

having to do with specific problems in the congregation. Even the
τοιοῦτος named in 2 Cor. 2.6 is to be understood simply as οὗτος
'weakened to a more vague description'.[101]

But it is nevertheless difficult to determine the incident mentioned
in 2.5ff. Even if Paul is here alluding to a specific person his
discussion of the case is stylized, using exemplary/fictitious language
and with the intention of general Christian instruction (2.10).

Fourth, Paul could have chosen the aorist forms in 2 Cor. 2 because
he sees himself still in the context of the beginning of the letter. Then
the epistolographic aorist at the beginning of the letter would have a
function similar to that at the end of the letter; the writer looks back
in conclusion at the process of the writing.

Fifth, ἔγραψα can finally be so interpreted that Paul, by using this
aorist, is specifically referring to the emotional event 'which is the
reason for his writing the letter'.[102]

Hence on balance we may justify the interpretation of the aorist forms in 2
Cor. 2 as follows: in contrast to 2 Cor. 7.12, where Paul in the context
(7.8) is explicitly speaking of another letter (see above) and correspondingly uses a temporal aorist, the tense of the aorist in 2 Cor. 2.3f., 9 can be
understood as epistolographic with a reflexive character: here Paul is
reflecting on the process of his current letter-writing. Therefore 2 Cor. 2
represents a part of the so-called plaintive letter.

(4) Paul writes about his writing. The statements which Paul makes about
this in the first person singular (or plural) present and aorist perform
various functions[103] which are drawn up in the table below. With the
present Paul makes statements in a *durative* or *iterative* aspect upon the
epistolary hermeneutical meaning of the writing.

The *epistolographic aorist* relates to the current writing and can have an
autographic function. Paul also uses the epistolographic aorist in
conjunction with the *beginning of a letter* or at its end or when he *is
reflecting upon* the process of writing. The *temporal aorist* certainly refers
to an earlier letter.

And yet epistolographic and temporal aorist in common reflect specific
aspects of the 'aorist' tense: 'The epistolary use is not very different from
that of the aorist in past narrative, for the effect is essentially a distancing
of the writer from the event, and because this is done by forward

---

101. BDR §304.2.

102. Koskenniemi, *Studien*, p. 194.

103. This differentiation can be supported by observations on the 'aspect' character of
the temporal forms. ('Verbal aspect in NT Greek is that category in the grammar of the verb
which reflects the focus or viewpoint of the speaker in regard to the action or condition which
the verb describes ...', Fanning, *Aspect*, p. 84.)

projection, the time of event (more important to us than to the speakers of ancient Greek) becomes relatively past.'[104]

Present	*durative*	*iterative*
	Gal. 1.20	2 Cor. 1.13
	1 Cor. 4.14; 14.37	(first person plural!)
	2 Cor. 13.10	
Aorist	*temporal* 1 Cor. 5.9; (1 Cor. 7.1); 2 Cor. 7.12	

Aorist	*epistolographic*		
	autograph	**letter beginning/end**	**reflexive**
	Phlm. 19	Rom. 15.15	1 Cor. 5.11; 9.15
	Gal. 6.11	Phlm. 21	2 Cor. 2.3, 4, 9

4.4.3. Λέγειν, λαλεῖν, λόγος *in 2 Corinthians*

How does Paul understand his speaking (λέγειν or λαλεῖν) or his λόγος in relation to the scribality of 2 Cor.? The various instances of the lexemes λέγειν, λαλεῖν, λόγος in 2 Cor. reveal that Paul sees himself primarily as a 'speaking' Apostle in his communication with the Corinthians.

In 2 Cor. Paul uses λόγος to refer to the apostolic message, i.e. the gospel authorized by God (2.17; 4.2; 5.19; 6.7; 8.7). But λόγος is also a term for Paul's speaking in general (1.18), for the way he speaks (10.10; 11.6) and for the spoken message which can also occur in the letter (10.11). Hence for Paul there is initially no difference between his oral λόγος (10.10) and that which is written in the letter (10.11). This corresponds to the normal general polysemantic usage of the term 'λόγος' in antiquity. Consequently there exists a terminological indifference as to whether speech is defined as oral or written. Nevertheless orality was more highly thought of than scribality.

The verb λέγειν can refer to God's speaking (e.g. 4.6). But in 2 Cor. Paul uses λέγειν essentially in relation to his speaking to the Corinthians in meta-argumentation or in performative statements (6.13; 7.3; 8.8). In so doing he is referring to the current communication situation (likewise in 11.16, 21) – i.e. he thinks of the present letter-writing as if he were speaking or he is referring to previous or forthcoming speeches (9.3). Common to the verbs λέγειν and λαλεῖν is the fact that in 2 Cor. they are used predominantly in the first person singular or plural. The difference between λέγειν and λαλεῖν consists in the fact that λαλεῖν can only rarely be followed by a statement or direct speech. Hence λαλεῖν, which is classed as a lexeme of the lower Koine, is a non-specific description of 'speech' in general. With λαλεῖν Paul names the basic process of Christian

---

104. McKay, 'Observations', p. 155, where he scrutinizes the epistolographic use of the aorist in 2 Cor. 8.17, 18, 22.

(4.13) or apostolic (12.19) speaking or Christ's speaking through the Apostle (13.3). Here Paul finds himself on the defensive or he is defending himself polemically against his opponents and their accusations (2.17) – in this connection λαλεῖν can also introduce meta-argumentative statements (11.17, 23). But the speaking can also be transitive and related to the Corinthian congregation (7.14). Finally, within his apocalyptic/autobiographical *narratio* Paul uses λαλεῖν to describe the words spoken there as words (ῥήματα)[105] which mankind may not utter (12.4).

Paul considers himself in the first instance as a 'speaking' person – this is clear from the performative or meta-argumentative statements introduced by λέγειν or λαλεῖν. The propositional content of what Paul 'writes' or 'speaks' is indifferent. This being so, in Paul's view writing is a specific way of speaking. The specifics of 'speaking' as opposed to 'writing' can be characterized as follows: when he uses γράφειν Paul is reflecting upon the process of letter-writing; when using λέγειν or λαλεῖν he is describing the fact of spoken communication in general. But this also means that in his verbal communication Paul is primarily considering the oral statement and looks upon letter-writing – i.e. the written statement – as a special case of communication, but one which he explicitly reflects upon in an epistolary hermeneutical way.

4.4.4. *Autobiographical passages in Paul*

If we now ask about autobiographical passages in Paul we simultaneously register that Paul wrote his letters as a literary productive 'author', since the term 'autobiography', anchored in the field of literary studies, requires a literary 'author' as the writer of his own life-story. Hence in the following we must emphasize the fact that Paul is an author.

The term 'autobiography' appeared at the beginning of the nineteenth century and in the field of literary studies denotes the description 'of one's own life-story'.[106] 'Autobiography' in the narrower sense is defined as follows: 'Autobiography is a form of text in which its author verbally and in narrative form articulates inner and outer experiences in the past together with actions he has personally performed in a document which gathers them together in such a way that he actively puts himself in a particular relationship to his environment.'[107] In the broader sense, however, autobiographical writing can be defined as follows: '... any statement about oneself, whether in poetry or in prose, can be regarded as autobiographical'.[108] According to this definition autobiographical writ-

---

105.   In 2 Cor. ῥῆμα only appears elsewhere in 13.1, in a quotation from the LXX (Deut. 19.15) and there means a 'matter'.

106.   Wuthenow, 'Autobiographie', p. 169.

107.   Lehmann, *Bekennen*, p. 36.

108.   Momigliano, *Biography*, p. 23.

ing begins in the Greek or Ionian world with the travel reports of *Scylax of Karyanda* who, around 519 BCE led the first circumnavigation of Arabia. Biographical and autobiographical reports arise in the Greece of the fifth century together with historical writing.

Paul is not only the earliest Christian author but – alongside the autobiographical notes of John, the writer of the Apocalypse – the only author who writes autobiographically in the first three generations of early Christianity. The records of the Carthaginian martyr, *Vibia Perpetua* from the beginning of the third century count as the oldest autobiographical notes made by a woman in the history of Christianity. In early Judaism *Josephus* (37/38–100 CE) with his *Vita* (after 93/94) comes on stage as an author who writes autobiographically. Types of autobiography – partly within the field of letters – also existed in the Roman world from the time of the Republic. But already in the autobiographical letters of the Graeco-Hellenistic period 'propaganda and self-justification' are central.[109]

If we look for autobiography in the area of ancient rhetoric this can be found in the shape of the *encomium*. Here, however, the rhetorical effect is what is taken into consideration, not the literary components of the authorship of a written text as found in the Pauline epistles. From the viewpoint of literary studies autobiography exists in various forms including that of a *letter*[110] to the extent in which it contains shorter or longer passages of narrative self-portrayal. Autobiographical writing takes place mainly in the first person singular.

In Paul[111] there are – as we shall see – autobiographical passages not only in the first person singular (particularly in 2 Cor. 10–13) but also in the first person plural (6.4ff.) or in the third person singular (12.2ff.). In this connection we must differentiate the various functions: while the first person singular has a confessional function (see below), the first person plural pursues an inter-communicative purpose. In the case of the third person singular we are dealing particularly with an autobiographical *narratio*[112] where Paul names himself as narrator in the first person singular but then speaks of himself as a protagonist in the third person singular. By so doing Paul distances himself from his experience of ecstasy and puts it on an apocalyptic plane.

---

109. Thus Momigliano, *Biography*, p. 110 with regard to Plato's *Seventh Letter* and the *Alexander* letters.

110. See e.g. Müller, 'Brief', p. 61: 'In its connection to the personal context of its author's life the l[etter] is akin to autobiography but differs from this in its relationship to the addressees ...'.

111. Research into 'autobiography' in Paul is mostly related to Galatians and 1 Thessalonians. See e.g. Lyons, *Autobiography*, pp. 123ff., 177ff.; Malina/Neyrey, *Portraits*, pp. 55ff. examine encomiastic motifs within 2 Cor. 11.21–12.10.

112. See O. Wischmeyer, '2. Korinther', p. 34.

Autobiographical writing takes place with an *apologetic* or *educational* intention 'to transmit example and warning'.[113] Consequently it is *directed toward the addressees* and *hermeneutically* directed to the extent in which it is concerned with the understanding of the person. 'Where one person dwells on the story of his sufferings and persecutions, another wishes to know why he has been spared such things. The one desires to show how his own history is interwoven with his epoch ..., the other his independence and self-assertion in resistance to his times.'[114] Paul describes his experiences e.g. within the catalogues of *peristases* (2 Cor. 4.7–12; 6.4ff.; 11.23)[115] or in the 'disclosure' formula in 2 Cor. 1.8ff.

Autobiographical writing is consequently connected to *self-reflection* which is then articulated and communicated. Put another way: autobiography can be seen as a way 'to construct or reconstruct one's own identity, to build up one's own spiritual and moral personality'.[116]

Autobiographies take account of the current *situation in which they are written* and often contain 'details about the physical, emotional and intellectual state of the author at the time of writing'.[117] This motif is found for Paul in 2 Cor. 2.3f.; 7.8f., 12f. At the same time the author frequently reflects upon his autobiographical text in a *meta-argumentative* fashion or introduces it performatively. Autobiographical statements need *acceptability* which depends less 'upon the possibilities the recipients have of verifying them than on the credibility of the one who is writing'.[118] Paul consequently frequently has to justify himself (2 Cor. 1.12f., 18, 23; 4.2). In the case of the *explicit reader* or the addressees of the letter the author then assumes knowledge of his life-story when he simply alludes to it. Paul does this with regard to his illness (2 Cor. 12.7). At the same time autobiographical texts also have *religious* aspects: hence an autobiography is 'not simply a description of the author's previous religious experiences; rather in itself it represents a deeply religious action, an attempt to grasp the workings of God ... and to give a new orientation to the life of the author and his readers'.[119]

To describe the *pragmatics* of the language used in autobiographical passages we can suggest for Paul the type of 'confession', particularly within 2 Cor. 10–13. The author speaks in the first person singular for what he says is known to him alone and may contain personal facts which are probably explosive for the recipients: 'For confession the conditions of

---

113. Wuthenow, 'Autobiographie', p. 171.
114. Wuthenow, 'Autobiographie', p. 171.
115. Josephus describes the dangers he encountered on his travels in a similar way in *Vita* 15.
116. Dalfen, 'Autobiographie', p. 198.
117. Lehmann, *Bekennen*, p. 39.
118. Lehmann, *Bekennen*, p. 42.
119. Barbour, 'Autobiographie', p. 1604.

the duty to defend, of sincerity but above all those of consistency are absolute.'[120] Looked at stylistically this is a 'confidence' which Paul expresses above all through the 'I' and 'you' forms.[121]

In Paul only the 'I'-passages can be cited as being *autobiographically confessional.* We shall now glance at the autobiographical passages in 2 Cor. 10–13 – which have an apologetic character – using the criteria of literary studies.

First, Paul makes his statements out of a process of *self-reflection* (11.5). Second, he gives details about his current *situation when writing* (11.30; 12.7) and introduces these performatively (10.1; 11.5, 11). Third, he forms his self-reflection in a *productive literary* manner (12.1ff. or 11.23ff.). Autobiographies cannot give a 'faithful reproduction of past events' for one simple reason – 'because they *give an account* and consequently give the past a form which it in itself does not possess'.[122] Fourth, he writes autobiographically with a *pragmatic intention* which is specially directed at the situation in Corinth: the Corinthians should relieve Paul of accusations and criticism (*apologetic* intention, 10.1f.); they should understand why he boasts of his weakness (11.30) just as he can refer to revelations (*hermeneutic* intention); they should learn from and be taught by him (*educational* intention, 11.12ff.).

Individual sections in 2 Cor. 10–13 can therefore be called *'confessing autobiographies'.* This form then attained its own literary genre in Christian autobiography (e.g. the *Confessions* of Augustine).

Finally we must remember that Paul, in so far as he can be designated a writer of letters who writes autobiographically, encounters us even more clearly as a literary *author* – i.e. as a letter-writer who deliberately fashions literature.

4.4.5. *Performative and meta-argumentative statements in 2 Corinthians*
(a) *A brief description of the 'speech act' theory using the example of 2 Corinthians*

Speech act theory analyses acts of speaking which are initially performed orally. The 'production or issuance of a sentence token under certain conditions is a speech act and speech acts ... are the basic or minimal units of linguistic communication ... Talking is performing acts according to rules.'[123] In so far as the 'letter' can be compared to a conversation, even if in written form, one should be able to detect speech acts within a letter such as 2 Cor.

Austin designates as *performative* – as opposed to affirmative or

---

120. Lehmann, *Bekennen*, p. 60.
121. See Zmijewski, *Stil*, p. 112.
122. De Bruyn, *Ich*, p. 66.
123. Searle, *Speech Acts*, p. 16 and p. 22.

descriptive – particular statements which cannot be true or false; for they perform actions. The speech act then presents itself as *illocutive* or illocutionary.

Searle distinguishes within a speech act between the *act of utterance*, the *propositional act* and the *illocutionary act*, and indicates with this differentiation that in a speech act utterances are physically expressed, have a propositional content and in addition perform particular actions.[124]

Austin allows a distinction between *implicit* and *explicit* performative statements. While implicit or primary performative statements reveal 'in general no lexical illocutionary indicators', explicit performative statements usually have a structure which consists of a matrix clause 'with a *performative verb*[125] in the first person present indicative, an object which is usually indirect (indicating the addressee) and an embedded clause' – each case may also be amplified with a 'hereby'.[126]

Austin suggests a subdivision of 'utterance ... according to their illocutionary force'[127] into *verdictive, exercitive, commissive, behabitive* and *expositive* statements and describes their pragmatic function, without fixing it definitively, as follows: 'To sum up, we may say that the verdictive is an exercise of judgment, the exercitive is an assertion of influence or exercising of power, the commissive is an assuming of an obligation or declaring of an intention, the behabitive is the adopting of an attitude, and the expositive is the clarifying of reasons, arguments, and communications.'[128]

Searle takes up Austin's subdivision of the speech act but develops it in a modified form. Thus Searle differentiates between assertive, directive, commissive, expressive and declarative illocutionary acts: with assertive illocutionary acts the question of the truth of a proposition is in the foreground; directive illocutionary acts bring an influence to bear on the action of the listener. The concept of the commissive act corresponds essentially with Austin's definition. Expressive speech acts express the speaker's emotional attitude towards the content of the proposition, and in the case of declarative speech acts their implementation establishes 'the correspondence between the propositional content and reality'.[129]

Consequently the significant difference between the terminologies of Austin and Searle is that in differentiating between the propositional and the illocutionary act (see above) Searle attempts to determine the relationship between the propositional content stated and the action

124. Cf. Searle, *Speech Acts*.

125. Bußmann, *Sprachwissenschaft*, p. 568.

126. Bußmann, *Sprachwissenschaft*, p. 568. The example usually cited is 'I (hereby) baptize you in the name ...'.

127. Austin, *How to Do Things with Words*, p. 151.

128. Austin, *How to Do Things with Words*, p. 163.

129. Searle, 'Taxonomy', p. 16.

accomplished in the speech act. Austin for his part bases his classification of the speech act on the respective action-oriented aspects which are relevant to the different performative verbs which introduce the speech act. The differentiations in the speech acts mentioned or types of illocution can be particularly meaningfully applied in 2 Cor. (see the following table) if in so doing we start by discerning the performative verbs. This perception must then be related to the observation that in 2 Cor. we have meta-communicative statements.

Illocutionary speech acts and consequently explicit performative statements are constituted in 2 Cor. by various such performative verbs.

Reference in 2 Cor.	*performative verb*	*type of statement*
1.8[130]	οὐ γὰρ θέλομεν . . . ἀγνοεῖν	expositive
1.23	μάρτυρα τὸν θεὸν ἐπικαλοῦμαι	commissive (Austin/Searle)
5.12	συνιστάνομεν	exercitive
6.1	παρακαλοῦμεν	exercitive
7.3[131]	πρὸς κατάκρισιν οὐ λέγω	exercitive
8.1	γνωρίζομεν δέ	expositive
8.3	μαρτυρῶ	expositive
10.1f.	παρακαλῶ	exercitive
10.12f.	τολμῶμεν ἐγκρῖναι ἢ συγκρῖναι	verdictive
11.2	ζηλῶ	expressive (Searle)
11.3	φοβοῦμαι	expressive (Searle)
11.5	λογίζομαι	verdictive
11.16	λέγω . . .	commissive
11.17	ὃ λαλῶ. . ., ἀλλ' ὡς	verdictive
12.14	ἑτοίμως ἔχω ἐλθεῖν . . .	commissive
12.20	φοβοῦμαι	commissive (Austin/Searle)
13.2	προείρηκα καὶ προλέγω . . .	expositive/ exercitive

In addition the εὐχαριστῶ-constructions which represent behabitive statements can also be cited as performative phrases, i.e. as 'explications or at least indicators of the illocution executed in the text'. These phrases are conditioned by the 'operational requirements of the "letter" form of communication'.[132]

---

130. See also 1 Cor. 10.1; 11.3; 12.1; 1 Thess. 4.13.

131. The two passages in italics are also considered to be meta-communicative statements (see below).

132. Bickmann, *Kommunikation*, pp. 46f.

(b) *Appreciation, criticism, continuation: speech act theory and meta-communication*

What is the significance of such statements in 2 Cor. which can be described as performative within the frame of the speech act theory? The understanding of these forms of speech as 'performative utterances' is not yet found in ancient rhetoric. Here we have a means of approach stamped by the modern philosophy of language which starts from the premise that 'speech is essentially speaking, i.e. is an activity'.[133] Hence the concept of 'performance' has meanwhile become an appropriate terminus in philology and cultural studies. At the same time the speech act theory opens up a *communication-oriented* perspective to the extent to which it endeavours to differentiate communicative functions.

Here, however, a description with the help of communication theory can be helpful over and above the descriptive perspectives on linguistic statements opened up by the speech act theory. For the speech act theory describes the function of speech acts – particularly on the basis of syntactical, semantic and pragmatic criteria – but neither the actual 'author's intention' nor the 'reception' by the 'reader' or 'listener' can be checked: 'It is... difficult to differentiate between success and failure when we have no insight into the minds of the people participating ...'.[134] This difficulty is exacerbated in the analysis of an ancient text, e.g. of a Pauline epistle, which is viewed from an historical distance.

Hence the descriptive perspective of meta-communication should accompany the description of linguistic utterances by the speech act theory, for it allows us to recognize *meta-communicative statements* as well as performative statements. For in 2 Cor. Paul reflects meta-communicatively – admittedly from *his* perspective as a letter-writer – on the one hand on his *intention* as a letter-writer. On the other hand he expresses himself retrospectively and contemporarily on his relationship to the Corinthians and thereby indicates whether *earlier speech acts* were successful (2 Cor. 7.8ff. and whether *current speech acts* may succeed from his point of view (2 Cor. 2.3ff.).

What *relationship* then do performative and meta-communicative statements have to one another? This can be made clear using the examples given in the table above.

First, some linguistic expressions are here specifically described as performative – which has as yet not been taken into account in previous exegesis – e.g. 2 Cor. 8.1. In this verse the performative expression γνωρίζομεν δὲ ὑμῖν ... introduces what then happens: for in 8.2ff. Paul describes the readiness in Macedonia to contribute to the collection.

But second, in the table above two comments are listed as performative

133. Simon, *Sprachphilosophie*, p. 234.
134. Simon, *Sprachphilosophie*, p. 236.

which in the exegesis are also examined in depth as meta-communicative statements (7.3; 11.17). These two remarks are performative in so far as Paul, speaking in what follows, carries through what he announces in the performative expression: in 7.3ff. he really does not condemn; in 11.17ff. he speaks ἐν ἀφροσύνῃ. But the statements are at the same time meta-communicative or meta-argumentative in that Paul uses these expressions to reflect and comment on the current argumentation: in 7.3ff. he does not wish to be understood as one who condemns; in 11.17 he refuses to make an apostolic claim for what he is saying and sees himself as one speaking like a fool. Third, some other meta-communicative statements of 2 Cor. are missing in the table above (e.g. 11.6; 13.10): 11.6 is meta-communicative to the extent that here Paul is reflecting upon his communicative competence; in 13.10 he is reflecting upon the purpose of his letter-writing. But neither statement is introduced performatively.

Hence the balance between performative and meta-communicative statements can be shown on the example of 2 Cor. in a threefold way:

performative (e.g. 8.1)	performative *and* meta-communicative (7.3; 11.17)	meta-communicative (e.g. 11.5; 13.10)
action-oriented function	action-oriented *and* reflexive/commenting function	reflexive/commenting function

To sum up: The description of epistolary statements derived from the speech act theory consequently stands *alongside* their description as meta-communicative statements. Both forms of characterization are descriptive. The description made by the speech act theory sees the linguistic statements in their inherent linguistic connection. The pragmatic function of performative expressions consists in their *orientation towards action*. If an epistolary statement is meta-communicative, it departs from the flow of the discourse in reflecting and commenting upon the current communication or communication in general. The pragmatic function of a meta-communicative statement is that of *reflection*. Consequently on a reflexive level one may ask about the speaker's or letter-writer's intention, about the writer's disposition during the communication-process and finally about the success of the communication with regard to the relationship of the writer to the addressees.

Hence the examination of performative expressions in 2 Cor. leads us to an awareness of the letter's orientation towards action; on the other hand asking about the meta-communication aims to understand the reflexivity of the speech or writing and in so doing to grasp the explicated epistolary hermeneutics.

Chapter 5

EXEGETICAL AND HISTORICAL PERSPECTIVES

5.1. *Meta-communicative statements in 1 Corinthians 7–8*

5.1.1. *Translation of 1 Corinthians 8.1–6*

1a *Now* with regard to the food sacrificed to idols –
1b we know that all of us possess knowledge.
1c Knowledge puffs up, but love builds up.
2   If anyone thinks he knows something, he does not yet have the necessary knowledge.
3   But anyone who loves God is known by him.

4a *Consequently*, with regard to eating meat offered to idols -
4b we know that no false gods in the world really exist and that there is no god apart from the One God.

5a For even though there may be so-called gods – be it in heaven or on earth -
5b just as there are many gods and many lords –
6a for us there is *one* God, the Father
6b from whom are all things and for whom we exist
6c and *one* Lord, Jesus Christ,
6d through whom are all things and through whom we exist.
7   But not everyone has the knowledge ...

5.1.2. *Exegetical observations*
(a) *1 Corinthians 8.1–6 in its context*
Although *Literarkritik* maintains that 1 Cor. as a whole is not a unit but a compilation of several separate letters, in the various hypotheses of division the sections 1 Cor. 7.1ff. and 8.1ff. are considered to be parts of *one* common letter.[1] This has a twofold significance for the interpretation of 1 Cor. 8.1–6: the question of the literary unity of 1 Cor. is irrelevant to the interpretation of 1 Cor. 8.1–6; and the analysis of the context of 1 Cor.

---

1.   For a survey of the question in *Literarkritik* see e.g. Merklein, *Brief*, pp. 164ff.

8.1ff. – regardless of the judgement of *Literarkritik* – can include 1 Cor. 7.1ff.

On the other hand 1 Cor. 8 contains semantic references to the macrotext of the letter as a whole which support the literary unity of the letter: ch. 8 refers back to 6.13a; 8.10 relates to 10.14–22; 8.13 refers to 9.1–23. Whether one defends the unity of 1 Cor. or thinks that it is a compilation of separate letters – one can still take 1 Cor. 7 and 1 Cor. 8 as being from the start parts of the same text.

An important factor for the analysis of the structure of the argumentation in 1 Cor. 8.1–6 is its relation to 7.39f. and what appear to be structural parallels to 7.1 and 7.25. Consequently for the interpretation of 1 Cor. 8.1–6 my observations on the context concentrate on 1 Cor. 7–8.

The transition from 7.39f. to 8.1 reveals a clear break in grammar, in semantics and in the purpose of the text. Paul grounds his consideration of the remarriage of a widow on his personal opinion (7.40b), which he justifies by stating that he has the Spirit of God (7.40c). In 7.40bc we have a *meta-argumentative* statement. Paul is talking about the manner of his argumentation. 8.1 can be separated from 7.39f. by the changes in person and topic. Paul takes up a new theme, namely εἰδωλόθυτον, and uses the first person plural, i.e. the general Christian 'we'.

As to the pragmatics or function of the text, 1 Cor. 8.1 can be read as both convergent with *and* divergent from 7.40. The change of theme in 8.1 is combined with the phrase: οἴδαμεν ὅτι πάντες γνῶσιν ἔχομεν. When he says this Paul is reflecting in a fundamental way on the process of his communication with the Corinthians. Hence this is a *meta-communicative* statement which differs from the communicative type of the meta-argumentative statement in 7.40c. In 7.40 Paul compares the apostolic opinion authorized by the Spirit of God with the general Christian certainty of knowledge in 8.1. While in 7.39f. Paul is giving his opinion on a specific question addressed to him as Apostle, in 8.1ff. a series of questions begins which needs to be discussed on the basis of general Christian knowledge:

> 7.40c   I *think* that I have the <u>Spirit of God;</u>
> 8.1b   <u>we</u> *know* that all of us possess <u>knowledge.</u>

The convergence of 7.40c and 8.1b consists in that both statements depart from the train of the argument onto the level of meta-communicative communication whence they consider the actual argumentation at a distance. The divergence of the two statements consists in their meta-communicative type: 7.40c is related to the preceding argumentation (at least to 7.39f. or perhaps even to 7.25f.) and can therefore be more narrowly defined as a meta-argumentative statement. In 8.1 on the other hand the meta-communicative expression οἴδαμεν ὅτι πάντες γνῶσιν ἔχομεν is placed directly against the newly opened discussion on the food sacrificed to idols. Here we have a general meta-communicative statement which, initially not classifiable, itself then becomes in what follows (8.1c, 2) the starting-point for theological differentiations.

Hence, first, 1 Cor. 8.1b – convergent with 7.40 – states on a meta-communicative level the initial requirements for the theological-ethical discussion. But then, second, 1 Cor. 8.1b – and here it is divergent from 7.40 – develops an independent theological thesis (8.1c) which does not merely reflect the progress of the argument in 8.1ff. but also determines its theological course. This theological thesis can also be described as a meta-communicative surplus: this term is used to characterize statements and forms of speech which have an independent theological content and which arise in the context of meta-communicative reflections.

(b) *The double function of 1 Corinthians 8.1b in the text*
The pattern of reasoning in 1 Cor. 8.1–6 is introduced by περὶ δέ – here used in the cataphoric and not in the concessive sense. This widens the separation from the previous course of the argument. In 1 Cor. 7.1ff. περὶ δέ signals a change of topic and consequently also marks off the individual pericopes and the course of their reasoning from one another. Consequently 8.1 might appear to be parallel to 7.1 and 7.25. But we can detect significant differences from the uses of περὶ δέ in 7.1, 25: in 7.1 Paul is explicitly reacting to a written question from the Corinthians; in 7.25 it is no longer clear whether Paul is again responding to a specific question from Corinth or whether he for his part of his own accord in view of the shortness of time takes up the question of the marriage of man and woman.

Common to 7.1, 25 and 8.1 is their function in the text, for all three statements are found in *meta-communicative* sections: in 7.1 Paul refers to the writing from the Corinthians and makes this the basis of his reflections. This, then, is a *meta-textual* statement. In 7.25 Paul refers to the fact that he has *no* ἐπιταγή from the Lord, and instead, in a manner similar to 7.40c, mentions his γνώμη and qualifies it in more detail – again as in 7.40c. Hence in 7.25, 40c we have the type of meta-communicative statements which relate to the actual course of the argument (*meta-argumentative* statements).

In 8.1b on the other hand Paul does not introduce his remarks with a meta-argumentative statement intended to take the context into consideration and/or to authorize his speaking as an apostle. Rather in 8.1b he returns with the Christian 'we' to knowledge which represents the legitimizing authority for the following reflections on the meat offered to idols (8.1–13). The ὅτι in 8.1b should be understood as explicative since the expression οἴδαμεν ὅτι serves to 'introduce a generally known and acknowledged fact' (cf. 2 Cor. 5.1; Rom. 2.2; 3.19; 7.14; 8.22, 28).[2] Paul uses a similar construction for rhetorical questions (cf. 1 Cor. 3.16; 5.6; 6.2f.; 9.13, 24).

In 1 Cor. 8.1a Paul is presumably taking up a topic provided by the Corinthians – the introductory περὶ δέ seems to indicate this. But this does not necessarily mean that in 8.1b Paul is introducing a connected quotation as is often debated in research.[3] The assumption that in 1 Cor. 8.1b Paul is repeating a quotation from Corinth is important from the viewpoint of the history of religion and the theory of communication and consequently must be given careful consideration. For if in 1 Cor. 8.1b Paul takes up a phrase current in Corinth, this would provide information about the factions there and their theological beliefs. This would also mean, for the theory of linguistics and communication, that in 8.1bff. Paul is not actively articulating in his own words but has taken up a pre-text lying before him. Then the wording of the Corinthian letter could possibly even be reconstructed here.[4]

On the basis of linguistic and structural observations I advance the contrary thesis and assume that 1 Cor. 8.1, 4 are Pauline formulations in the course of argumentation lying before us. The indications that in 8.1 we do *not* have a Corinthian quotation but a Pauline expression can be supported by two observations on Pauline style. First, Paul normally introduces quotations, i.e. meta-textual statements, in a recognizable way (cf. Rom. 3.8; 1 Cor. 15.12; 2 Cor. 10.10; 1 Thess. 5.3) in order to engage in critical debate with opposing views. Second, the expression εἰδέναι ὅτι must be seen as 'the most important Pauline formula for introducing teaching'.[5] Hence both observations speak *against* the assumption that the quotation of a Corinthian motto lies behind 1 Cor. 8.1b. Furthermore, no party is indicated in 8.1–6. Such only appears in 8.7 (τίνες ... ἀσθενής) and in 8.9 (τοῖς ἀσθενέσιν), for this is the first time Paul mentions the group of weaker Christians for whom the aforementioned beliefs are offensive. In 8.1, 4 by contrast Paul does not simply 'neutrally' repeat the view of a group in Corinth but identifies himself with their reasoning. Thus in 1 Cor. 8.1bff. he formulates an introductory *propositio* of his own on the topic of meat sacrificed to idols which – at least we cannot exclude the possibility – was in circulation in a similar form in Corinth. In the context of the Pauline argumentation this statement has a meta-

---

2. See Bauer/Aland, p. 1127.

3. Thus e.g. Lietzmann, *Korinther*, p. 37. Lietzmann constructs the following wording: 'We find nothing offensive in enjoying meat sacrificed to idols'; Wolff, *Erste Brief*, p. 168; Schrage, *Brief*, pp. 220f.; Conzelmann, *Brief*, p. 166 sees in 8.1ff. the maxim of the Corinthians, which gives the 'theoretical basis for the freedom practised'.

4. Thus in Lietzmann, *Korinther*, p. 37.

5. O. Wischmeyer, *Weg*, p. 67 n. 145.

communicative function *and* moreover expounds an eminently theological propositional content which I have called its meta-communicative surplus.

The phrase οἴδαμεν ὅτι in 8.1b has, as we have seen, a meta-communicative function. It states the legitimizing authority upon which Paul formulates the following observations on meat offered to idols. In addition to this communicative function 1 Cor. 8.1b – with its appeal to general Christian knowledge (οἴδαμεν) – also develops *propositionally* the material content of this legitimizing authority: 'We all possess *gnosis*.' With this statement Paul establishes the *theological* starting-point of the discussion which now follows on the consumption of meat offered to idols.

Yet Paul immediately makes a critical correction of this statement (8.1b) without substantially eradicating the *gnosis*. In placing *agape above gnosis* (see also 13.2, 4) he narrows down the relevant scope of *gnosis*. In 8.3, 4 Paul continues this critical correction of *gnosis* on the level of speech related to action, here simply using verbal forms: 'If anyone claims to know something ...', in which Paul formulates this possibility in an 'exemplary-fictitious' way (τις) in the form of a realistic conditional clause. The verbal form δοκεῖ in 8.2 *corrects* and *individualizes* the οἴδαμεν in v. 1. While the general Christian 'we' in 8.1a know that they have *gnosis*, in 8.2 the talk is of the possible case that someone, an individual, thinks he has understood something. But this type of recognition does not correspond to the *necessary* (δεῖ) form of knowledge. Although the Christian community can be certain that they have knowledge, in the individual case where an individual Christian refers to his knowledge, he cannot affirm that this is so. The personal opinion or the individual claim to have knowledge is consequently, in the language of Pauline argumentation, virtually the condition of not yet (οὔπω) having begun to have knowledge. Only when someone – the δέ here is used concessively – loves 'God' does he fulfil the condition of real knowledge. Real knowledge does not consist in one's being able to know of oneself but in being known by God or being already known (the resultative perfect in 8.2a is taken up again in the ἔγνωσται in 8.3b). Although the Christian community can act in theological and ethical controversies on the basis of the charisma of *gnosis*, Paul excludes in a twofold way any possible *instrumentalization* of gnosis in the process of theological and ethical decisions: *agape* has precedence over *gnosis* as a principle of οἰκοδομεῖν; and the individual claim to have *gnosis* outwith the relationship-structure 'God–man–Christian community' is per se without significance.

Consequently 1 Cor. 8.1–3 and 8.4 do not in the first place represent only the spiritual attitude of the so-called 'strong' party in Corinth.[6] In the

---

6. In 1 Cor. 8.1–13 – as in Romans 14 – Paul mentions the 'weak' but not the 'strong'. This allows us to suspect that Paul identified with those who are rarely designated as the 'strong' (e.g. Rom. 15.1).

general Christian sense Paul can accord *gnosis* to *all* (πάντες) Christians in Corinth. Only in the specific application of γνῶσις in relation to dealing with meat sacrificed to idols (8.7ff.) is a deficiency of knowledge seen among the 'weak Christians'. Paul addresses 8.1–3 to the 'strong' *and* the 'weak' in Corinth, but already here delimits the sphere of influence and the effectiveness of *gnosis* by reference to the love which is set above it.

(c) *The redundancy and clarification of 1 Corinthians 8.1 in 8.4*

What is the content and function of that *gnosis* which Paul speaks of in 1 Cor. 8.1ff.? If one disregards the meta-communicative function of 8.1b, the expression οἴδαμεν ὅτι πάντες γνῶσιν ἔχομεν develops a theological proposition in which *gnosis* appears as a *theologoumenon* and is defined in greater detail. In the Corinthian correspondence and elsewhere Paul formulates aspects of his understanding of '*gnosis*': *gnosis* belongs in the sphere of the *charismata* (see 1 Cor. 12.8), it relates to God (2 Cor. 4.6; 10.5) and is God-given (2 Cor. 2.14). In the ecclesiological respect (1 Cor. 8.1) and in the anthropological respect (1 Cor. 13.2) as well as in the apocalyptic perspective (1 Cor. 13.8) it is subordinate to ἀγάπη. Paul's theological understanding and evaluation of *gnosis* can be seen in a connected form in Romans: 'For Paul Christian γνῶσις is … suffused by the doctrine of justification [see Rom. 10.2f.; Gal. 2.16] … It is determined by the Christological interpretation of the OT-Jewish εἶς θεός-gnosis … The classical formulation of this fundamental re-evaluation of γνῶσις is to be found already in 1 Cor. 8.3: Man no longer knows God through his own γνῶσις nor wins salvation in this way, but God has known man …'.[7] Because a human being responds to God's *gnosis* which takes place in love with just such an *agape, gnosis* is not in Paul's eyes an important soteriological factor. It is subordinate and subject to *agape* which represents the acme of the eschatologically relevant goods of salvation (1 Cor. 13.13).

In 1 Cor. 8.1–3 Paul develops *gnosis* as a theological proposition. His knowledge of the general Christian *gnosis* develops alongside the meta-communicative function of the text a theological proposition which defines and criticizes *gnosis* in its relationship to *agape*. In 8.4f. there is added as it were 'belatedly' to the Pauline understanding of *gnosis* a further aspect which stems from the Judaeo-Hellenistic tradition. Judaeo-Hellenistic theologians and philosophers such as Philo teach that 'the εἶς θεός is the proper γνῶσις θεοῦ'.[8]

If one understands 1 Cor. 8.1ff. on the basis of 8.4ff. – which can be justified on the basis of linguistic, syntactic and semantic observations – the *theologoumenon* of *gnosis* (8.1b) is related to the confession of the εἶς

---

7. O. Wischmeyer, *Weg*, pp. 63f.
8. O. Wischmeyer, *Weg*, p. 60.

θεός (8.4b). 'What is meant by γνῶσις here is the fundamental knowledge of monotheism with all its consequences,'[9] or, put with more historical precision: the basic insight of *Jewish* monotheism.

In 8.4 Paul takes up again the structure: περὶ ... τῶν εἰδωλοθύτων (...) οἴδαμεν ὅτι ... from 8.1. Here, too, we are *not* dealing with a Corinthian quotation; rather Paul is returning – in a similar fashion to 8.1 – to a matter of general Christian knowledge. The subject in 8.4 is no longer the εἰδωλόθυτον but specifically the βρῶσις of the meat offered to idols. In contrast to the cataphoric significance of δέ in 8.1 we find in 8.4 the consecutive particle οὖν, and in contrast to the πάντες of 8.1 in 8.4 we have οὐδέν and οὐδείς. Hence 8.4 from a formal, linguistic and semantic viewpoint *is parallel, continues, puts in more specific terms* and *is antithetical* to 8.1. Initially 8.4 is *redundant* to 8.1 in these four aspects. As in 8.1b the ὅτι in 8.4b should be understood as explicative: Paul classifies the statement οὐδὲν εἴδωλον ἐν κόσμῳ καὶ ὅτι οὐδεὶς θεὸς εἰ μὴ εἷς as being a matter of general Christian knowledge (οἴδαμεν). Here, too, Paul is not thinking of the so-called 'strong' party but attributes the statements to the knowledge and profession of *all* the Corinthian Christians. Precisely with the antithetical structure of πάντες (8.1b) and οὐδὲν ... οὐδείς (8.4b) Paul emphasizes his statements that *all* Christians share in the knowledge of the *non*-existence of the world of the gods.

If we compare verses 1 and 4 we observe a further detail which gives us information about the theological significance of *gnosis* in 8.1ff.: what is contained in the ὅτι-clause in 8.4b can be seen – particularly because of the parallel structure – as an *explanation* of the γνῶσις in 8.1b (see also Rom. 1.21–23). The following structure of reasoning emerges:

8.1 With regard to the food sacrificed to idols	we know (positive) that all of us possess γνῶσις.
(...)	
8.4 With regard to eating meat sacrificed to idols	we know (negative) that no false gods ... and no god ... (exists).

The *gnosis* in 8.1b is elucidated in 8.4 in the statement οὐδὲν εἴδωλον ἐν κόσμῳ καὶ ὅτι οὐδεὶς θεὸς εἰ μὴ εἷς. Hence from the standpoint of 8.4 *gnosis* in v. 1 is to be understood as an 'enlightened attitude' in which in principle *all* the Christians in Corinth could participate. In terms of tradition history the ὅτι-clause in 8.4 can be taken as referring back to OT statements which express the recognition of the One God (Deut. 4.35; Isa. 44.8; 45.5).

9. Wolff, *Erste Brief*, p. 169.

To sum up: The concept of γνῶσις is used three-dimensionally in 1 Cor. 8.1–4. With regard to the discussion which has arisen on meat offered to idols it has in the first instance a meta-communicative function in the text. Second, in 8.1–3 it develops a theological propositional content which is defined by its relationship to *agape*. Third, in 8.4 Paul retrospectively explains the content of *gnosis* in the specific discussion of the eating of meat offered to idols – *gnosis* consists in the acknowledgment of the One God. In principle all the Corinthian Christians have a part in this *gnosis*.

5.1.3. *Epistolary hermeneutical aspects*

In 1 Cor. 8.1 Paul opens the discussion – presumably raised by the Corinthians themselves – on meat offered to idols in such a way that he initially places it on the level of meta-communicative argumentation. Hence initially the reference to Christian *gnosis* has a meta-communicative function. In a second step *gnosis* becomes the subject of a theological proposition critically correcting it in its relationship to *agape* (8.2f.). The statements on *gnosis* form a meta-communicative surplus. In a third step the content of *gnosis* is explicated positively (8.4): it embraces the confession of the 'One God'. This monotheistic statement is qualified (8.5) by the reference to the experienced knowledge of the non-Christian external perspective.

Accordingly in 1 Cor. 8.1–6 the Pauline argumentation on the subject of meat offered to idols takes place in several steps: after the explicit statement of the topic Paul chooses a meta-communicative level of speech which develops a meta-communicative surplus and leads into a pointed monotheistic statement.[10] This in turn is amended with reference to empirical experience.

Hence Paul does not use his writing to introduce an authoritative decision in the discussion on the consumption of meat offered to idols. Through employing the level of meta-communication he draws *all* the Corinthian Christians – regardless of their individual attitude to meat offered to idols – into the course of his reasoning. In what follows, *gnosis* – through the establishment of its relationship to *agape* and its fundamentally monotheistic affirmation – builds a theologically relevant meta-communicative surplus and receives at each point critical theological correction of its scope.

Consequently we can see how Paul develops precise formulations in dealing with current problems in the context of his correspondence with a congregation: in the discussion on meat offered to idols he does not endeavour to make an authoritative decision but draws his readers into

---

10. See E.-M. Becker, 'ΕΙΣ ΘΕΟΣ'.

the process of reasoning on the level of meta-communication. The concept of *gnosis*, however, does not remain in its meta-communicative function but develops the content of a theological proposition which in the end is aimed at its own critical amendment. Consequently whether meat offered to idols may be eaten or not is not in the end decided on theologically responsible knowledge but on the criterion of brotherly conscience (8.7–13). For, since its range surpasses that of *gnosis, agape* is the highest form of theologically responsible thought and action.

5.2. 2 Corinthians from the first to the fourth century

5.2.1. *The* Literarkritik, Literargeschichte *and reception of 2 Corinthians*
I have suggested a model for the emergence of the canonical 2 Cor. which estimates that 2 Cor. originally consisted of four or five individual letters (2 Cor. 1.1–7.4; 7.5–16; ch. 8/ch. 9; chs 10–13). Where these individual letters are joined can be seen from the analysis of so-called meta-communicative statements in 2 Cor. which reveal the different situations in which the communication took place. The resulting reconstruction of the correspondence contained in 2 Cor. can be supported by particular exegetical observations. But *literarcritical* considerations are not sufficient to explain the emergence of the canonical 2 Cor. as we have it. The question arises as to how a 'compilation' of the canonical 2 Cor. from four or five originally separate letters could have come about.

I have reconstructed the process of the compilation of letters with the help of a '*literarhistorical* model'. Following this model, the compilation of the letter-parts into *one* letter came about less through a so-called 'editing' of the Pauline letters than by individual letters becoming attached to one another in the course of their being 'copied'. It is conceivable that Paul's lively correspondence with the Corinthian congregation was written on wooden or wax tablets which – if the letters were to be preserved and put into the archives – would have to be copied. Such wooden or wax tablets could be joined together into so-called polyptychs and consequently represent an early form of the later codex so highly regarded by the Christians. If, then, Paul's letters, brought to Corinth by personal colleagues or couriers, were to be handed down and preserved, they had to be copied – perhaps originally onto scrolls then later into codices, initially on papyrus then on parchment. In the course of this copying, several documents were put together so that out of four or five individual letters there arose one composite letter which found its way as such into the history of the NT text and canon.

The process of copying the individual letters which led to their being placed one after the other must have taken place at a very early date (*c*.70–90 CE) and was completed at the latest at the end of the first century. For at that time there presumably already existed 'small corpora' of Pauline letters relating to the congregation which grew into '*Urcorpora*' through increasing exchange outwith the congregation – a process of proto-canonization of Pauline epistles which in the early canon-like collections or canonical selections (Marcion, P^{46} and the Muratorian Canon) reached its preliminary completion at the latest at the end of the second century. These canonical lists at the same time form the *terminus ad quem* for the extensive attestation or representation of the 'canonical' 2 Cor.

Hence the *literarhistorical* model which I suggested attempts, on the basis of the individual letters contained in 2 Cor. which reveal diverse situations of communication, to throw light upon this process of compilation – i.e. the period between the writing of the part-letters in '2 Cor.' (the beginning to the middle of the 50s) and the first certain widespread attestation of 2 Cor. at the end of the second century. Yet with this not all the questions on the early history of the reception of 2 Cor. in the transition from the early Christian transmission and reception down to the patristic exegesis and commentaries have been sufficiently discussed. The observations made by *Literarkritik* and the history of literature on the original form of the individual letters in 2 Cor. and on the emergence of the canonical 2 Cor. raise further questions relating to the history of their reception which are of importance historically and for literary studies. *Historically* we must examine whether we can prove that 2 Cor. was generally known and used in the period between the emergence of 2 Cor. and its first positive attestation. What kinds of reception and documentary proof of 2 Cor. can we distinguish in the process?

This question leads on to an important aspect for *literary studies*: for in the documentary proof or literary adaptation of texts – be it in the form of an allusion or a quotation – one can speak of the phenomenon of intertextuality, i.e. the capacity of a text 'to be related to other texts'.[11] Allusions to or quotations from pre-texts can be described more exactly as 'palintextual' statements or texts.[12] When we differentiate the various forms of palintextuality in the early history of the reception of Pauline letters we see at the same time the extent to which the Pauline epistles were regarded and used as literarily and theologically binding.

At the latest in the third century the Pauline letters are recognized as canonical, which is also apparent from the fact that commentaries are written on them, i.e. they are examined and interpreted exegetically and philologically. We must ask to what extent the Church Fathers paid particular attention to the interpretation of 2 Cor. In view of the

11. Aczel, 'Intertextualität', p. 287.
12. Stocker, *Theorie*, particularly pp. 53ff.

literarcritical problem of 2 Cor. formulated at the beginning of this work it would be interesting to know whether the patristic exegetes stumbled upon such problems of incohesion as form the basis of our modern *literarcritical* hypotheses.

5.2.2. *The reception of 2 Corinthians up to the end of the second century – allusion, attestation and quotation*

The end of the second century at the latest forms the *terminus ad quem* for the existence of the canonical 2 Cor. as we know it. Now we must examine whether and how far we can check back before this date and what earlier references we can find for the knowledge of the *synthesized* 2 Cor. Here we must first make a distinction important for the history of reception. The reception of ancient texts takes place in a process of 'literary adaptation'. This adaptation occurs in various literary forms which can be differentiated as allusion, attestation and quotation. NT or patristic studies of the history of the reception of NT texts and of the formation of the canon frequently do not suggest such distinctions[13] which are useful for the philological assessment of the *process of literary adaptation*, at most part pointing only to those distinctions which aim at a *historical-theological* evaluation of the *historical impact* of NT texts.[14]

The distinctions suggested above turn out not only to be significant for philological and literary historical observation of the history of reception and interpretation; they are also important in respect of the history of the

---

13.   In Stuhlhofer, *Gebrauch*, particularly pp. 38ff. there is a remarkable lack of objective differentiation in his statistical investigations of quotations e.g. in the second century.

14.   See Looks, *Das Anvertraute*, pp. 8ff. He takes a critical look at the existing differentiations of forms of reception but he himself simply distinguishes between 'indicated' and 'not indicated' reception (p. 12). The distinctions suggested by Nagel, *Rezeption*, pp. 34ff. serve primarily to give an historical-theological assessment of the historical effect of John's Gospel, and in like manner – although methodically considerably less thought through and dealing with the reception of the Pauline epistles – Aleith, *Paulusverständnis*.

Over and above the literature reviewed in the latest studies let me refer to such works as suggest distinctions helpful for a *literary assessment* of the processes of reception: Rathke, *Ignatius*, pp. 28ff., considering the letters of Ignatius, distinguishes between 'obvious quotations' from the Pauline epistles and 'shorter echoes' of the same. According to Rathke Ignatius used Paul's letters 'independently' since he probably had no copies of the epistles at his disposal and he 'had to quote from memory' (p. 40). Koch, *Schrift*, pp. 11 and 17 classifies Paul's use of scripture *inter alia* with the following: a *quotation* 'represents the deliberate adoption of someone else's written … formulation, which is, however, fully integrated into one's own account'. In contrast to Koch, although comparable in its formulation of the question, the recently published work of Powery, *Jesus*, particularly on pp. 22ff., mentions criteria for differentiating the concept of quotation which emphasize 'narrative use' and 'narrative function' and thereby are directed at a purely theological evaluation of Jesus' use of scripture.

canon. For they confirm that the various literary forms in which the reception of a Pauline letter took place indicate varying degrees of literary and theological authority ascribed to the Pauline epistles. Traversing the NT and non-NT Christian literature up to the end of the second century reveals that the form of an introduced *quotation* from the Pauline epistles such as 2 Cor. is first encountered in the early third century (Tertullian, Irenaeus, etc.). The earliest compilations of the canon might be recruited to reveal that there was a general knowledge and reproduction of 2 Cor. – i.e. for its *clear attestation*. In the rest of the Christian literature in the period from the end of the first to the end of the second century, however, we can at the most perceive *allusions* to 2 Cor.

5.2.2.1. *Allusions to 2 Corinthians in the transition from the first to the second century*

The question of the reception of the Pauline epistles within the NT has frequently been the subject of examination both in the field of the history of reception and in that of tradition.[15] Now we must ask specifically about the NT-internal reception of 2 Cor. In the so-called *Deutero-* or *Trito-Paulines* or the *Catholic Epistles* we can, if only occasionally, establish allusions to 2 Cor. Thus in Eph. 1.3 or also in 1 Pet. 1.3 there is a eulogy which is similar to that in 2 Cor. 1.3.[16] How can we interpret this? We either reckon with an established tradition to which the post-Pauline authors had recourse as did Paul himself before them; or we presuppose a direct literary dependence of the Deutero- and Trito-Paulines on the authentic Pauline epistles. Only if we start from the last-mentioned assumption of a literary dependency could we prove a knowledge of the authentic Pauline letters in the pseudepigraphical Paulines.[17] In isolated cases there is a possible third solution: several expressions coined by Paul (e.g. πᾶν ἔργον ἀγαθόν, 2 Cor. 9.8) might have set a stylistic pattern so

---

15. See e.g. Aejmelaeus, *Rezeption*. Here, however, it is mainly questions of tradition and *motif* which are examined. See also Wolter, *Pastoralbriefe* and Gese, *Vermächtnis* with regard to the reception of Pauline theology in Ephesians. Standhartinger, *Studien* looks at the relationship of Colossians to the orthonymous Pauline epistles in respect of the literary prerequisites for the production of Colossians.

16. Gese, *Vermächtnis*, p. 32 understands Eph. 1.3–14 as a copy of the introductory epistolary eulogy in 2 Cor. 1.3–7. He suspects that in 2 Cor. 1.3ff. Paul 'created …' an introductory epistolary eulogy 'on the pattern of the Jewish eulogy, which was then taken over by the letter to the Ephesians and 1 Peter' (p. 57). Gese thus opposes Lindemann, *Paulus im ältesten Christentum*, p. 122. Lindemann sees in 2 Cor. 1.3 an established traditional introductory formula which lay before both authors independently of one another.

17. Gese, *Vermächtnis*, p. 73 attempts to prove that this is so, and consequently sees Eph. 1.13f. as a reference to 2 Cor. 1.22 and Eph. 6.20 as an incorporation of 2 Cor. 5.20 (pp. 65ff.).

that they were reused in the Deutero- and Trito-Paulines as established expressions (cf. Col. 1.10; 2 Tim. 2.21; 3.17; Tit. 1.16; 3.1) or they continued to be used in post-Pauline literature and theology as motifs of Pauline biography.[18] The relationship of Acts 9.25 to 2 Cor. 11.33 must, however, be interpreted differently: The lexeme τεῖχος is singular in the *Corpus Paulinum* so that its use in Acts can be seen as a reflection of Paul's flight from Damascus described in 2 Cor. 11.

In the post-Pauline NT writings we do find isolated allusions to expressions in 2 Cor., but we cannot conclude from this either that 2 Cor. was generally known or that there had been a literary reception of it either as a whole or at least in parts. Likewise we cannot necessarily presuppose knowledge and theological or literary adaptation of 2 Cor. in the writings which go under the collective name of 'the Apostolic Fathers': *1 Clem.* (after 96)[19] contains no palintextual elements which would allow us to conclude unequivocally that the author knew and used 2 Cor.[20] This

---

18.　Wolter, *Pastoralbriefe*, p. 76 n. 32 sees such an after-effect of 2 Cor. 1.6 in 2 Tim. 2.10. Such after-effects can be conveyed through the 'personal tradition of Paul' and then relate to Pauline biography.

19.　On the dating see also Eusebius, *Hist. Eccl.* III.15f.

20.　An acquaintance with 2 Cor. cannot be conclusively proved in 1 Clement. Thus Lindemann, 'Paulus in den Schriften', p. 262: 1 Clem. 13.1 relates rather to 1 Cor. 1.31, similarly the formulation in 2 Cor. 10.17 – on this see Lindemann, *Clemensbriefe*, p. 54 – and therefore not compellingly to 2 Cor. The formulation in 1 Clem. 2.7; 33.1 and 34.4 (πᾶν ἔργον ἀγαθόν) which could be taken as an incorporation of 2 Cor. 9.8 is not sufficient to prove that he knew 2 Cor. (see here Lindemann, *Clemensbriefe*, p. 103 and p. 106) since this expression is also found in 2 Tim. 2.21; 3.17, in Tit. 1.16; 3.1 and in a similar form in Phil. 1.6. This, to be sure, does not prove that 1 Clement did *not* know 2 Cor. The situation is similar with regard to 1 Clem. 36.2 which does not explicitly relate to 2 Cor. 3.7, 13 (contrary to Lona, *Clemensbrief*, p. 506) or to 2 Cor. 3.18. Even 1 Clem. 38.2 is at most a 'first reflection' of 2 Cor. 9.12 – see Schnelle, *Einleitung*[4], p. 94 or Furnish, *Corinthians*, p. 451 – but cannot count as evidence for the knowledge of 2 Cor. For the same concepts appear both in 1 Clement and in 2 Cor. in other places (ὑστέρημα in 2 Cor. 8.14 and 1 Clem. 2.6; or (προσ)ἀναπληρόω in 2 Cor. 11.9, cf. also 1 Cor. 16.17; Phil. 2.30, both connected to ὑστέρημα – hence it was clearly a common Pauline expression – whereas in 1 Clem. 63.1 it stands alone. Likewise the similar expression in 1 Clem. 34.2 ... ἐξ αὐτοῦ γάρ ἐστιν τὰ πάντα and 2 Cor. 5.18 (τὰ δὲ πάντα ἐκ τοῦ θεοῦ ...) is not sufficient to allow us to see here a derivation, contrary to *Biblia Patristica*, p. 478. The same is true for 1 Clem. 5.6 and 2 Cor. 11.24–25 (contrary to *Biblia Patristica*, p. 480). Both passages are only comparable to the extent that here we are dealing with peristases which are, however, different linguistically and in content. Likewise 1 Clem. 47.1f. contains no reference to a knowledge of 2 Cor. – contrary to K. Aland, 'Entstehung', p. 326: '1 Clem. 47.1–2 ... appears to be ... a reference to the fact that a second Corinthian epistle was also known in Rome ...'. In 1 Clem. 47.1f. it is particularly clear from the context of 47.3f. that the reference here is to 1 Cor. – see Lindemann, *Clemensbriefe*, p. 138. This does not mean to say that we can exclude any

observation is reinforced by the fact that 1 Clement either makes explicit reference to 1 Cor. (47.1ff.) or reflects it above and beyond particular expressions in extended thematic allusions (37.5; 49.5). All these observations, however, do not allow us to conclude vice versa that 1 Clement did *not* know or use 2 Cor.

An examination of the so-called *2 Clement* (mid-second century)[21] or the letters of *Ignatius* (beginning of the second century)[22] leads to similar conclusions. In these letters there are diverse extensive references to 1 Cor. as opposed to 2 Cor.[23] Finally in *Polycarp* (around 135)[24] and in the

---

knowledge of 2 Cor. in 1 Clement since the singular τὴν ἐπιστολὴν does not necessarily mean the actual knowledge of only *one* Corinthian letter (see also Origen, *Contra Celsum* I.63; III.20). To this extent we can agree with Lona, *Clemensbrief*, p. 506. The depiction of Paul in 1 Clement 5.5–7 suggests rather that the author was unaware of the range of the peristases in 2 Cor. 11.23–27, see Lindemann, *Paulus im ältesten Christentum*, p. 76. Hence 1 Clement on the one hand gives no indisputable documentary evidence of 2 Cor., but on the other hand it must remain open whether he *did* know it – whereby one need not necessarily think of a 2 Cor. which had already been edited, contrary to Lindemann, 'Paulus im 2. Jahrhundert', pp. 43f. and n.18.

21.   On the so-called 2 Clement see Lindemann/Paulsen, *Väter*, p. 152. 2 Clem. 9.13 does not explicitly reflect 2 Cor. 6.16, contrary to *Biblia Patristica*, p. 479.

22.   The letters of Ignatius probably should be related to his martyrdom at the time of Trajan (98–117, see Eusebius, *Hist. Eccl.* III.36); see also Lindemann/Paulsen, *Väter*, p. 176. On the discussion about the dating of the Ignatian writings see Hübner, 'Thesen', pp. 44–72; Lindemann, 'Antwort', pp. 185–94 and Schöllgen, 'Ignatianen', pp. 16–25. On the relationship of Ignatius to Paul see also Lindemann, 'Paulus in den Schriften', pp. 267ff. Ign. *Trall.* 13.3 (πιστὸς ὁ πατήρ . . .) cannot be understood as an obvious quotation of 2 Cor. 1.18 (πιστὸς δὲ ὁ θεός); see also 1 Cor. 1.9. Ign. *Trall.* 9.2 is similar to 2 Cor. 4.14 in content but not in language. Neither can Ign. *Phild.* 6.3 be a quotation from 2 Cor. 11.9 or 2 Cor. 12.16 – in both cases contrary to the listing in *Biblia Patristica*, p. 474ff.; or Lindemann, *Paulus im ältesten Christentum*, p. 211, who sees here a hint at 2 Cor. 11.9; 12.16 and 1.12 but comes to a similar conclusion: Ign. *Phild.* 6.3 is not sufficient 'as proof for the assumption that Ignatius . . . knew 2 Cor.', p. 212.

23.   See here the index in Lindemann/Paulsen, *Väter*.

24.   The letter of Polycarp also has no reference to 2 Cor. In ch. 6.2 the wording suggests an allusion to Rom. 14.12 rather than to 2 Cor. 5.10, contrary to Schnelle, *Einleitung*[4], p. 399 and Lindemann, *Paulus im ältesten Christentum*, p. 226 or Lindemann, 'Paulus im 2. Jahrhundert', p. 50, who conjectures that here, perhaps, we may have 'the earliest evidence for the use of 2 Cor. in the early church'; likewise contrary to Lindemann, 'Paulus in den Schriften', p. 277, where he speaks of a 'quotation' here. Lindemann consequently conjectures in 'Paulus in den Schriften', p. 277 that Polycarp might have been 'familiar with both Corinthian epistles'. It is more likely that ch. 2.2 (ὁ δὲ ἐγείρας αὐτὸν ἐκ νεκρῶν καὶ ἡμᾶς ἐγειρεῖ) points to 2 Cor. 4.14 – but this allusion is linguistically neutral and could just as well relate to 1 Cor. 6.14 or Rom. 6.11. Pol. *Phil.* 4.1 is also insufficient as evidence for the knowledge of 2 Cor. 6.7. This is even more obvious in the case of Pol. *Phil.* 6.1 in relation to 2 Cor. 8.21 – in both cases against the listing in *Biblia Patristica*, pp. 478f. Pol. *Phil.* 3.2, however, reflects the knowledge of several Pauline epistles.

Epistle of Barnabas (around 130–132)[25] we find no concepts or expressions which conclusively demand the knowledge and reception of 2 Cor. But the inverse conclusion cannot definitively be ruled out that there was a knowledge and reception of 2 Cor. in individual writings of the Apostolic Fathers.[26] We can prove at the most allusions, not quotations. If a Pauline expression is used verbatim (e.g. πᾶν ἔργον ἀγαθόν in 1 Clem. 2.7) this should not be considered as proof of the knowledge and use of a particular Pauline epistle such as 2 Cor. but rather that at the time of 1 Clement – i.e. at the end of the first century – common phrases from the Pauline letters had an effect on language and style beyond the Deutero- and Trito-Pauline generations (see also Col. 1.10; 2 Tim. 2.21 or Tit. 1.16) and that the 'Apostolic Fathers' presumably already possessed a collection of Pauline letters in '*Urcorpora*'. The letter of *Diognetus* is usually dated rather towards the end of the second century.[27] This letter, too, contains at most allusions to 2 Cor.[28] and is thus comparable to the written corpus of the Apostolic Fathers as a testimony to knowledge and use of 2 Cor.

It remains difficult to define what can be considered as a quotation in the sense of an unquestionable proof that 2 Cor. was known in the second century.[29] All we can say with certainty is that only where something is explicitly quoted – i.e. a pre-text is repeated verbatim and possibly introduced – can the knowledge of a Pauline epistle be clearly established. But this does not mean that in all the places where individual expressions

---

25.   On the dating see Prostmeier, *Barnabasbrief*, p. 118. Barn. 4.12 is thematically similar to 2 Cor. 5.10 but can also – contrary to *Biblia Patristica*, p. 477 – not be taken as an obvious reception of 2 Cor. Likewise for Dassmann, *Stachel*, pp. 223f. the 'traces' in the Epistle of Barnabas are not enough to assume 'an assured dependence' of the epistle on the Pauline letters.

26.   Against e.g. Bornkamm, 'Philipperbrief', p. 202 or Schneemelcher, 'Paulus', p. 6 in relation to Ignatius' knowledge of a collection of Pauline letters.

27.   See Wengst, 'Diognetbrief', p. 201; Schöllgen, 'Diognetbrief', p. 858. Lindemann, 'Diognet', p. 282 would like to date the letter of Diognetus in the mid-second century. Chapters 11 and 12, however, are unanimously considered to be a postscript, see Lindemann/Paulsen, *Väter*, p. 304 and Wengst, 'Diognetbrief', p. 201.

28.   *Biblia Patristica* mentions various references in *Ep. Diog.* which may be understood as allusions to 2 Cor.: *Ep. Diog.* 6.8 in relation to 2 Cor. 5.1; 5.12 in connection with 2 Cor. 6.9f.; see also Dassmann, *Stachel*, p. 254, who sees 2 Cor. 6.9f.; 10.3 (but also 1 Cor. 4.10–13 and Phil. 3.20) as being 'close' to *Ep. Diog.* 5.8–16. For Lindemann, 'Diognet', p. 284, 5.11–16 'touches closely upon' 2 Cor. 6.9f.; *Ep. Diog.* 5.16 might then be an allusion to 2 Cor. 6.10; *Ep. Diog.* 7.2 is only connected to 2 Cor. 6.18 by the (LXX) concept παντοκράτωρ. *Ep. Diog.* 5.8 is a 'direct reminder of Pauline statements' such as 2 Cor. 10.3, but also Rom. 8.12f. – thus Lindemann, 'Diognet', p. 283. But it could also refer to Romans 8 – thus Lindemann, *Paulus im ältesten Christentum*, p. 345.

29.   On this see the varied conclusions which are drawn by e.g. Schneemelcher, 'Paulus', pp. 6ff.; K. Aland, 'Entstehung', e.g. 324ff. or Lindemann, 'Paulus im 2. Jahrhundert', pp. 40ff.

in Pauline letters are taken up or ignored they were not also known or available in smaller collections. One can hardly speak of quotations in the writings of the Apostolic Fathers[30] but rather of hints in motifs, theme or language, i.e. allusions.[31]

Up until the earliest definite witness for the extensive knowledge of 2 Cor., namely Marcion (see below) – i.e. up to the middle of the second century – the knowledge of 2 Cor. could also in theory be established from the writings or bodies of writing which in the period following stand rather on the borders of Christian literature.[32] But here, too, the findings produce no proofs which go beyond allusions. In *gnostic literature* up to the middle or end of the second century there are no clear quotations. The reference in Epiphanius (*Haer.* 38.2.5) to a gnostic group of *Cainites* who were said to have written a document on the Ἀναβατικὸν Παύλου incorporating 2 Cor. 12.4 is not dependable.[33] Whether the *Apocalypse of Paul* from Nag Hammadi (NHC v/2) can be evidence for the knowledge of 2 Cor. in the second century[34] is doubtful.[35] In Hippolytus, *Refutatio* v.8.25 there is no direct reference to the group of the Naassenes, for what is under discussion here is the confrontation with the Phrygians (as already in *Refutatio* v.7.20ff. and v.8.13ff.).[36] Moreover the evidence can be introduced rather as an example of how Hippolytus quoted 2 Cor. (see below). In the *Evangelium Aegyptiorum copticum*[37] no connection to 2 Cor. can be found. In the *Gospel of Philip* (possibly the second half of the second century) we can see occasional 'weak traces of Paul' in respect of 2 Cor.[38] Other texts from Nag Hammadi – e.g. the *Evangelium Veritatis* (NHC I.3/XII.2) and the so-called *Letter to Rheginus* (NHC I.4) – can at

---

30. Lindemann for example in 'Paulus in den Schriften', p. 275, describes Pol. *Phil.* 11.2, 3 as 'an explicit quotation formula' from 1 Cor. 6.2.

31. Compare on the use of the concept corresponding examinations in the fields of the history or science of literature such as Jacoff, *Poetry*; Wilss, *Anspielungen*, or Pasco, *Allusion*.

32. Here I cite only the writings which can be dated with the 'evidence' which is generally called allusions.

33. See here Lindemann, *Paulus im ältesten Christentum*, pp. 97f.

34. Lindemann, 'Paulus im 2. Jahrhundert', p. 56 sees in the *Apocalypse of Paul* an adoption of 2 Cor. 12.2ff. See also Lindemann, *Paulus im ältesten Christentum*, p. 332 and n. 237: '2 Cor. 12.2–4 was at any rate the occasion for the drafting of the Apc. Pl. Admittedly the passage is not cited.'

35. The dating of this document is very controversial. While MacRae *et al.*, 'Apocalypse of Paul', p. 257 take the second century as the time of its emergence, Funk, 'Koptisch-gnostische Apokalypse des Paulus': Schneemelcher, *Apokryphen* II, pp. 628f. suspects a period of time between the second and fourth centuries as the date of its composition.

36. See Lindemann, *Paulus im ältesten Christentum*, p. 309.

37. This writing was probably drafted in gnosticizing circles in the second or third century; see also Schenke, 'Ägypter Evangelium'.

38. See Dassmann, *Stachel*, p. 198 and n. 24.

the most be introduced as instances of allusions to particular phrases from 2 Cor.[39]

Yet on the whole those gnostic texts which most likely include allusions to 2 Cor.[40] make virtually no use of other Pauline epistles.[41] Iustinus Gnosticus (end of second century)[42] contains only weak allusions to 2 Cor. and should be dated long after Marcion.

An examination of the rest of the early Christian literature up to the end of the second century and the more or less contemporary so-called *apocryphal* writings which belong to the texts from Nag Hammadi, leads to similar results. Here at best we can show allusions to 2 Cor. Neither in Hegesippus[43] (after 160) nor in Justin Martyr[44] (d. between 162 and 168) can the knowledge or use of 2 Cor. be clearly established. At most they contain isolated allusions. On the other hand Justin (e.g. *Dialogus cum Tryphone*) makes more frequent and more extensive use of 1 Cor.[45]

---

39. See the recently published *Nag Hammadi Deutsch.* In the *Evangelium Veritatis* (second century), NHC I.3/XII.2, 33–44 we can detect allusions to 2 Cor. 2.14; 5.4, 9; 8.9. In their edition Malinine *et al.,* *Evangelium Veritatis,* mention allusions to 2 Cor. 1.21; 2.14–16; 5.2–4; 5.4; 5.9.

In *Ad Rheginum de resurrectione* (NHC I.4, 2nd century) – cf. *Nag Hammadi Deutsch,* pp. 49–52 – no references to 2 Cor. are offered. Malinine, *De resurrectione (Epistula ad Rheginum)* names allusions to 2 Cor. 5.4 in *Ad Rheg.* 7.14; 9.1 and to 2 Cor. 10.2 in *Ad Rheg.* 15.11. Particularly in regard to 2 Cor. 10.2 a literary dependence cannot be assumed; cf. also Lindemann, *Paulus im ältesten Christentum,* p. 321.

40. The following other writings are named in *Biblia Patristica* in connection with 2 Cor.: *Liber Secundus Seth Magni* (NHC VII/2) 149 in relation to 2 Cor. 6.14 and the *Interpretatio animae* (Codex 2 and 6) – references to 2 Cor. 3.6 in *Int. An.* 80; 2 Cor. 7.1 in *Int. An.* 74.

41. Here compare the concluding assessment in Lindemann, *Paulus im ältesten Christentum,* pp. 341ff.

42. Iustinus Gnosticus should be dated towards the end of the second century, since in Hippolytus, *Refutatio* V.23.1–27.6 one can find the gnostic *Book of Baruch,* see von Harnack, *Chronologie,* p. 566. See also Speyer, 'Baruch', p. 190. In *Refutatio* V.26.23 we can detect a reference alluding to 2 Cor. 11.3 – here see Marcovich, *Refutatio.*

43. Hegesippus (post-160), *Memorabilia* (as handed down in Eusebius, *Hist. Eccl.* IV.22.1ff.), see Preuschen, *Antilegomena,* pp. 107–13. 110.9 and 111.38 are considered as referring to 2 Cor. 11.2. But the written record is too 'thin' to allow us to judge that he knew Pauline letters; thus Lindemann, *Paulus im ältesten Christentum,* pp. 295f.

44. Marcovich, *Dialogus* 35.3 might refer to 2 Cor. 11.3 but also to 1 Cor. 11.18f. – see Lindemann, *Paulus im ältesten Christentum,* p. 360. 2 Cor. 3.14 might lie behind 55.3. But Lindemann simply draws the conclusion: 'Justin had knowledge of Pauline letters, at least of Romans, 1 Cor. and Galatians, and consulted them when drafting the *Dialogus ....*', p. 366.

45. See also the relevant index in Marcovich, *Dialogus,* pp. 329f.

The *Epistula Apostolorum* (after 170)[46], the *Ascensio Isaiae* (second century)[47], the *Odae Salomonis* (second century)[48] and the *Oracula Sibyllina*[49] offer no evidence for the knowledge and use of 2 Cor. which goes beyond occasional allusions. Finally in Theophilus of Antioch (end of the second century)[50] in the *Apocryphon Iacobi*,[51] Melito of Sardis (d. before 190)[52] and Julius Cassianus (around 170)[53] we can establish only faint allusions to 2 Cor. Theophilus makes obvious allusions in both theme and language to 1 Cor. but not to 2 Cor.[54]

'Echoes' of 2 Cor. are seen in the *Evangelium Thomae copticum* (at the latest mid-second century)[55], in Tatianus Syrus (after 165)[56] and in

---

46.   The *Biblia Patristica* names *Ep. Ap.* 26 (37) as referring to 2 Cor. 5.10 and *Ep. Ap.* 30 (41) to 2 Cor. 12.12, biblical details according to Schneemelcher, *Apokryphen I*, pp. 205ff. Lindemann, *Paulus im ältesten Christentum*, p. 373 reaches the conclusion: 'The author perhaps (!) knew Pauline letters; he presumably did not make explicit use of them.'

47.   Schneemelcher, *Apokryphen II*, pp. 547ff. *Asc. Isa.* 10.12 can at best merely allude to 2 Cor. 4.4.

48.   *Papyrus Bodmer X–XII*, 60–69. In the *Odae Salomonis.* there are references seen to 2 Cor. 2.14, 15; 3.1; 4.13 and 6.7. Lindemann, *Paulus im ältesten Christentum*, p. 378 gives the following judgement: 'We cannot completely rule out the idea that the parallels to Pauline statements can be traced back to the influence of the Pauline epistles. But the uncertainty is so great that the *Odae Salomonis* (like the *Oracula Sibyllina*) must be left out of account as proofs of an early use of Paul.'

49.   This holds good for the question of an incorporation of 2 Cor. 5.10 in *Or. Sib.* 2.38, 2.39; 2 Cor. 6.15 in *Or. Sib.* 2.35; 3.50 and 2 Cor. 11.2 in *Or. Sib.* 8.160.

50.   This is true e.g. for *Ad Autolycum* I.8 in relation to 2 Cor. 1.22; I.12 related to 2 Cor. 1.21 and I.2 as reflecting 2 Cor. 7.1. Theophilus, too, makes more frequent and more extensive reference to 1 Cor.; see also the index in Marcovich, *Ad Autolycum*.

51.   The *Epistola Iacobi Apocrypha* (NHC I.2) was probably written around the end of the second century, see Hartenstein/Plisch,'Brief', p. 12. But in the *Epistola Iacobi* we can assume that 1 Cor. was known rather than 2 Cor., see Kirchner, 'Brief', p. 235.

52.   This is true of *De Fide* 244.43 in relation to 2 Cor. 11.2 and for the compilation of the evidence in Dassmann, *Stachel*, pp. 287f. Fragment XIV.9 is taken to be a recapitulation of 2 Cor. 8.9 but also of Phil. 2.6f., see on this Angstenberger, *Christus*, pp. 27f., who here – with a reservation as to its authenticity – sees 'an echo' of 2 Cor. 8.9; Fragment *Papyrus Bodmer* XII.4f. is held to be a reference to 2 Cor. 11.2 but also to Eph. 5.25–32; ΠΕΡΙ ΠΑΣΧΑ 7 counts as a reference to 2 Cor. 5.17; see Dassmann (as above).

53.   This applies to 2 Cor. 11.3 in connection with *De continentia* 239.

54.   See e.g. *Ad Autolycum* I.7 in relation to 1 Cor. 15.53f. See also the index in Marcovich, *Ad Autolycum*, p. 145.

55.   This applies to 2 Cor. 8.9 in Log. 29 and 2 Cor. 5.3 in Log. 21, see Guillaumont *et al.*, *Evangelium nach Thomas*, p. 59.

56.   Applying to 2 Cor. 6.16 in *Oratio ad Graecos* 15.16 and 2 Cor. 10.4 in 16.18. See Schwartz, *Tatiani oratio*, pp. 1–43.

Athenagoras[57] but these findings, too, when examined more closely, must remain ambiguous.

5.2.2.2. *Clear documentary proof of 2 Corinthians*

2 Cor. as a connected letter is first attested to in the earliest canonical lists. There 2 Cor. can be found in a proto-canonical corpus of Pauline letters. Marcion[58], the Canon Muratori[59] and Papyrus 46 [60] are named as the earliest undisputed witnesses to the knowledge or citation of the combined 2 Cor. from the second century. This simultaneously marks the dates relevant to the history of the canon.[61] Yet these findings can only be accepted with reservations, since in the meantime the dating of the *Muratorian Fragment* has become highly controversial[62] so that as witness for 2 Cor. in the second century we can only use, alongside P[46], Marcion's *Apostolikon*.[63] Here, however, we must take into consideration that *Adversus Marcionem V* – 'the most important aid in analyzing Marcion's text of Paul'[64] which appeared between 207 and 211 CE[65] – reflects the view of Tertullian. Consequently the question of the size, language and text of Marcion's *Apostolikon* in the middle of the second century becomes exceedingly difficult on this basis. Nevertheless, on the basis of *Adversus Marcionem V* Marcion can be enlisted as a 'substantial witness to the text of 1 and 2 Corinthians and as a proto-canonical editor of both letters'.[66]

---

57. In Athenagoras, *De resurrectione mortuorum* to the expression δεῖ ... ἀφθαρσίαν, ἵνα ... reminds us at most of 2 Cor. 5.10 (φανερωθῆναι ... ἵνα ...) or also 1 Cor. 15.53. See also Dassmann, *Stachel*, p. 250. A reference to 2 Cor. 5.10 might also lie behind the closing phrase in *De resurrectione mortuorum* (εἴτε ἀγαθὰ εἴτε κακά), here see Marcovich, *Athenagorae*.

58. See E.-M. Becker, 'Marcion', pp. 95–109.

59. See Lietzmann, *Das muratorische Fragment* and Schneemelcher, *Apokryphen I*, p. 29.

60. See K./B. Aland, *Text*, p. 92. On the individual deviations regarding the composition of the Corpus Paulinum see K. Aland, 'Entstehung', p. 327 and p. 346 as well as p. 336: 'The differences in the sequence of the letters... are clear proof that from the start diverse drafts were joined together in different ways.' But it is striking that despite differing drafts the same letters were known, named and cited.

61. See Schnelle, 'Bibel', pp. 1417f.

62. See Hahneman, *Muratorian Fragment*, especially pp. 215ff. He would like to date the fragment between 303 and 392. Eusebius', *Hist. Eccl.* (303–24) is assumed as the *terminus a quo*.

63. See E.-M. Becker, 'Marcion', particularly pp. 96f. Compare also Sellin, 'Hauptprobleme', p. 2981: 'The first certain witness to an acquaintance with 2 Cor. is Marcion.'

64. Lindemann, *Paulus im ältesten Christentum*, p. 380.

65. Here see E.-M. Becker, 'Marcion', *passim*.

66. E.-M. Becker, 'Marcion', p. 109.

5.2.2.3. *Quotations from 2 Corinthians in the Patristic Literature of the second and third centuries*

Theophilus of Antioch does indeed explicitly quote words from John's Gospel and introduces them as quotations (see *Ad Autolycum* II.22) – but we do not yet encounter in this work true quotations from Paul's letters which go beyond linguistic and thematic allusions.[67] Tertullian (d. around 220) knows – over and above *Adversus Marcionem V* – 1 and 2 Corinthians[68] and already registers differences between the two epistles to the Corinthians.[69] He, Irenaeus (d. around 200)[70] and Hippolytus (d. around 170) as well as Origen (d. 254, see below) and Clement of Alexandria (d. around 220)[71] are the first of Paul's interpreters to exegete 2 Cor. using the form of quotation. In Irenaeus quotations from Paul can generally be recognized because they contain specific introductory formulae.[72] Hippolytus' *Refutatio* v.8.25 proves to be a quotation from 2 Cor. 12.2–4, for he explicitly refers to Paul and there follows a verbatim reproduction of the text:

... Παῦλος οἶδεν ὁ ἀπόστολος...
καὶ εἰπὼν ἡρπάσθαι ὑπὸ ἀγγέλου καὶ γεγονέναι
ἕως δευτέρου καὶ τρίτου οὐρανοῦ εἰς τὸν παράδεισον ...[73].

Our observations on the rise of the practice of quoting show, for the evaluation of the history of the reception of the Pauline epistles *as a whole*, that the patristic authors only began to quote from Pauline texts when they saw their form of literary adaptation as an exegetical act. In so doing they combine various motives: if quotations were originally introduced for apologetic reasons (e.g. Tertullian), Origen uses the quotation to analyse it exegetically and philologically. Both ways of using the quotation – the apologetic and the philological – reflect the fact that, and the way in which, the Pauline letters are coming to acquire a binding – i.e. canonical – literary and theological authority. In a reciprocal fashion the literary adaptation in the form of quotation drives forward the process of canonization.

---

67. Contrary to Dassmann, *Stachel*, pp. 251f., who sees in *Ad Autolycum* III.15 a connection to Rom. 13.7f. Even the reference to 2 Cor. 11.6 in *Ad Autolycum* II.1 (ἰδιώτης ὢ τῷ λόγῳ) does not go much beyond an allusion. Compare also Nagel, *Rezeption*, pp. 55f.

68. Tertullian, *De praescriptione haereticorum* 36.

69. See Tertullian, *De pudicitia* 13–14. He notices the discrepancy between 1 Cor. 5 and 2 Cor. 2.5–6; 7.5–6. Compare also Heinrici, *Brief*, pp. 11ff.

70. See e.g. Noormann, *Irenäus*, p. 517. Eighteen quotations from 2 Cor. can be found in Irenaeus. See Dassmann, *Stachel*, p. 295 and Werner, *Paulinismus*, p. 7.

71. Here see the work by Mees, *Zitate*, particularly I.143ff. and II.171ff.

72. See Noormann, *Irenäus*, pp. 63f. This basic formula largely consists of the naming of Paul and a reference to the letter being quoted.

73. See Marcovich, *Refutatio* on this passage.

These observations tell us three things about the history of the reception of 2 Cor. *in particular*.

(a) 2 Cor. is not one of the Pauline epistles to which the clearest allusions are made or which are most often quoted.

(b) The comprehensive literary reception of 2 Cor. only then becomes evident when the initially non-binding intertextual references taking up 2 Cor. in the form of allusions in the post-NT literature lead on to a literary and theologically binding – i.e. practically canonical – reception of the text, driven forward on the one hand by the emergence of canonical lists and on the other by the use of quotation. Only then is 2 Cor. too comprehensively and verbally received and attested.

(c) This is where the literary genus of the commentary comes into being.

5.2.3. *The patristic interpretation of 2 Corinthians in the third and fourth centuries*

5.2.3.1. *Examples of the patristic reception and interpretation of 2 Corinthians*

We must now ask *how* 2 Cor. was perceived in the *early church* in so far as this is reflected in the extant fragmentary patristic commentaries. Can we find hints in these commentaries that already in the interpretation of 2 Cor. in the early church the possible disunity of the letter was considered to be a problem? The following observations simply list some aspects of the early history of commentaries on 2 Cor. in their *literarcritical* perspectives.

It has already been explained above that up until the end of the second century 2 Cor. was adopted in the form of allusions, mentioned in canonical lists and was then cited in the third century in the form of quotations. At this period it is possible that, in terms of the history of the canon, there was also an ongoing interpretation of the letter. Pieces of evidence from commentaries or homilies[74] on 2 Cor. are only preserved in *catenae*.[75] The catenae for the most part represent fragmentary mediaeval collections of important individual passages and serve a double purpose. They serve to safeguard the tradition of the Church Fathers at a later date and prepare the way for a continuous interpretation of biblical writings.

---

74.   On the form of the homily see Lang, 'Bibelkommentare', pp. 203ff.

75.   For the definition see Neuschäfer, 'Katene'[3], p. 424: A characteristic of this genre is 'the compilation of the verse-for-verse commentary of a biblical book out of verbatim excerpts. These are excerpted from individual commentaries, homilies or exegetical explanations of a different literary type from selected Church Fathers, noted down in consecutive sequence and differentiated one from the other by a particular style of writing and with the appended name of the author.'

The direct transmission of early church biblical commentaries was superseded by the catenae.[76]

Which fragments of patristic exegesis of 2 Cor. are preserved for us in such catenae? Can we already detect critical reflections on the passages in 2 Cor. which we with our modern feeling for cohesion perceive as 'breaks' (2 Cor. 2.13, 14; 6.14–7.1; 7.4, 5; 8.23; 9.1)? Origen (see above) wrote *inter alia* homilies on the Corinthian epistles[77] and placed them in a historical relationship to one another as well as in a theological.[78] Origen also made a critical examination of the style of Paul (and John). He confirms that the Epistle to the Romans is difficult to understand[79] and gives as the ground for the flawed ἀκολουθία of Pauline texts Paul's own statement in 2 Cor. 11.6 (ἰδιώτης τῷ λόγῳ). In this way Origen uses 2 Cor. 11.6 to show that Paul's authority was not based on his rhetorical competence. Rather scripture should lead to ἀλήθεια and κοινωφέλεια, and the ἰδιωτεία in the sense of a general comprehensibility can help precisely for this purpose.[80]

The following aspects of an awareness of 2 Cor. can also be taken from the catenae of patristic exegetes.[81] In his exegesis of 2 Cor. 7.1 Didymus of Alexandria (d. around 398)[82] refers to a variant reading.[83] He considers the transition from 2 Cor. 7.4 to 7.5 to be cohesive and interprets it with γάρ. As in Theodore and Severian below there is also in Didymus no extant fragment of exegesis of 2 Cor. 9. Theodore of Mopsuestia [84] is concerned with style and consequently endeavours to prove the 'logical consistency of thought', the ἀκολουθία of biblical texts.[85] He, too, observes a lack of rhetorical competence in Paul's style,[86] making a critical remark about the style of 2 Cor. 8.23;[87] looking at 2 Cor. 12.1–4 he interprets Paul as an apocalyptic writer on the lines of OT prophecy.[88] But Theodore does not stop at philological observations and assessments. On

76. See also Mühlenberg, 'Katenen', p. 14 and also Hagedorn, 'Katenen'.

77. *CPG* I.1458.

78. See Markschies, 'Origenes', p. 87.

79. See *CPG* I.60.1f.

80. See Neuschäfer, *Origenes*, p. 256.

81. Here see the bibliography in Bieringer/Lambrecht, *Studies,* pp. 4f. and Windisch, *Korintherbrief*, p. 1.

82. *CPG* 2560; see also Ὑπόμνημα εἰς τὴν δευτέραν ἐπιστολὴν Παύλου ἀποστόλου πρὸς Κορινθίους. Commentarius in epistolam secundam ad Corinthios, *PG* 39, cols 1679–1732. Compare Staab, *Pauluskommentare*, pp. 14–44.

83. See Staab, *Pauluskommentare*, pp. 32f. He contrasts the version ἐπιτελέσαι ἡμᾶς ἐν φόβῳ κυρίου ἁγιωσύνην with the variant καὶ πνεύματος ἐπιτελοῦντες ἁγιωσύνην.

84. See *PG* 3847 and Staab, *Pauluskommentare*, pp. 196–200.

85. Thus in Theodore's Commentary on the Psalms, Schäublin, *Untersuchungen*, p. 143.

86. See Schäublin, *Untersuchungen*, p. 146.

87. See Staab, *Pauluskommentare*, p. 199: he considers the figure of speech εἴτε … εἴτε in Paul to be a common linguistic expression (συνήθως).

88. See Staab, *Pauluskommentare*, p. 200.

the contrary, it is 'remarkable how in *Theodore* philological precision and psychological observation are united'.[89] Theodore interprets the leaps in thought and fluctuations in Galatians as stemming from Paul's emotional disposition and his zeal for the gospel.[90] Hence Theodore is aware of a lack of cohesion in the text but he interprets these breaks either theologically or psychologically.

We have a comprehensive interpretation of 2 Cor. by Severian of Gabala (d. around 408).[91] Hence in Severian's commentary we can examine all the possible breaks in 2 Cor. to see whether possible incohesions in the form of 2 Cor. were observed and evaluated. Severian, however, proves to be an interpreter of the content of those passages in 2 Cor. which we find to be incohesive (2.12, 13 and 2.14) and makes no critical observations on the style.[92] In spite of the extensive records in catenae no exegesis of 2 Cor. 6.14–7.8 or ch. 9 has been handed down. But we cannot draw any really well-grounded conclusions from this fact.

There exist both a connected commentary[93] and homilies on individual verses[94] by *John Chrysostom* (around 349–407). We have also commentaries by *Cyril of Alexandria* (d. 444)[95] and *Theodoret of Cyrus* (around 393–466).[96] Only a fragment on 2 Cor. 10.7 is known from Gennadius of Constantinople (around 400–71).[97] In *Oecumenius* (first half of the sixth century) there are fragments of Pauline commentaries including some on 2 Cor.[98] In the Latin area of the early church there are commentaries on 2

---

89. Wickert, 'Persönlichkeit', p. 57.

90. See Wickert, 'Persönlichkeit', p. 56 or Swete, *Commentaria*, I.71.23 on Gal. 4.21. Theodore interprets the phenomenon of prophecy as being similarly psychological. Hence the 'revelation which the prophet receives' is 'not simply considered as a supernatural communication of the future; it is – and Theodore in no way wants to exclude the fact that God may have a supernatural efficacy – far more an inner awareness of the divine will and action in an intensified spiritual state', Bultmann, *Exegese*, pp. 102f. Theodore also relates to this the revelation which Paul mentions in 2 Cor. 12.4, see Bultmann, as above, p. 104.

91. See *CPG* 4219 and Staab, *Pauluskommentare*, pp. 278–98.

92. See Staab, *Pauluskommentare*, pp. 282f.

93. See *CPG* 4429, Ὑπόμνημα εἰς τὴν πρὸς Κορινθίους δευτέραν ἐπιστολήν. In secundam ad Corinthios epistolam commentarius (Homiliae), *PG* 61, cols 381–610.

94. Thus on 2 Cor. 4.13 see *CPG* 4383; on 2 Cor. 5.17 see *CPG* 4701; on 2 Cor. 11.1 see *CPG* 4384; on 2 Cor. 12.9 see *CPG* 4576. Added to these there is a new fragment, see Noret, 'Fragment', p. 182.

95. See *CPG* 5209.2, Ἑρμηνεία εἰς τὴν πρὸς Κορινθίους ἐπιστολήν β. Explanatio in epistulam II ad Corinthios, *PG* 74, cols 915–52.

96. See *CPG* 6209/ Ἑρμηνεία τῆς δευτέρας ἐπιστολῆς πρὸς Κορινθίους. Interpretatio secundae epistolae ad Corinthios, *PG* 82, cols 375–460.

97. See *CPG* 5973 and Staab, *Pauluskommentare*, p. 419.

98. See *CPG* 7471 and Staab, *Pauluskommentare*, pp. 444–46.

Cor. by *Ambrosiaster* (mid- to end fourth century)[99] and *Pelagius* (350/360–418/431).[100] There is also a commentary on 2 Cor. by *Ephraim the Syrian* (306–73).[101]

5.2.3.2. *Observations on the hermeneutics of the patristic exegesis of 2 Corinthians*

Patristic philology knows of *critical* methods – such as textual criticism and the κρίσις ποιημάτων. These critical methods serve to prove the authority, authenticity and aestheticity of biblical writings. *Literarkritik* in the modern sense – i.e. in the sense of a historical criticism of sources – is as little known to the ecclesiastical authors at the time of the early church as it was in antiquity as a whole. Ancient textual interpretation is *historical* on the one hand to the extent in which it attempts to restore the original text but assumes that it is known and at most makes critical note of corruptions in the text and consequently can be characterized as 'criticism of the transmission'. On the other hand 'historical' interpretation in patristic exegesis means understanding the history of the document and the person of the Apostle, Paul. The Apostle lends authority to both the form and the content of his letters and gives cause neither for examining sources in a *literarcritical* fashion nor for extensive critical reflections on their content. In the realm of *hermeneutics* Paul's letters are interpreted theologically – e.g. allegorically, typologically, pneumatically and/or psychologically. In the ancient reception of the Pauline epistles the problem of the cohesion of the text is treated as an aspect of historical and theological interpretation and of the understanding of Paul the Apostle as he is present in the letters he left to posterity.

5.2.4. *A brief summary and prospect*

In early church and apocryphal Christian literature up to the end of the second century 2 Cor. was referred to at most in allusions. This does not necessarily mean that 2 Cor. was not known and used in this period; we may suppose that this was so but we cannot take this as certain. Only within the earliest drafts of the canon – i.e. in Marcion's *Apostolikon* and P[46] – is there clear proof of the general knowledge of 2 Cor. Only at the beginning of the third century when the transition to philological exegesis and commentaries also took place did 2 Cor. receive literary adaptation in clear quotations.

Thus the reception of 2 Cor. in the first to fourth centuries turns out to

---

99.   On Ambrosiaster see Geerlings, *Ambrosiaster*[3], p. 18. On the handing down of the commentary on 2 Cor. see *CPL* 184/ *CSEL* 81/1–3, H.J. Vogels.

100.   See *CPL* 728/ *Expositio in II Corinthios*, in: Souter, *Expositions*.

101.   The authenticity of this commentary is not certain. *Comm. in ep. Pauli*, Venice 1893, pp. 85–116.

be an exemplary, by no means exceptional, case of how Pauline letters are treated in the course of a developing process of canonization in which the literary and theological aspects of the corpus of Pauline epistles became more authoritative. We must, however, stress that in the history of the early Christian and early church reception and commentaries 2 Cor. is quoted less often and less comprehensively than 1 Cor. This can already be seen in Tertullian's clash with Marcion's *Apostolikon*.[102] This could perhaps be traced back to the fact that 2 Cor. reflects Paul's relationship to the Corinthian congregation much more intensively and is consequently less suited than 1 Cor. for e.g. theological, philosophical and ethical interpretations.

In the extant early Christian and early church writings we can find neither indications that 2 Cor. was available only in parts – as modern *literarcritical* hypotheses suggest – nor that, in the history of its reception, 2 Cor. was felt to be incoherent. Rather 2 Cor. is taken up initially in allusions, later in quotations and gains access to the early canonical lists as an undisputed part of the *Corpus Paulinum*. The exegetical-philological interpretation related to the quotation does occasionally contain literary criticism (see Origen and Theodore of Mopsuestia). The explanation for the lack of cohesion in Pauline letters, however, is not sought in the area of the reception and history of the text but in the person of Paul himself. To interpret the results of the philological exegesis of the text properly we must widen the inventory of philological methods with a hermeneutical one.[103]

5.3. *A retrospective review and a prospect*

The book you have before you is intended as an exegetical contribution to the hermeneutics of the Pauline epistles. The specific issues raised in Chapters 1–4 relate to Paul's epistolary hermeneutical conception. This is fundamental for the Second Letter to the Corinthians and for research into the original form of the individual letters which, in the course of their collection, were compiled and gathered together into the 2 Cor. which we have today.

For more than a hundred and fifty years the predominant question in the interpretation of 2 Cor. was that of its literary unity: do we have in the canonical 2 Cor. the text of one original letter, or does this letter represent a collection of what were initially several separate epistles? In research this *literarcritical* question either led, and still leads, to complex hypotheses of

---

102.   See E.-M. Becker, 'Marcion', especially p. 100.

103.   Fiedrowicz, *Prinzipien*, offers a provisional collection of texts on the hermeneutical principles of the early Church. Reference should be made to the volumes of the *Novum Testamentum Patristicum* which will appear in the near future.

division or it is ignored – which means that the historical development of the letter with its importance for the interpretation of the text is to a large extent left aside.

In this book the question of the *historical* development of 2 Cor. is considered as a *hermeneutical* question and is pursued constructively in two respects: first, the technical conditions which underlay the production, preservation and transmission of letters in antiquity were taken into consideration to aid the reconstruction of how Paul's letters were written and preserved. As a result we see that pre-canonical collections of letters, i.e. letter-compilations, could have come into being in the course of the copying of individual letters.

Second, with the help of exegesis and communication studies we achieve a differentiated picture from the extant Corinthian correspondence (1 and 2 Cor.) of the individual *phases* of Paul's communication with the Corinthian congregation. Hereby we may see how possible individual letters are chronologically related to each other.

In the course of this exegesis based on the theory of communication the concept of meta-communication is seen to be a valid description of the fact that not only various chronological *phases* but also diverse *levels* of Paul's communication can be inferred from 2 Cor. While the phases of communication permit a chronology of the Corinthian correspondence, the various levels of communication show how Paul in the course of his letter-writing begins to reflect *about* his communication with the Corinthians. Implicit Pauline epistolary hermeneutics can be deduced from this epistolary meta-communication since Paul writes in meta-communicative language about the intent and purpose of his letters. The two methods of research lead to an integrated model for understanding the Second Epistle to the Corinthians.

In the analysis of the meta-communicative texts we were able to reach a further conclusion. Paul's genuinely theological thought and speech – i.e. the Pauline theology of 2 Cor. – arise in the meta-communicative sections of the letter. For it is precisely at the points where Paul reflects upon his communication with the Corinthians that he sees himself provoked particularly to argue theologically.

Altogether five sections pursue topics of research in more detail or offer semantic studies on the central epistolary hermeneutical concepts of 2 Cor.

In two sections I have looked beyond Paul's epistolary hermeneutical conception in the various phases of his communication with the Corinthian congregation as they are documented in the collection which is the Second Letter to the Corinthians.

The question of the reception of 2 Cor. from the first to the fourth centuries looks for the *terminus ad quem* for the first preserved witness of 2 Cor. in its present form. I have also tested the importance of 2 Cor. in the context of the early Christian history of reception and in the context of the patristic exegesis of the Pauline epistles. On the example of 1 Cor. 8 I show that Paul's epistolary hermeneutical conception in 2 Cor., analysed on the basis of meta-communicative structures, can also be found in central sections of the First Letter to the Corinthians.

BIBLIOGRAPHY

1. *Sources*

Ambrosiaster in epistulam ad Corinthios secundam, ed. Vogels, H.J.; 1968 (*CSEL* 81.2), pp. 195–314.

Apocalypsis Henochi graeca, A.-M. Denis (ed. M. Black), *Fragmenta pseudepigraphorum quae supersunt graeca. Una cum historicorum et auctorum judaeorum hellenistarum fragmentis*, (Leiden: 1970) (PVTG 3b), pp. 5–44.

Aristotle, *Ars rhetorica* (ed. Kassel, R.; Berlin: 1976).

—*Divisiones quae vulgo dicuntur Aristoteleae* (ed. Mutschmann, H.; Leipzig: 1906).

Athenagoras, *De resurrectione mortuorum* (ed. Marcovich, M.; Leiden, etc.: 2000) (SVigChr 53).

Augustine, *Confessiones* (ed. Verheijen, L.; 1990) (CCSL 27).

—*De doctrina christiana* (ed. Martin, I.; 1962) (CCSL 32), pp. 1–167.

—*Epistulae* (ed. Goldbacher, A.; 1911) (CSEL 57).

—*Sermons pour la pâque* (ed. Poque, S.; Paris: 1996) (SC 116).

Augustus, *Res gestae. Das Monumentum Ancyranum* (ed. Volkmann, H.; Berlin[2]: 1964) (KlT 29/30).

Die syrische Baruch-Apokalypse: The Old Testament in Syriac, Part 4, Fasc. 3. *Apocalypsis Baruch. 4. Ezra* (eds. Deddering, S./R.J. Bidawind; Leiden: 1973).

M. Tullius Cicero, *De oratore* (ed. Kumaniecki, K.F.; Leipzig: 1969).

—*Epistulae ad Atticum* Vol. 1 (*Libri I–VIII*), Vol. 2 (*Libri IX–XVI*) (ed. Shackleton Bailey, D.R.; Stuttgart: 1987).

—*Epistulae ad Familiares Libri I–XVI* (ed. Shackleton Bailey, D.R.; Stuttgart: 1988).

—*Epistulae ad Familiares* Vol. 1 (*62–47 v. Chr.*), Vol. 2 (*47–43 v. Chr.*) (ed. Shackleton Bailey, D.R.; Cambridge: 1977).

—*Epistuale ad Quintum fratrem. Epistulae ad M. Brutum* (ed. Shackleton Bailey, D.R.; Stuttgart: 1988).

Clement of Alexandria, *Stromata Buch I–VI* (eds. Stählin, O./L. Früchtel; Berlin[3]: 1960) (GCS 2).

Caecilius Cyprianus, *Epistulae 1–57* (ed. Diercks, G.F.; 1994) (CCSL 3b).

Cyril of Alexandria, *Explanatio in epistulam II ad Corinthios*: PG 74 (1863), pp. 915–52.

Demetrii Phalerei qui dicitur de elocutione Libellus (ed. Radermacher, L.; Leipzig: 1901 = Stuttgart: 1967).

Didymus of Alexandria, *Commentarius in epistolam secundam ad Corinthios*: Staab, *Pauluskommentare*, pp. 14–44.

Dio Chrysostom, *Orations VII, XII and XXXVI* (Cambridge: 1992) (Cambridge Greek and Latin Classics. Imperial Library), pp. 62–88.

Dion von Prusa, *Olympische Rede. Eingeleitet, übersetzt und interpretiert von H.-J. Klauck* (Darmstadt: 2000) (Sapere 2).

Dionysius Halicarnassensis, *De compositione verborum: Opuscula 2* (eds. Usener, H./L. Radermacher; Stuttgart: 1965), pp. 1–143.

Dionysius Thrax, *Ars Grammatica* (ed. Uhlig, G.; Hildesheim: 1979) (Grammatici Graeci 1.1).

Das 4. Buch Esra: Biblia sacra iuxta vulgatam versionem (ed. Weber, R.; Stuttgart[3]: 1984), pp. 1931–74.

Eusebius, *Kirchengeschichte* (eds. Schwartz, E.; Kleine Ausgabe, Leipzig[5]: 1955).

Evangelium nach Thomas (eds. Guillaumont, A. *et al.*; Leiden: 1959).

Evangelium Veritatis (eds. Malinine, M. *et al.*; Zurich: 1956).

Evangelium Veritatis (Suppl.) (ed. Malinine, M. *et al.*; Zurich/Stuttgart: 1961).

Die Fragmente der Griechischen Historiker. Dritter Teil (ed. Jacoby, F.; Leiden: 1958) (abbreviated: FGrHist).

Gennadius of Constantinople, *Fragment zu 2 Kor 10,7*: Staab, *Pauluskommentare*, p. 419.

Hippolytus, *Refutatio omnium haeresium* (ed. Marcovich, M.; Berlin/New York: 1986) (PTS 25).

Homer, *Iliad* Vol. 1 (ed. West, M.L.; Stuttgart/Leipzig: 1998).

Horatius, *Opera* (ed. Shackleton Bailey, D.R.; Stuttgart: 1995).

John Chrysostom, *In secundam ad Corinthios epistolam commentarius*: PG 61 (1861), pp. 381–610.

Josephus, *Antiquitatum Iudaicarum: Flavii Josephi Opera* Vols. 1–4 (ed. Niese, B.; Berlin[2]: 1955).

—*Aus meinem Leben (Vita). Kritische Ausgabe, Übersetzung und Kommentar von F. Siegert et al.* (Tübingen: 2001).

—*The Jewish War I–III* (London/Cambridge, Massachusetts: 1927/1989).

Flavius Josephus, *Judean Antiquities* Vols 1–4 (eds. Feldman, L.H./S. Mason, *Flavius Josephus. Translation and Commentary* Vol. 3; Leiden etc.: 2000).

Justinus Martyr, *Apologiae pro christianis* (ed. Marcovich, M.; Berlin/New York: 1994) (PTS 38).

—*Dialogus cum Tryphone* (ed. Marcovich, M.; Berlin/New York: 1997) (PTS 47).

Klijn, A.F.J., *2 (Syriac Apocalypse of) Baruch: The Old Testament Pseudepigrapha* Vol. 1 (ed. Charlesworth, J. H.; New York: 1983), pp. 615–52.

Lietzmann, H., *Das muratorische Fragment und die monarchianischen Prologe zu den Evangelien* (Berlin[2]: 1933) (KlT I).

Lindemann, A./H. Paulsen, (eds.), *Die Apostolischen Väter* (Tübingen: 1992) (abbreviated: Lindemann/Paulsen, *Väter*).

Malherbe, A.J., *Ancient Epistolary Theorists* (Atlanta: 1988) (SBL.SBibSt 19).

M.V. Martial, *Epigrammaton Libri* (ed. Friedlaender, L.; Amsterdam: 1967).

Meliton de Sardes, *Sur la Pâque* (ed. Perler O.; Paris: 1966) (SC 123).

Nag Hammadi Deutsch Vol. 1: *NHC I.1—V.1* (eds. Schenke, H.-M. *et al.*; Berlin/New York: 2001) (GCS n.s. 8).

Cornelios Nepos, *Vitae cum fragmentis* (ed. Marshall, P.K.; Leipzig: 1977).

Novum Testamentum Graece (ed. Nestle, E.E./B.K. Aland *et al.*; Stuttgart[27]: 1995).

Oecumenicus, *Fragmente zum 2 Kor*: Staab, *Pauluskommentare*, pp. 444–46.

Die Oracula Sibyllina (ed. Geffcken, J.; Leipzig: 1902) (GCS 8).

Papyrus Bodmer X–XII (ed. Testuz, M.; Cologne/Geneva: 1959).

Paulinus von Nola, *Epistulae* (ed. Hartel, G. v.; 1894) (CSEL 29).

Pelagius, *Expositio in II Corinthios: Pelagius's Expositions of Thirteen Epistles of St Paul II* (ed. Souter, A.; Cambridge: 1926) (Text and Studies 9/2), pp. 231–305.

Philo of Alexandria, *De decalogo: Philonis Alexandrini. Opera quae supersunt IV* (ed. Cohn, L.; Berlin: 1902), pp. 269–307.

Plato, *Epistulae: Platonis Opera* Vol. 5.2 (ed. Burnet, I.; Oxford: 1907/1937).

—*Phaidros: Platonis Opera* Vol. 2 (ed. Burnet, I.; Oxford: 1901/1946).

Plinius Minor, *Epistularem Libri Novem. Epistularem ad Traianum Liber. Panegyricus* (eds. Schuster, M./R. Hanslik; Stuttgart/Leipzig: 1992).

Quintilian, *Institution Oratoire 3,5,6* (ed. Cousin, J.; Paris: 1976/1978/1979).

De resurrectione (Epistula ad Rheginum) (eds. Malinine, M. *et al.*; Zurich/Stuttgart: 1963).

Schneemelcher, W., *Neutestamentliche Apokryphen I–II* (Tübingen[6]: 1990/1997).

Seneca, *Dialogorum libri duodecim* (ed. Reynolds, L.D.; Oxford: 1977).

—*Epistulae morales ad Lucilium* (ed. Hense, O.; Leipzig: 1914).

Septuaginta. Id est Vetus Testamentum graece iuxta LXX interpretes (ed. Rahlfs, A.; Stuttgart: 1979).

Severian von Gabala, *Fragmente zum 2 Kor*: Staab, *Pauluskommentare*, pp. 278–98.

Sextus Empiricus, *Adversos Mathematicos Libros I–VI* (eds. Mutschmann, H./J. Mau; Stuttgart: 1961).

Staab, K., *Pauluskommentare aus der griechischen Kirche. Aus Katenenhandschriften gesammelt* (Münster[2]: 1984).

C. Suetoni Tranquilli Opera. Vol. I De Vita Caesarum Libri VIII (ed. Ihm, M.; Stuttgart: 1958).

P. Cornelius Tacitus, *Annales. Tomus I* (ed. Heubner, H.; Stuttgart/Leipzig[2]: 1994).

Tatiani oratio ad Graecos (ed. Schwartz, E.; Leipzig: 1888) (TU 4.1).

Tertullian, *Adversus Marcionem* (ed. Kroymann, A.; 1954) (CCSL 1), pp. 437–726.

—*De praescriptione haereticorum* (ed. Refoulé, R.F.; 1954) (CCSL 1), pp. 185–224.

—*De pudicitia* (ed. Dekkers, E.; 1954) (CCSL 2), pp. 1279–330.

The Nag Hammadi Library in English (ed. Robinson, J.M.; Leiden[4], etc.: 1996).

Theodor von Mopsuestia, *Fragmente zum 2 Kor*: Staab, *Pauluskommentare*, pp. 196–200.

Theodoret of Cyrus, *Interpretatio secundae epistolae ad Corinthios*: PG 82 (1864), pp. 375–460.

Theodori Episcopi Mopsuestui in Epistolas Beati Pauli Commentaria I–II (ed. Swete, H.B.; Cambridge: 1880–1882).

Theophilus Antiochenus, *Ad Autolycum* (ed. Marcovich, M.; Berlin/New York: 1995) (PTS 43).

Theophilus of Antioch, *Ad Autolycum. Text and Translation by R.M. Grant*; (Oxford: 1970).

Thukydides, *Historiae Libri I–IV* (eds. Jones, H.S./J.E. Powell; Oxford: 1942).

C. Iulius Victor, *Ars rhetorica* (eds. Giomini, R./M.S. Celentano; Leipzig: 1980).

Viereck, P./F. Zucker, (eds.), *Papyri, Ostraka und Wachstafeln aus Philadelphia im Fayûm* (Berlin: 1926) (Ägyptische Urkunden aus den Staatlichen Museen zu Berlin. Griechische Urkunden VII).

Neuer Wettstein, Texte zum Neuen Testament aus Griechentum und Hellenismus, Vol. II.1 *Texte zur Briefliteratur und zur Johannesapokalypse* (eds. Strecker, G./U. Schnelle; Berlin/New York: 1996).

2. Commentaries

Bachmann, P., *Der zweite Brief des Paulus an die Korinther* (Leipzig: 1909) (KNT VIII).

Barnett, P.W., *The Second Epistle to the Corinthians* (Grand Rapids/Cambridge: 1997) (NIC).

Barrett, C.K., *A Commentary on the Second Epistle to the Corinthians* (London: 1973) (BNTC).

Bauer, J.B., *Die Polykarpbriefe* (Göttingen: 1995) (KAV 5).

Betz, H.D., *2. Korinther 8 und 9. Ein Kommentar zu zwei Verwaltungsbriefen des Apostels Paulus* (Gütersloh: 1993).

—*2 Corinthians 8 and 9. A Commentary on Two Administrative Letters of the Apostle Paul* (Philadelphia: 1985) (Hermeneia).

Bultmann, R., *Der zweite Brief an die Korinther* (ed. Dinkler, E.; Göttingen^2: 1987) (KEK Sonderbd.).

Carrez, M., *La deuxième épître de Saint Paul aux Corinthiens* (Geneva: 1986) (CNT VIII).

Clarke, G.W., *The Letters of St. Cyprian of Carthage* Vol. 1 (*Letters 1–27*) and 2 (*Letters 28–54*) (New York/Ramsey: 1984) (Ancient Christian Writers 43 and 44).

Conzelmann, H., *Der erste Brief an die Korinther* (Göttingen: 1969) (KEK 5).

Dibelius, M., *Die Pastoralbriefe* (Tübingen^4: 1966) (HNT 13).

Furnish, V.P., *II Corinthians. A New Translation with Introduction and Commentary* (Garden City, New York: 1984) (AncB 32A).

Heinrici, C.F.G., *Der zweite Brief an die Korinther* (Göttingen^8: 1900) (KEK 6).

Holtzmann, H.J., *Die Pastoralbriefe. Kritisch und exegetisch behandelt* (Leipzig: 1880).

Hughes, P.E., *Paul's Second Epistle to the Corinthians* (Grand Rapids^4: 1973) (NIC).

Klauck, H.-J., *2. Korintherbrief* (Würzburg^3: 1994) (NEB 8).

Kremer, J., *2. Korintherbrief* (Stuttgart^2: 1998) (SKK.NT 8).

Lambrecht, J., *Second Corinthians* (Collegeville, Minnesota: 1999) (Sacra Pagina Series Vol. 8).

Lang, F., *Die Briefe an die Korinther. Übersetzt und erklärt* (Göttingen/Zurich: 1986) (NTD 7).

Lietzmann, H., *An die Korinther I/II (ergänzt von W.G. Kümmel)* (Tübingen^5: 1969) (HNT 9).

Lindemann, A., *Die Apostolischen Väter I. Die Clemensbriefe* (Tübingen: 1992) (HNT 17).

Lona, H.E., *Der erste Clemensbrief* (Göttingen: 1998) (KAV 2).

McCant, J.W., *2 Corinthians* (Sheffield: 1999).

Merkel, H., *Apokalypsen. Sibyllinen* (Gütersloh: 1998) (JSHRZ V/8).

Merklein, H., *Der erste Brief an die Korinther. Kapitel 5,1–11,1* (Gütersloh: 2000) (ÖTK 7/2).

Metzger, B.M., *The Fourth Book of Ezra. A New Translation and Introduction: The Old Testament Pseudepigrapha* Vol. 1: *Apocalyptic Literature and Testaments* (ed. Charlesworth, J.H.; New York: 1983), pp. 517–59.

Murphy-O'Connor, J., *The Theology of the Second Letter to the Corinthians* (Cambridge: 1991).

Prostmeier, F.R., *Der Barnabasbrief* (Göttingen: 1999) (KAV 8).

Roloff, J., *Der erste Brief an Timotheus* (Neukirchen-Vluyn: 1988) (EKK 15).

Sauer, G., *Jesus Sirach* (Gütersloh: 1981) (JSHRZ III/5).

Schoedel, W.R., *Die Briefe des Ignatius von Antiochien. Ein Kommentar* (Munich: 1990).

Schrage, W., *Der erste Brief an die Korinther (1 Kor 1,1–6,11)* (Neukirchen-Vluyn: 1991) (EKK VII/1).

Schreiner, J., *Das 4. Buch Esra* (Gütersloh: 1981) (JSHRZ V/4).

Scott, J.M., *2 Corinthians* (Peabody, Massachusetts: 1998) (NIBC).

Thrall, M., The *Second Epistle to the Corinthians* (Vol. 1, Edinburgh: 1994; Vol. 2, Edinburgh: 2000) (ICC).

Uhlig, S., *Das Äthiopische Henochbuch* (Gütersloh: 1984) (JSHRZ V/6).

Wendland, H.-D., *Die Briefe an die Korinther* (Göttingen: 1968) (NTD 7).

Windisch, H., *Der zweite Korintherbrief* (Neudruck der 9. Aufl. 1924; ed. Strecker, G.; Göttingen: 1970) (KEK 9).

Witherington, B., *Conflict and Community in Corinth. A Socio-Rhetorical Commentary on 1 and 2 Corinthians* (Grand Rapids: 1995).

Wolff, C., *Der erste Brief des Paulus an die Korinther* (Berlin/Leipzig: 1996) (ThHK 7).

—*Der zweite Brief des Paulus an die Korinther* (Berlin: 1989) (ThHK 8).

Zeilinger, F., *Krieg und Friede in Korinth. Kommentar zum 2. Korintherbrief des Apostels Paulus. Teil 1. Der Kampfbrief, der Versöhnungsbrief, der Bettelbrief* (Vienna, etc.: 1992).

—*Krieg und Friede in Korinth. Kommentar zum 2. Korintherbrief des Apostels Paulus, Teil 2. Die Apologie* (Vienna, etc.: 1997).

3. *Reference works*

Anderson, R.D., *Glossary of Greek Rhetorical Terms Connected to Methods of Argumentation, Figures and Tropes from Anaximenes to Quintilian* (Leuven: 2000) (Contributions to Biblical Exegesis and Theology 24).

Bauer, W./K. and B. Aland, *Griechisch-deutsches Wörterbuch zu den Schriften des Neuen Testaments und der frühchristlichen Literatur* (Berlin/New York[6]: 1988) (abbreviated Bauer/Aland).

Berkowitz, L./K.A. Squitiere, *Thesaurus Linguae Graecae. Canon of Greek Authors and Works* (New York/Oxford[3]: 1990).

Biblia Patristica. Index des citations et allusions bibliques dans la littérature patristique (ed. Pantler, A.; Paris: 1975–).

Blass, F./A. Debrunner/F. Rehkopf, *Grammatik des neutestamentlichen Griechisch* (Göttingen[17]: 1990) (abbreviated: BDR).

Concordance to the Novum Testamentum Graece (ed. Institut für Neutestamentliche Textforschung; Berlin/New York[3]: 1989).

A Concordance to the Septuagint and the Other Greek Versions of the Old Testament (Including the Apocryphal Books) (Vol. 1 and 2; eds. Hatch, E./H.A. Redpath; Graz: 1954; Oxford: 1897).

Das Neue Testament auf Papyrus II. Die paulinischen Briefe, Teil 1. *Röm., 1. Kor., 2. Kor.* (arranged by Junack, K. *et al.*; Berlin/New York: 1989) (ANTF 12).

Dekkers, E., *Clavis Patrum Latinorum. Corpus Christianorum. Series latina* (Steenbrugis[3]: 1995) (abbreviated: CPL).

Frede, H.J., *Kirchenschriftsteller. Verzeichnis und Sigel* (Freiburg[4]: 1995) (VL 1/1).

Geerard, M., *Clavis Patrum Graecorum I–V. Corpus Christianorum* (Turnhout: 1983–1987) (abbreviated: CPG).

Haubeck, W./H. v. Siebenthal, *Neuer sprachlicher Schlüssel zum griechischen Neuen Testament. Römer – Offenbarung* (Gießen: 1994).

Hoffmann, E.G./H. v. Siebenthal, *Griechische Grammatik zum Neuen Testament* (Riehen[2]: 1990) (abbreviated: HS).

Lausberg, H., *Elemente der literarischen Rhetorik. Eine Einführung für Studierende der klassischen, romanischen, englischen und deutschen Philologie* (Ismaning[10]: 1990).

—*Handbuch der literarischen Rhetorik. Eine Grundlegung der Literaturwissenschaft* (Stuttgart[3]: 1990).

Lehnardt, A., *Bibliographie zu den Jüdischen Schriften aus hellenistisch-römischer Zeit. Supplementa* (eds. Lichtenberger, H./G.S. Oegema; Gütersloh: 1999) (JSHRZ VI/2).

Liddell, H.G./R. Scott/H.S. Jones, *A Greek-English Lexicon. With a Revised Supplement* (Oxford: 1996) (abbreviated: LS).

Louw, J.P./E.A. Nida *et al.*, *Greek-English Lexicon of the New Testament Based on Semantic Domains* (Vols. 1 and 2; New York[2]: 1989).

Mayser, E., *Grammatik der Griechischen Papyri aus der Ptolemäerzeit*. Band II *Satzlehre. Analytischer Teil Erste Hälfte* (Berlin/Leipzig: 1926).

Meyers Enzyklopädisches Lexikon (Vol. 14; 1975).

Rahlfs, A., *Verzeichnis der griechischen Handschriften des Alten Testament für das Septuaginta-Unternehmen* (Göttingen: 1914) (MSK 2).

Zundel, E., *Clavis Quintilianae. Quintilians 'Institutio oratoria'* (Darmstadt: 1989).

4. Studies

Aczel, R., 'Intertextualität und Intertextualitätstheorien': *Metzler Lexikon Literatur- und Kulturtheorie. Ansätze – Personen – Grundbegriffe* (ed. Nünning, A.; Stuttgart/ Weimar[2]: 2001), pp. 287–89.

Adewuya, J.A., *Holiness and Community in 2 Cor 6.14–7.1. Paul's View of Communal Holiness in the Corinthian Correspondence* (Frankfurt/Berlin: 2001) (Studies in Biblical Literature 40).

Aejmelaeus, L., *Die Rezeption der Paulusbriefe in der Miletrede (Apg 20:18–35)* (Helsinki: 1987).

—*Streit und Versöhnung. Das Problem der Zusammensetzung des 2. Korintherbriefes* (Helsinki: 1987) (SESJ 46).

Agnew, F.H., 'The Origin of the NT Apostle-Concept: A Review of Research': *JBL* 105/1 (1986), pp. 75–96.

Ahlzweig, C., 'Geschichte des Buches': *Schrift und Schriftlichkeit. Writing and Its Use. Ein interdisziplinäres Handbuch internationaler Forschung. An Interdisciplinary Handbook of International Research* (Vol. 1; eds. Günther, H./O. Ludwig; Berlin/New York: 1994), pp. 85–102.

Aland, B., 'Die Rezeption des neutestamentlichen Textes in den ersten Jahrhunderten': *The New Testament in Early Christianity. La réception des écrits néotestamentaires dans le christianisme primitif* (ed. Sevrin, J.-M.; Leuven: 1989) (BEThL 86), pp. 1–38.

—'Neutestamentliche Handschriften als Interpreten des Textes? P[75] und seine Vorlagen in Joh 10': *Jesu Rede von Gott und ihre Nachgeschichte im frühen Christentum* (Festschrift W. Marxsen; eds. Koch, D.-A. *et al.*; Gütersloh: 1989), pp. 379–97.

—'Textgeschichte/Textkritik der Bibel II. Neues Testament': *TRE* 33 (2002), pp. 155–68.

Aland, K., 'Die Entstehung des Corpus Paulinum': *Neutestamentliche Entwürfe* (Munich: 1979) (TB 63), pp. 302–50.

—'Methodische Bemerkungen zum Corpus Paulinum bei den Kirchenvätern des zweiten Jahrhunderts': *Kerygma und Logos. Beiträge zu den geistesgeschichtlichen Beziehungen zwischen Antike und Christentum* (Festschrift C. Andresen; ed. Ritter, A.M.; Göttingen: 1979), pp. 29–48.

—*Repertorium der griechischen christlichen Papyri. I. Biblische Papyri. Altes Testament, Neues Testament, Varia, Apokryphen* (Berlin/New York: 1976) (PTS 18).

Aland, K./B., *Der Text des Neuen Testaments. Einführung in die wissenschaftlichen Ausgaben sowie in Theorie und Praxis der modernen Textkritik* (Stuttgart[2]: 1989).

Albrecht, M. v., *Geschichte der römischen Literatur von Andronicus bis Boëthius. Mit Berücksichtigung ihrer Bedeutung für die Neuzeit* (Munich[2]: 1997).

Aleith, E., *Paulusverständnis in der Alten Kirche* (Berlin: 1937) (BZNW 18).

Alexander, L., 'The Living Voice. Scepticism towards the Written Word in Early Christian and in Graeco-Roman Texts': *The Bible in three Dimensions. Essays in celebration of forty years of Biblical Studies in the University of Sheffield* (Clines, D.J.A. *et al.* (eds.); Sheffield: 1990) (JSOT Suppl. 87), pp. 221–47.

Alexander, P.S., 'Epistolary Literature': *Jewish Writings of the Second Temple Period. Apocrypha, Pseudepigrapha, Qumran Sectarian Writings, Philo, Josephus* (ed. Stone, M. E.; Assen/Philadelphia: 1984) (CRI Sect. 2), pp. 579–96.

Alkier, S./A. Cornils, 'Bibliographie Mündlichkeit – Schriftlichkeit': *Logos und Buchstabe. Mündlichkeit und Schriftlichkeit im Judentum und Christentum der Antike* (eds. Sellin, G./F. Vouga; Tübingen/Basel: 1997) (TANZ 20), pp. 235–65.

Amador, J.D.H., *Academic Constraints in Rhetorical Criticism of the New Testament. An Introduction to a Rhetoric of Power* (Sheffield: 1999) (JSNT 174).

—'Revisiting 2 Corinthians: Rhetoric and the Case for Unity': *NTS* 46 (2000), pp. 92–111.

—'Socio-Rhetorical Criticism and the Parable of the Tenants': *New Testament Interpretation and Methods* (eds. Porter, S.E./C.A. Evans; Sheffield: 1997) (BiSe 45), pp. 221–49.

Anderson, C.P., 'Epistle to the Laodiceans': *ABD* 4 (1992), pp. 231–33.

Anderson, R.D., *Ancient Rhetorical Theory and Paul* (Leuven[2]: 1998) (Contributions to Biblical Exegesis and Theology 18).

Angstenberger, P., *Der reiche und der arme Christus. Die Rezeptionsgeschichte von 2 Kor 8,9 zwischen dem zweiten und dem sechsten Jahrhundert* (Bonn: 1997) (Hereditas 12).

Antos, G., 'Ansätze zur Erforschung der Textproduktion': *Text- und Gesprächslinguistik. Linguistics of Text and Conversation. Ein internationales Handbuch zeitgenössischer Forschung. An International Handbook of Contemporary Research* (Vol. 1; eds. Brinker, K. *et al.*; Berlin/New York: 2000), pp. 105–12.

Arzt, P., 'The "Epistolary Introductory Thanksgiving" in the Papyri and in Paul': *NovTest* 36 (1994), pp. 29–46.

Ascough, R.S., 'The Completion of a Religious Duty. The Background of 2 Cor 8,1–15': *NTS* 42 (1996), pp. 584–99.

Assmann, J., *Fünf Stufen auf dem Wege zum Kanon. Tradition und Schriftkultur im frühen Judentum und in seiner Umwelt. Mit einer Laudatio von H.-P. Müller* (Münster: 1999) (MTV 1).

—'Schrift, Tod und Identität. Das Grab als Vorschule der Literatur im alten Ägypten': Assmann, A. and J./C. Hardmeier (eds.), *Schrift und Gedächtnis. Archäologie der literarischen Kommunikation I* (Munich[3]: 1998), pp. 64–93.

Assmann, J./A., 'Schrift – Kognition – Evolution. Eric A. Havelock und die Technologie kultureller Kommunikation': E. A. Havelock, *Schriftlichkeit. Das griechische Alphabet als kulturelle Revolution* (Weinheim: 1990), pp. 1–35.

Attridge, H.W., 'Josephus and His Works': *Jewish Writings of the Second Temple Period. Apocrypha, Pseudepigrapha, Qumran Sectarian Writings, Philo, Josephus* (ed. Stone, M. E.; Assen/Philadelphia: 1984) (CRI. Sect. 2), pp. 185–232.

Aune, D.E., *Greco-Roman Literature and the New Testament* (Atlanta, Georgia: 1988).

Aune, D.E. (ed.), *The Westminster Dictionary of New Testament and Early Christian Literature and Rhetoric* (Louisville/London: 2003).

Austin, J.L., *How to Do Things with Words* (London, etc.: 1976).

Baird, W., 'Biblical Criticism. New Testament Criticism:' *ABD* 1 (1992), pp. 730–36.

—'Letters of Recommendation. A Study of II Cor 3,1–3': *JBL* 80 (1961), pp. 166–72.

Ballaira, G., *Esempi di scrittura latina dell'età romana*. Vol. 1: *dal III–II seculo a.C. al I seculo d.C.* (Alessandria: 1993) (Corso Universitari 4).

Bammel, E., 'Zum Testimonium Flavianum': *Josephus-Studien. Untersuchungen zu Josephus, dem antiken Judentum und dem Neuen Testament* (Festschrift O. Michel; eds. Betz, O. *et al.*; Göttingen: 1974), pp. 9–22.

Barbour, J.D., 'Biographie III. Autobiographie und Religion': *RGG* 1 (1998)[4], pp. 1603f.

Barnett, P.W., 'Second Corinthians: Why Paul Wrote It': *Ancient History in a Modern University*. Vol. 2 *Early Christianity, Late Antiquity and Beyond* (eds. Hillard, T.W./ R.A. Kearsley *et al.*; Michigan/Cambridge: 1998), pp. 138–52.

Barthes, R., 'Der Tod des Autors': *Texte zur Theorie der Autorschaft* (eds. Jannidis, F. *et al.*; Stuttgart: 2000) (RUB 18058), pp. 185–93.

Barton, J., *The Spirit and the Letter. Studies in the Biblical Canon* (London: 1997).

Baum, D.A., 'Literarische Echtheit als Kanonkriterium in der alten Kirche': *ZNW* 88 (1997), pp. 97–110.

—*Pseudepigraphie und literarische Fälschung im frühen Christentum. Mit ausgewählten Quellentexten samt deutscher Übersetzung* (Tübingen: 2001) (WUNT 2.138).

Baumgarten, J., 'ἀναστροφή, ἀναστρέφω': *EWNT* 1 (1980), pp. 222–24.

Bayer, O., *Gott als Autor. Zu einer poietologischen Theologie* (Tübingen: 1999).

Beardslee, W.A., 'What Is It About? Reference in New Testament Literary Criticism': *The New Literary Criticism and the New Testament* (eds. Malbon, E.S./E.V. McKnight; Sheffield: 1994) (JSNT.S 109), pp. 367–86.

De Beaugrande, R.-A./W.U. Dressler, *Einführung in die Textlinguistik* (Tübingen: 1981) (Konzepte der Sprach- und Literaturwissenschaft 28).

Becker, E.-M., 'ΕΙΣ ΘΕΟΣ und 1 Kor 8. Zur frühchristlichen Entwicklung und Funktion des Monotheismus': Brucker, R./W. Popkes (eds.), *Monotheismus im Neuen Testament* (Neukirchen-Vluyn: 2004) (BThSt).

—'Marcion und die Korintherbriefe nach Tertullian, Adversus Marcionem V': May, G./K. Greschat (eds.), *Marcion und seine kirchengeschichtliche Wirkung. Marcion and His Impact on Church History* (Berlin/New York: 2002) (TU 150), pp. 95–109.

—'Was ein Text sein kann. Zur Beschreibung eines Textinventars': *Was ist ein Text?* (eds. Wischmeyer, O./E.-M. Becker; Tübingen/Basel: 2001) (NET 1), pp. 159–69.

—'Was ist "Kohärenz"? Ein Beitrag zur Präzisierung eines exegetischen Leitkriteriums': *ZNW* 94 (2003), pp. 97–121.

Becker, J., 'Der Völkerapostel Paulus im Spiegel seiner neuesten Interpreten': *ThLZ* 122 (1997), pp. 977–90.

Beckheuer, B., *Paulus und Jerusalem. Kollekte und Mission im theologischen Denken des Heidenapostels* (Frankfurt, etc.: 1997) (EHS.T 611).

Beier, P., *Geteilte Briefe? Eine kritische Untersuchung der neueren Teilungshypothesen zu den paulinischen Briefen*, Dissertation (Halle: 1984).

Beilner, W., 'ἐπιστολή': *EWNT* 2 (1981), pp. 95–99.

Belleville, L.L., 'A Letter of Apologetic Self-Commendation. 2 Cor. 1:8–7:16': *NT* 31 (1989), pp. 142–63.

Berger, K., 'Apostelbrief und apostolische Rede. Zum Formular frühchristlicher Briefe': *ZNW* 65 (1974), pp. 190–231.

—'χαρά': *EWNT* 3 (1992)[2], pp. 1087–90.

—'Die impliziten Gegner. Zur Methode des Erschließens von "Gegnern" in neutestamentlichen Texten': *Kirche* (Festschrift G. Bornkamm; eds. Lührmann, D./G. Strecker; Tübingen: 1980), pp. 73–400.

—*Exegese des Neuen Testaments* (Heidelberg[2]: 1984) (UTB 658).

—*Formgeschichte des Neuen Testaments* (Heidelberg: 1984).

—'Hellenistische Gattungen im Neuen Testament': *ANRW* 25.2 (1984), pp. 1031–432.

Betz, H.D., 'Apostle': *ABD* 1 (1992), pp. 309–11.

—*Der Apostel Paulus und die sokratische Tradition. Eine exegetische Untersuchung zu seiner 'Apologie' 2 Korinther 10–13* (Tübingen: 1972) (BHTh 45).

—'Korintherbriefe': *EKL* 2 (1989), pp. 1448–53.

Beyer, K., *Semitische Syntax im Neuen Testament* Band I: *Satzlehre Teil 1* (Göttingen: 1962) (StUNT 1).

Bickmann, J., *Kommunikation gegen den Tod. Studien zur paulinischen Briefpragmatik am Beispiel des Ersten Thessalonicherbriefes* (Würzburg: 1998) (fzb 86).

Bieringer, R., '2 Korinther 6,14–7,1 im Kontext des 2. Korintherbriefes. Forschungsüberblick und Versuch eines eigenen Zugangs': Bieringer, R./J. Lambrecht (eds.), *Studies on 2 Corinthians* (Leuven: 1994) (BEThL 62), pp. 551–70.

—'Der 2. Korintherbrief als ursprüngliche Einheit. Ein Forschungsüberblick': Bieringer, R./J. Lambrecht (eds.), *Studies on 2 Corinthians* (Leuven: 1994) (BEThL 62), pp. 107–130.

—'Die Liebe des Paulus zur Gemeinde in Korinth. Eine Interpretation von 2 Korinther 6,11': *SNTU* 23 (1998), pp. 193–213.

—'Plädoyer für die Einheitlichkeit des 2. Korintherbriefes. Literarkritische und inhaltliche Argumente': Bieringer, R./J. Lambrecht (eds.), *Studies on 2 Corinthians* (Leuven: 1994) (BEThL 62), pp. 131–79.

—'Teilungshypothesen zum 2. Korintherbrief. Ein Forschungsüberblick': Bieringer, R./J. Lambrecht (eds.), *Studies on 2 Corinthians* (Leuven: 1994) (BEThL 62), pp. 67–105.

—'Zwischen Kontinuität und Diskontinuität. Die beiden Korintherbriefe in ihrer Beziehung zueinander nach der neueren Forschung': Bieringer, R. (ed.), *The Corinthian Correspondence* (Leuven: 1996) (BEThL 75), pp. 3–38.

Bieringer, R. (ed.), *The Corinthian Correspondence* (Leuven: 1996) (BEThL 75).

Bieringer, R./J. Lambrecht (eds.), *Studies on 2 Corinthians* (Leuven: 1994) (BEThL 62).

Bierwisch, M., 'Linguistik als kognitive Wissenschaft': *Zeitschrift für Germanistik* 8 (1987), pp. 645–67.

Bischoff, B., *Paläographie des römischen Altertums und des abendländischen Mittelalters* (Berlin[2]: 1986) (Grundlagen der Germanistik 24).

Blanck, H., *Das Buch in der Antike* (Munich: 1992).

Blänsdorf, J., 'Die Werwolf-Geschichte des Niceros bei Petron als Beispiel literarischer Fiktion mündlichen Erzählens': *Strukturen der Mündlichkeit in der römischen Literatur* (ed. Vogt-Spira, G.; Tübingen: 1990) (Script Oralia 19), pp. 193–217.

Bloomquist, L.G., 'A Possible Direction for Providing Programmatic Correlation of Textures in Socio-Rhetorical Analysis': Porter, S.E./D.L. Stamps (eds.), *Rhetorical Criticism and the Bible* (Sheffield: 2002) (JSNT.S 195), pp. 61–96.

Bornkamm, G., 'Der Philipperbrief als paulinische Briefsammlung': *Geschichte und Glaube. Zweiter Teil. Ges. Aufsätze* (Vol. 4; Munich: 1971) (BEvTh 53), pp. 195–205.

—'Die Vorgeschichte des sogenannten Zweiten Korintherbriefes': *Geschichte und Glaube. Zweiter Teil. Ges. Aufsätze* (Vol. 4; Munich: 1971) (BEvTh 53), pp. 162–94.

Bosenius, B., *Die Abwesenheit des Apostels als theologisches Programm. Der zweite Korintherbrief als Beispiel für die Brieflichkeit der paulinischen Theologie* (Tübingen/ Basel: 1994) (TANZ 11).

Bowman, A.K./J.D. Thomas, *Vindolanda. The Latin Writing-Tablets* (London: 1983) (Britannia Monograph Series No. 4).

Brandenburger, E., *Die Verborgenheit Gottes im Weltgeschehen. Das literarische und theologische Problem des 4. Esrabuches* (Zurich: 1981) (AthANT 68).

Brandt, A. v., *Werkzeug des Historikers. Eine Einführung in die historischen Hilfswissenschaften* (Stuttgart[16]: 2003).

Breuer, D., *Einführung in die pragmatische Texttheorie* (Munich: 1974) (UTB 106).

Breytenbach, C., *Nachfolge und Zukunftserwartung nach Markus. Eine methodenkritische Studie* (Zurich: 1984) (AthANT 71).

Brinker, K., *Linguistische Textanalyse. Eine Einführung in Grundbegriffe und Methoden* (Berlin: [4]1997/[5]2001) (Grundlagen der Germanistik 29).

—'Textstrukturanalyse': *Text- und Gesprächslinguistik. Linguistics of Text and Conversation. Ein internationales Handbuch zeitgenössischer Forschung. An International Handbook of Contemporary Research* (Vol. 1; eds. Brinker, K. *et al.*; Berlin/New York: 2000), pp. 164–75.

Brinkmann, H., 'Der Satz und die Rede': *Wirkendes Wort* 16 (1966), pp. 376–90, repr.: *Sprache als Teilhabe. Aufsätze zur Sprachwissenschaft* (ed. Scherner, M.; Düsseldorf: 1981) (Sprache der Gegenwart Vol. LV), pp. 89–110.

—'Die Konstituierung der Rede': *Wirkendes Wort* 15 (1965), pp. 157–62.

Broer, I., *Einleitung in das Neue Testament* Vol. 2; *Die Briefliteratur, die Offenbarung des Johannes und die Bildung des Kanons* (Würzburg: 2001) (NEB Ergbd. 2/II).

Brucker, R., *'Christushymnen' oder 'epideiktische Passagen'? Studien zum Stilwechsel im Neuen Testament und seiner Umwelt* (Göttingen: 1997) (FRLANT 176).

Brunkhorst, H., 'Kommunikation I. Philosophisch': *RGG*[4] 4 (2001), pp. 1509–10.

de Bruyn, G., *Das erzählte Ich. Über Wahrheit und Dichtung in der Autobiographie* (Frankfurt/Main: 1995).

Bühner, J.-A., 'ἀπόστολος': *EWNT* 1 (1980), pp. 342–51.

Bullmore, M.A., *St. Paul's Theology of Rhetorical Style. An Examination of 1 Corinthians 2.1–5 in the Light of First Century Graeco-Roman Rhetorical Culture* (San Francisco, etc.: 1995).

Bultmann, R., 'γινώσκω, γνῶσις κτλ.': *ThWNT* 1 (1933), pp. 688–719.

—'καυχάομαι κτλ.': *ThWNT* 3 (1938), pp. 646–54.

—*Der Stil der paulinischen Predigt und die kynisch-stoische Diatribe* (Göttingen: 1910).

—*Die Exegese des Theodor von Mopsuestia* (Posthum eds. Feld, H./K.H. Schelkle; Stuttgart, etc.: 1984).

—*Exegetische Probleme des zweiten Korintherbriefes: Exegetica. Aufsätze zur Erforschung des Neuen Testaments* (ed. Dinkler, E.; Tübingen: 1967), pp. 298–322.

—*Theologie des Neuen Testaments* (Tübingen[9]: 1984) (UTB 630).

Burfeind, C., 'Wen hörte Philippus? Leises Lesen und lautes Vorlesen in der Antike': *ZNW* 93 (2002), pp. 138–45.

Burke, T.J./J.K. Elliott (eds.), *Paul and the Corinthians. Essays in Honour of M. Thrall* (Leiden/Boston: 2003).

Bußmann, H., *Lexikon der Sprachwissenschaft* (Stuttgart[2]: 1990) (KTA 452).

Byrskog, S., 'Co-Senders, Co-Authors and Paul's Use of the First Person Plural': *ZNW* 87 (1996), pp. 230–50.

—*Story as History – History as Story. The Gospel Tradition in the Context of Ancient Oral History* (Tübingen: 2000) (WUNT 123).

Camassa, G., 'Buch': *DNP* 2 (1997), pp. 809–16.

Carrez, M., 'Le "Nous" en 2 Corinthiens': *NTS 26* (1980), pp. 474–86.

Cavallo, G., 'Codex I. Kulturgeschichte': *DNP* 3 (1997), pp. 50–53.

Cavallo, G./F. Hild, 'Buch': *DNP* 2 (1997), pp. 809–16.

Chadwick, H., *Antike Schriftauslegung. Pagane und christliche Allegorese. Activa und Passiva im antiken Umgang mit der Bibel* (Berlin/New York: 1998).

Cizek, A.N., *Imitatio et tractatio. Die literarisch-rhetorischen Grundlagen der Nachahmung in Antike und Mittelalter* (Tübingen: 1994) (Rhetorik-Forschungen 7).

Clabeaux, J.J., *A Lost Edition of the Letters of Paul. A Reassessment of the Text of the Pauline Corpus Attested by Marcion* (Washington: 1989) (CBQ.MS 21).

Classen, C.J., 'Paulus und die antike Rhetorik': *ZNW* 82 (1991), pp. 1–33.

—'Philologische Bemerkungen zur Sprache des Apostels Paulus: ΣΦΑΙΡΟΣ': WSt 107/108 (1994/95), pp. 321–35.

—'Rhetoric and Literary Criticism. Their Nature and their Functions in Antiquity': *Mn.* 48 (1995), pp. 513–35.

—*Rhetorical Criticism of the New Testament* (Tübingen: 2000) (WUNT 128).

—'Zur rhetorischen Analyse von Paulusbriefen': *ZNW* 86 (1995), pp. 120–21.

Collins, J.N., *Diakonia. Re-interpreting the Ancient Sources* (New York/Oxford: 1990).

Collins, R.F., 'Reflections on 1 Corinthians as a Hellenistic Letter': *The Corinthian Correspondence* (ed. Bieringer, R.; Leuven: 1996), pp. 39–61 (BEThL 125).

Conte, G.B./G.W. Most, 'Imitatio'*: OCD*[3] (1996), p. 749.

Conzelmann, H./A. Lindemann, *Arbeitsbuch zum Neuen Testament* (Tübingen[12]: 1998) (UTB 52).

Conzelmann, H., 'χαίρω κτλ.': *ThWNT* 9 (1973), pp. 350–62.

—'Die Schule des Paulus': *Theologia Crucis – Signum Crucis* (Festschrift E. Dinkler; eds. Andresen, C./G. Klein; Tübingen: 1979), pp. 85–96.

—*Grundriß der Theologie des Neuen Testaments* (Tübingen[4]: 1987) (UTB 1446).

—'Paulus und die Weisheit': *Theologie als Schriftauslegung* (Munich: 1974) (BevTh 65), pp. 177–90.

Cornelius, E.M., 'The Relevance of Ancient Rhetoric to Rhetorical Criticism': *Neotest.* 28 (1994), pp. 457–67.

Coseriu, E., *Textlinguistik* (Tübingen/Basel[3]: 1994) (UTB 1808).

Crafton, J.A., *The Agency of the Apostle. A Dramatic Analysis of Paul's Responses to Conflict in 2 Corinthians* (Sheffield: 1991) (JSNT.S 51).

Crake, J.E.A., 'Die Annalen des Pontifex Maximus': Pöschl, V. (ed.), *Römische Geschichtsschreibung* (Darmstadt: 1969) (WdF 90), pp. 256–71.

Dalfen, J., 'Autobiographie und Biographie': *GrB* 23 (2000), pp. 187–211.

Dassmann, E., *Der Stachel im Fleisch. Paulus in der frühchristlichen Literatur bis Irenäus* (Münster: 1979).

Dautzenberg, G., 'Der zweite Korintherbrief als Briefsammlung. Zur Frage der literarischen Einheitlichkeit und des theologischen Gefüges 2 Kor 1–8': *ANRW* 25.4 (1987), pp. 3045–66.

Davis, C.W., 'Oral Biblical Criticism. Raw Data in Phillipians': *Linguistics and the New Testament. Critical Junctures* (eds. Porter, S.E./D.A. Carson; Sheffield: 1999) (JSNT.S 168), pp. 96–124.

Debrunner, A., 'λέγω κτλ.': *ThWNT* 4 (1942), pp. 69–76.

Deissmann, A., *Licht vom Osten. Das Neue Testament und die neuentdeckten Texte der hellenistisch-römischen Welt* (Tübingen[4]: 1923).

Delling, G., 'τάσσω, τάγμα κτλ.': *ThWNT* 8 (1969), pp. 27–49.

—'Zum steigernden Gebrauch von Komposita mit ὑπέρ bei Paulus': *NT* 11 (1969), pp. 127–53.

Deuser, H., *Kleine Einführung in die Systematische Theologie* (Stuttgart: 1999).

Dewey, J., 'Textuality in an Oral Culture: A Survey of the Pauline Traditions': *Semeia* 65 (1994), pp. 37–65.

DiCicco, M.M., *Paul's Use of Ethos, Pathos, and Logos in 2 Corinthians 10–13* (Mellen: 1995) (Mellen Biblical Press Series Vol. 31).

Van Dijk, T.A., *Textwissenschaft. Eine interdisziplinäre Einführung* (Tübingen: 1980).

Di Lella, A.A./P.W. Skehan, *The Wisdom of Ben Sira* (New York: 1987) (AncB 39).

Dinkler, E., 'Bibelkritik II': *RGG* 1 (1957), pp. 1188–90.

Divjak, J., 'Epistulae': *Augustinus-Lexikon* (Vol. 2; ed. Mayer, C.; Basel: 2001), pp. 893–1057.

Dodd, B., *Paul's Paradigmatic 'I'. Personal Example as Literary Strategy* (Sheffield: 1999) (JSNT.S 177).

Döpp, S., 'Augustinus Confessiones': *Strukturen der Mündlichkeit in der römischen Literatur* (ed. Vogt-Spira, G.; Tübingen: 1990) (Script Oralia 19), pp. 271–84.

Dorandi, T., 'Tradierung der Texte im Altertum. Buchwesen': *Einleitung in die griechische Philologie* (ed. Nesselrath, H.-G.; Stuttgart/Leipzig: 1997), pp. 1–16.

Dorandi, T./S. Sohn, 'Abschrift': *DNP* 1 (1996), pp. 34–39.

Dörrie, H., 'Zur Methodik antiker Exegese': *ZNW* 65 (1974), pp. 121–38.

Doty, W.G., *Letters in Primitive Christianity* (Philadelphia: 1973).

Drescher, M., 'Textkonstitutive Verfahren und ihr Ort in der Handlungsstruktur des Textes': *Ebenen der Textstruktur. Sprachliche und kommunikative Prinzipien* (ed. Motsch, W.; Tübingen: 1996) (RGL 164), pp. 81–101.

Eagleton, T., *Einführung in die Literaturtheorie* (Stuttgart/Weimar[4]: 1997) (Sammlung Metzler 246).

Eckstein, H.-J., *Der Begriff Syneidesis bei Paulus. Eine neutestamentlich-exegetische Untersuchung zum 'Gewissensbegriff'* (Tübingen: 1983) (WUNT 2.10).

Eco, U., 'Porträt des Älteren als Jüngerer Plinius': Eco, U., *Über Spiegel und andere Phänomene. Aus dem Italienischen von B. Kroeber* (Munich[6]: 2001) (dtv 12924), pp. 223–43.

Egger, W., 'Faktoren der Textkonstitution in der Bergpredigt': *Laurentianum* 19 (1978), pp. 177–90.

—*Methodenlehre zum Neuen Testament. Einführung in linguistische und historisch-kritische Methoden* (Freiburg[5], etc.: 1999).

Ehler, C./U. Schaefer (eds.), *Verschriftung und Verschriftlichung. Aspekte des Medienwechsels in verschiedenen Kulturen und Epochen* (Tübingen: 1997) (Script Oralia 94).

Ehlich, K., 'Funktion und Struktur schriftlicher Kommunikation': *Schrift und Schriftlichkeit. Writing and Its Use. Ein interdisziplinäres Handbuch internationaler Forschung. An Interdisciplinary Handbook of International Research* (Vol. 1; eds. Günther, H./O. Ludwig; Berlin/New York: 1994), pp. 18–41.

Von Elderen, B., 'Early Christian Libraries': *The Bible as Book. The Manuscript Tradition* (eds. Sharpe, J.L. III/K. Van Kampen; Michigan: 1998), pp. 45–59.

Elliott, J.K., *A Bibliography of Greek New Testament Manuscripts* (Cambridge: 2000) (MSSNTS 109).

Ermert, K., *Briefsorten. Untersuchungen zu Theorie und Empirie der Textklassifikation* (Tübingen: 1979) (RGL 20).

Faintham, E., *Literarisches Leben im Antiken Rom. Sozialgeschichte der römischen Literatur von Cicero bis Apuleius* (Stuttgart/Weimar: 1998).

Fanning, B.M., *Verbal Aspect in New Testament Greek* (Oxford: 1990).

Feldmann, E., 'Psalmenauslegung der Alten Kirche: Augustinus': *Der Psalter in Judentum und Christentum* (ed. Zenger, E.; Freiburg, etc.: 1998), pp. 297–322.

Fenske, W., *Arbeitsbuch zur Exegese des Neuen Testaments. Ein Proseminar* (Gütersloh: 1999).

Fiedrowicz, M., *Prinzipien der Schriftauslegung in der Alten Kirche* (Bern, etc.: 1998) (TC X).

Figge, U.L., 'Einige Prinzipien der Textgrammatik': *Kohäsion, Kohärenz, Modalität in Texten romanischer Sprachen. Akten der Sektion 'Grundlagen für eine Textgrammatik der romanischen Sprachen' des XXIV. Deutschen Romanistentages Münster (25.-28.9.1995)* (ed. Gil, A.; Bonn: 1996).

Findeis, H.-J., *Versöhnung – Apostolat – Kirche. Eine exegetisch-theologische und rezeptionsgeschichtliche Studie zu den Versöhnungsaussagen des Neuen Testaments (2 Kor, Röm, Kol, Eph)* (Würzburg: 1983) (fzb).

Fitzgerald, J.T., 'Paul, the Ancient Epistolary Theorists, and 2 Corinthians 10–13. The Purpose and Literary Genre of a Pauline Letter': *Greeks, Romans, and Christians. Essays in Honor of A.J. Malherbe* (eds. Balch, D.L. *et al.*; Minneapolis: 1990), pp. 190–200.

Fitzmyer, J.A., 'Some Notes on Aramaic Epistolography': *JBL* 93 (1974), pp. 201–25.

Fögen, M.T., *Römische Rechtsgeschichten. Über Ursprung und Evolution eines sozialen Systems* (Göttingen: 2002) (Veröffentlichungen des Max-Planck-Instituts für Geschichte 172).

Forbes, C., 'Paul's Boasting and Hellenistic Rhetoric': *NTS* 32 (1986), pp. 1–30.

Foucault, M., 'Was ist ein Autor?': *Texte zur Theorie der Autorschaft* (eds. Jannidis, F. *et al.*; Stuttgart: 2000), pp. 198–229.

Frank, K.S., 'Sapienter et eloquenter dicere': *Strukturen der Mündlichkeit in der römischen Literatur* (ed. Vogt-Spira, G.; Tübingen: 1990) (Script Oralia 19), pp. 257–69.

Frankemölle, H., *Biblische Handlungsanweisungen. Beispiele pragmatischer Exegese* (Mainz: 1983).

Franz, M., 'Wahrheit, ästhetische': *Europäische Enzyklopädie zu Philosophie und Wissenschaften* 4 (1990), pp. 760–65.

Frede, D., 'Mündlichkeit und Schriftlichkeit: Von Platon zu Plotin': *Logos und Buchstabe. Mündlichkeit und Schriftlichkeit im Judentum und Christentum der Antike* (eds. Sellin, G./F. Vouga; Tübingen/Basel: 1997) (TANZ 20), pp. 33–54.

Frey, J., 'Der implizite Leser und die biblischen Texte. Der 'Akt des Lesens' nach Wolfgang Iser und seine hermeneutische Relevanz': *Theologische Beiträge* 23 (1992), pp. 266–90.

Fritz, G., *Bedeutungswandel im Deutschen. Neuere Methoden der diachronen Semantik* (Tübingen: 1974).

—*Kohärenz. Grundfragen der linguistischen Textanalyse* (Tübingen: 1982) (Tübinger Beiträge zur Linguistik 164).

Fuhrmann, M., *Das systematische Lehrbuch. Ein Beitrag zur Geschichte der Wissenschaften in der Antike* (Göttingen: 1960).

—*Die Dichtungstheorie der Antike. Aristoteles – Horaz – 'Longin'. Eine Einführung* (Darmstadt²: 1992).

—'Mündlichkeit und fiktive Mündlichkeit in den von Cicero veröffentlichten Reden': *Strukturen der Mündlichkeit in der römischen Literatur* (ed. Vogt-Spira, G.; Tübingen: 1990) (Script Oralia 19), pp. 53–62.

Funk, W.-P., 'Koptisch-gnostische Apokalypse des Paulus': Schneemelcher, W., *Neutestament-liche Apokryphen II* (Tübingen: 1989), pp. 628–33.

Fürst, A., 'Pseudepigraphie und Apostolizität im apokryphen Briefwechsel zwischen Seneca und Paulus': *JAC* 41 (1998), pp. 77–117.

Gadamer, H.-G., 'Text und Interpretation': *Gadamer Lesebuch* (ed. Grondin, J.; Tübingen: 1997) (UTB 1972), pp. 141–71.

Gall, D., *Zur Technik von Anspielung und Zitat in der römischen Dichtung. Vergil, Gallus und die Ciris* (Munich: 1999) (Zet. 100).

Gamble, H.Y., *Books and Readers in the Early Church. A History of Early Christian Texts* (New Haven/London: 1995).

—'The Redaction of the Pauline Letters and the Formation of the Pauline Corpus': *JBL* 94 (1975), pp. 403–18.

Gärtner, H.A./W.-L. Liebermann, 'Cento': *DNP* 2 (1997), pp. 1061–64.

Geerlings, W., 'Ambrosiaster': *Lexikon der antiken christlichen Literatur* (1998), pp. 12–13.

—'Ambrosiaster': *Lexikon der antiken christlichen Literatur* (2002)³, pp. 18–19.

Geffcken, J., 'Zur Entstehung und zum Wesen des griechischen wissenschaftlichen Kommentars': *Hermes* 67 (1932), pp. 397–412.

Georgi, D., *Die Gegner des Paulus im 2. Korintherbrief. Studien zur religiösen Propaganda in der Spätantike* (Neukirchen-Vluyn: 1964) (WMANT 11).

—*Die Geschichte der Kollekte des Paulus für Jerusalem* (Hamburg: 1965) (ThF 38).

Gese, M., *Das Vermächtnis des Apostels. Die Rezeption der paulinischen Theologie im Epheserbrief* (Tübingen: 1997) (WUNT 2.99).

Gil, A. (ed.), *Kohäsion, Kohärenz, Modalität in Texten romanischer Sprachen. Akten der Sektion 'Grundlagen für eine Textgrammatik der romanischen Sprachen' des XXIV. Deutschen Romanistentages Münster (25.-28.9.1995)* (Bonn: 1996).

Goody, J., 'Funktionen der Schrift in traditionalen Gesellschaften': *Entstehung und Folgen der Schriftkultur* (Frankfurt/M.³: 1997), pp. 25–61.

Goody, J./I. Watt, 'Konsequenzen der Literalität': *Entstehung und Folgen der Schriftkultur* (Frankfurt/M.³: 1997), pp. 63–122.

Görgemanns, H., 'Epistel A.-F.': *DNP* 3 (1997), pp. 1161–64.

—'Epistolographie': *DNP 3* (1997), pp. 1166–69.

Göttert, K.-H., *Einführung in die Rhetorik. Grundbegriffe – Geschichte – Rezeption* (Munich[2]: 1994) (UTB 1599).

Goulder, M., '2 Cor. 6:14–7:1 as an Integral Part of 2 Corinthians': *NT* 36 (1994), pp. 47–57.

Gräßer, E., 'Der Schatz in irdenen Gefäßen (2 Kor 4,7). Existentiale Interpretation im 2. Korintherbrief?': *ZThK* 97 (2000), pp. 300–16.

Grewendorf, G./F. Hamm/W. Sternefeld, *Sprachliches Wissen. Eine Einführung in moderne Theorien der grammatischen Beschreibung* (Frankfurt: 1987, [7]1994).

Grimm, R.R., 'Kompilation': *Metzler Literatur Lexikon. Begriffe und Definitionen* (eds. Schweikle, G. and I.; Stuttgart[2]: 1990), p. 248.

Gruber, M.M., *Herrlichkeit in Schwachheit. Eine Auslegung der Apologie des Zweiten Korintherbriefes 2 Kor 2,14–6,13* (Würzburg: 1998) (FzB 89).

Gülich, E./W. Raible, *Linguistische Textmodelle. Grundlagen und Möglichkeiten* (Munich: 1977) (UTB 130).

Gülzow, H., 'Caecilius Cyprianus': *Die Literatur des Umbruchs. Von der römischen zur christlichen Literatur 117 bis 284 n. Chr. Handbuch der lateinischen Literatur der Antike* (Vol. 4; ed. Sallmann, K.; Munich: 1997) (HAW VIII,4), pp. 532–75.

Haacker, K., *Paulus. Der Werdegang eines Apostels* (Stuttgart: 1997) (SBS 171).

Habermann, M., 'Ein Nürnberger Flugblatt von 1583. Ein Gebrauchstext aus sprachwissenschaftlicher Sicht': *Was ist ein Text?* (eds. Wischmeyer, O./E.-M. Becker; Tübingen/Basel: 2001) (NET 1), pp. 145–57.

Habermas, J., *Theorie des kommunikativen Handelns* Vol. 2: *Zur Kritik der funktionalistischen Vernunft* (Frankfurt/M.[3]: 1999) (stw 1175).

Hadot, P., *'Wege zur Weisheit' oder: Was lehrt uns die antike Philosophie?* (Frankfurt/M.: 1999).

Van Haelst, J., 'Les origines du codex': *Bibliologia* 9 (1989), pp. 13–35.

Hafemann, S.J., *Suffering and Ministry in the Spirit. Paul's Defense of His Ministry in II Corinthians 2:14–3:3* (Grand Rapids, Michigan: 1990) [cf.: Hafemann, S.J., *Suffering and the Spirit. An Exegetical Study of II Cor. 2:14–3:3 within the Context of the Corinthian Correspondence* (Tübingen: 1986) (WUNT 2.19)].

Hagedorn, D., 'Katenen': *RGG*[4] 4 (2001), pp. 875–76.

Hagemann, W., *Wort als Begegnung mit Christus. Die christozentrische Schriftauslegung des Kirchenvaters Hieronymus* (Trier: 1970) (TThSt 23).

Hahn, F., 'Apostel I. Neues Testament': *RGG*[4] 1 (1998), pp. 635–38.

Hahneman, G.M., *The Muratorian Fragment and the Development of the Canon* (Oxford: 1992).

Halford, B.K./H. Pilch (eds.), *Syntax gesprochener Sprachen* (Tübingen: 1990) (Script Oralia 14).

Halliday, M.A.K./R. Hason, *Cohesion in English* (New York: 1976).

Hanson, A.T., 'The Midrash in 2 Corinthians 3. A Reconsideration': *The Pauline Writings* (eds. Porter, S.E./C.A. Evans; Sheffield: 1995) (BiSe 34), pp. 98–123.

Haran, M., 'Codex, Pinax and Writing Slat': *SCI* 15 (1996), pp. 212–22.

Harnack, A.v., *Die Chronologie der altchristlichen Litteratur bis Eusebius. Erster Band. Die Chronologie der Litteratur bis Irenäus nebst einleitenden Untersuchungen* (Leipzig: 1897).

Hartenstein, J./U.-K. Plisch, 'Der Brief des Jakobus': *Nag Hammadi Deutsch*, pp. 11–26.

Hartman, L., 'A Sketch of the Argument of 2 Cor 10–13': *Text-Centered New Testament Studies. Text-Theoretical Essays on Early Jewish and Early Christian Literature* (ed. Hellholm, D.; Tübingen: 1997) (WUNT 102), pp. 235–52.

—'Doing Things With the Words of Colossians': *Text-Centered New Testament Studies. Text-Theoretical Essays on Early Jewish and Early Christian Literature* (ed. Hellholm, D.; Tübingen: 1997) (WUNT 102), pp. 195–209.

Hauck, F., 'περισσεύω κτλ.': *ThWNT* 6 (1959), pp. 58–63.

Havelock, E.A., *The Literate Revolution in Greece and Its Cultural Consequences* (Princeton, New Jersey: 1982).

Hawthorn, J., *Grundbegriffe moderner Literaturtheorie. Ein Handbuch* (Tübingen/Basel: 1994) (UTB 1756).

Heath, M., *Unity in Greek Poetics* (Oxford: 1989).

Heckel, T.K., *Vom Evangelium des Markus zum viergestaltigen Evangelium* (Tübingen: 1999) (WUNT 120).

Heckel, U., *Kraft in Schwachheit. Untersuchungen zu 2. Korinther 10–13* (Tübingen: 1993) (WUNT 2.56).

Heilmann, M., 'Brief, Briefliteratur': *DNP* 13 (1999), pp. 541–45.

Heinemann, W./D. Viehweger, *Textlinguistik. Eine Einführung* (Tübingen: 1991) (RGL 115).

Heither, T., *Translatio Religionis, Die Paulusdeutung des Origenes in seinem Kommentar zum Römerbrief* (Cologne/Vienna: 1990) (BoBKG 16).

Hengel, M., 'Die Septuaginta als "christliche Schriftensammlung", ihre Vorgeschichte und das Problem ihres Kanons': *Die Septuaginta zwischen Judentum und Christentum* (eds. Hengel, M./A.M. Schwemer; Tübingen: 1994) (WUNT 72), pp. 182–284.

Hengel, M./H. Löhr, (eds.), *Schriftauslegung im antiken Judentum und im Urchristentum* (Tübingen: 1994) (WUNT 73).

Heyworth, S.J./N.G. Wilson, 'Autorenvarianten': *DNP* 2 (1997), pp. 361–63.

Hezser, C., *Jewish Literacy in Roman Palestine* (Tübingen: 2001) (TSAJ 81).

Hofius, O., *Paulusstudien* (Tübingen: 1989) (WUNT 51).

Holtz, T., 'Das Selbstverständnis des Apostels Paulus': *Geschichte und Theologie des Urchristentums. Ges. Aufsätze* (eds. Reinmuth, E./C. Wolff; Tübingen: 1991), pp. 129–39.

—'Zum Selbstverständnis des Apostels Paulus': *ThLZ* 91 (1966), pp. 321–30.

Holtzmann, H.J., *Lehrbuch der historisch-kritischen Einleitung in das Neue Testament* (Freiburg³: 1892).

Honoré, T., 'Codex': *OCD*³ (1996), pp. 354–55.

Hoppe, R., 'Der erste Thessalonicherbrief und die antike Rhetorik. Eine Problemskizze': *BZ* 41 (1997), pp. 229–37.

Hornig, G., 'Textinterpretation und Hermeneutik des Einverständnisses. Kritische Anmerkungen zu den Theorien von Hans-Georg Gadamer und Peter Stuhlmacher': *Eschatologie und Schöpfung.* (Festschrift E. Gräßer; eds. Evang, M. *et al.*; Berlin/New York: 1997), pp. 123–37.

Hotze, G., *Paradoxien bei Paulus. Untersuchungen zu einer elementaren Denkform in seiner Theologie* (Münster: 1997) (NTA 33).

Hübner, H., 'λαλέω': *EWNT* 2 (1981), pp. 827–29.

—*Biblische Theologie des Neuen Testaments*, Vol. 1: *Prolegomena* (Göttingen: 1990); Vol. 2: *Die Theologie des Paulus* (Göttingen: 1993); Vol. 3: *Hebräerbrief, Evangelien und Offenbarung, Epilegomena* (Göttingen: 1995).

Hübner, R.M., 'Thesen zur Echtheit und Datierung der sieben Briefe des Ignatius von Antiochien': *ZAC* 1 (1997), pp. 44–72.

Hülsmann, H., 'Kohärenz': *HWPh* 4 (1976), pp. 877–78.

Hultgren, S.H., '2 Cor 6.14–7.1 and Rev 21.3–8. Evidence for the Ephesian Redaction of 2 Corinthians': *NTS* 49 (2003), pp. 39–56.

Hunger, H., 'Antikes und mittelalterliches Buch- und Schriftwesen': *Geschichte der Textüberlieferung* (Vol. 1; eds. Hunger, H. *et al.*; Zurich: 1961), pp. 25–147.

Hyldahl, N., 'Die Frage nach der literarischen Einheit des Zweiten Korintherbriefes': *ZNW* 64 (1973), pp. 289–306.

—*Die Paulinische Chronologie* (Leiden: 1986) (AThD XIX).

Iser, W., *Der Akt des Lesens. Theorie ästhetischer Wirkung* (Munich[4]: 1994) (UTB 636).

—*Der implizite Leser. Kommunikationsformen des Romans von Bunyan bis Beckett* (Munich[3]: 1994) (UTB 163).

Jacoff, R. (ed.), *The Poetry of Allusion. Virgil and Ovid in Dante's Comedia* (Stanford: 1991).

Jannidis, F. *et al.* (eds.), *Texte zur Theorie der Autorschaft* (Stuttgart: 2000).

Jaspers, K., *Philosophie 2: Existenzerhellung* (Berlin[3], etc.: 1956).

Jeanrond, W.G., *Text und Interpretation als Kategorien theologischen Denkens* (Tübingen: 1986) (HUTh 23).

Jegher-Bucher, V., *Der Galaterbrief auf dem Hintergrund antiker Epistolographie und Rhetorik. Ein anderes Paulusbild* (Zurich: 1991) (AThANT 78).

—'Der Pfahl im Fleisch. Überlegungen zu II Kor 12,7–10 im Zusammenhang von 12,1–13': *ThZ* 52 (1996), pp. 32–41.

Kabisch, R., *Das vierte Buch Esra auf seine Quellen untersucht* (Göttingen: 1889).

Kalverkämper, H., 'Vorläufer der Textlinguistik. Die Rhetorik': *Text- und Gesprächslinguistik. Linguistics of Text and Conversation. Ein internationales Handbuch zeitgenössischer Forschung. An International Handbook of Contemporary Research* (Vol. 1; eds. Brinker, K. *et al.*; Berlin/New York: 2000), pp. 1–17.

Kasch, W., 'συνίστημι, συνιστάνω': *ThWNT* VII (1964), pp. 895–96.

Käsemann, E., 'Die Legitimität des Apostels. Eine Untersuchung zu II Korinther 10–13': *ZNW* 41 (1942), pp. 33–71.

Kelber, W.H., 'Modalities of Communication, Cognition, and Physiology of Perception. Orality, Rhetoric, Scribality': *Semeia* 65 (1994), pp. 193–216.

—*The Oral and the Written Gospel. The Hermeneutics of Speaking and Writing in the Synoptic Tradition, Mark, Paul, and Q* (Philadelphia: 1983).

Kertelge, K., 'Das Apostelamt des Paulus, sein Ursprung und seine Bedeutung': *BZ* 14 (1970), pp. 161–81.

Keseling, G., 'Probleme der inhaltlichen und verbalen Planung beim Schreiben. Bericht über ein Forschungsprojekt': *Linguistische Studien* 173 (1988), pp. 65–86.

Keyes, C.W., 'The Greek Letter of Introduction': *AJP* 56 (1935), pp. 28–44.

Kienzler, K., 'Apologie': *Historisches Wörterbuch der Rhetorik* 1 (1992), pp. 809–21.

Kirchner, D., 'Brief des Jakobus': Schneemelcher, W. (ed.), *Neutestamentliche Apokryphen* I, (Tübingen: 1990), pp. 234–44.

Kirner, G.O., 'Apostolat und Patronage (II)': *ZAC* 7 (2003), pp. 27–72.

Klarer, M., *Einführung in die neuere Literaturwissenschaft* (Darmstadt: 1999).

Klauck, H.-J., 'Compilation of Letters in Cicero's Correspondence': *Early Christianity and Classical Culture. Comparative Studies in Honor of A.J. Malherbe* (eds. Fitzgerald, J.T. *et al.*; Leiden/Boston: 2003) (NT.S 110), pp. 131–55.

—*Die antike Briefliteratur und das Neue Testament* (Paderborn: 1998) (UTB 2022).

—'Mit Engelszungen? Vom Charisma der verständlichen Rede in 1 Kor 14': *ZThK* 97 (2000), pp. 276–99, repr.: Klauck, H.-J., *Religion und Gesellschaft im frühen Christentum. Neutestamentliche Studien* (Tübingen: 2003) (WUNT 152), pp. 145–67.

Kleberg, T., *Buchhandel und Verlagswesen in der Antike* (Darmstadt: 1969).

Klein, G., *Die zwölf Apostel. Ursprung und Gehalt einer Idee* (Göttingen: 1961) (FRLANT 77).

Kleinschmidt, E., *Autorschaft. Konzepte einer Theorie* (Tübingen/Basel: 1998).

Klijn, A.F.J., 'Die syrische Baruch-Apokalypse': *JSHRZ* V/2 (1976), pp. 103–84.

Koch, D.-A., *Die Schrift als Zeuge des Evangeliums. Untersuchungen zur Verwendung und zum Verständnis der Schrift bei Paulus* (Tübingen: 1986) (BHTh 69).

—'"…bezeugt durch das Gesetz und die Propheten". Zur Funktion der Schrift bei Paulus': *Sola scriptura. Das reformatorische Schriftprinzip in der säkularen Welt* (eds. Schmid, H.H./J. Mehlhausen; Gütersloh: 1988), pp. 169–79.

—'Schriftauslegung II. Neues Testament': *TRE* 30 (1999), pp. 457–71.

Koch, P., 'Briefkunst/Ars dictaminis': *DNP* 13 (1999), pp. 545–51.

Koch, P./W. Oesterreicher, 'Funktionale Aspekte der Schriftkultur. Functional Aspects of Literacy': *Schrift und Schriftlichkeit. Writing and Its Use. Ein interdisziplinäres Handbuch internationaler Forschung. An Interdisciplinary Handbook of International Research* (Vol. 1; eds. Günther, H./O. Ludwig; Berlin/New York: 1994) pp. 587–604.

—'Sprache der Nähe – Sprache der Distanz. Mündlichkeit und Schriftlichkeit im Spannungsfeld von Sprachtheorie und Sprachgeschichte': *Romanistisches Jahrbuch* 36 (1985/86), pp. 15–43.

König, H., 'Polykarp von Smyrna': *Lexikon der antiken christlichen Literatur* (1998), pp. 511–12.

Körtner, U.H.J., 'Literalität und Oralität im Christentum. Ein Beitrag zur biblischen Hermeneutik': *Text und Geschichte. Facetten theologischen Arbeitens aus dem Freundes- und Schülerkreis. D. Lührmann zum 60. Geburtstag* (eds. Maser, S./E. Schlarb; Marburg: 1999), pp. 76–88.

Kolb, A., *Transport und Nachrichtentransfer im Römischen Reich* (Berlin: 2000) (KLIO 2).

Kornemann, E., 'Die älteste Form der Pontifikalannalen': *Römische Geschichtsschreibung* (ed. Pöschl, V.; Darmstadt: 1969) (WdF 90), pp. 59–76.

Kositzke, B., 'Enthusiasmus': *Historisches Wörterbuch der Rhetorik* 2 (1994), pp. 1185–97.

Koskenniemi, H., *Studien zur Idee und Phraseologie des griechischen Briefes bis 400 n. Chr.* (Helsinki: 1956).

Krah, H., 'Kohärenz': *Metzler Lexikon Literatur- und Kulturtheorie. Ansätze – Personen – Grundbegriffe* (ed. Nünning, A.; Stuttgart/Weimar[2]: 2001), p. 316.

Krasser, H., 'Plinius Caecilius Secundus, C. (Der Jüngere)': *DNP* 9 (2000), pp. 1141–44.

Kraus, T.J., 'Der Artikel im Griechischen: Nutzen einer systematischen Beschäftigung anhand von ausgewählten Syntagmata (Hab 1,17; Jud 17; Joh 6,32)': *RB* 107 (2000), pp. 260–72.

Kröner, H.-O., 'Rhetorik in mündlicher Unterweisung bei Cicero und Plinius': *Strukturen der Mündlichkeit in der römischen Literatur* (ed. Vogt-Spira, G.; Tübingen: 1990) (Script Oralia 19), pp. 63–79.

Krug, J., *Die Kraft des Schwachen. Ein Beitrag zur paulinischen Apostolatstheologie* (Tübingen/Basel: 2001) (TANZ 37).

Kümmel, W.G., *Einleitung in das Neue Testament* (repr. of the 21st edition, Berlin: 1989).

Kullmann, W., 'Der Übergang von der Mündlichkeit zur Schriftlichkeit im frühgriechischen Epos': *Logos und Buchstabe. Mündlichkeit und Schriftlichkeit im Judentum und Christentum der Antike* (eds. Sellin, G./F. Vouga; Tübingen/Basel: 1997) (TANZ 20), pp. 55–75.

Kullmann, W./Reichel, M. (eds.), *Der Übergang von der Mündlichkeit zur Literatur bei den Griechen* (Tübingen: 1990) (Script Oralia 30).

Kuschnerus, B., *Die Gemeinde als Brief Christi. Die kommunikative Funktion der Metapher bei Paulus am Beispiel von 2 Kor 2–5* (Göttingen: 2002) (FRLANT 197).

Kytzler, B., 'Brief': *Lexikon der Alten Welt* (Zurich/Stuttgart: 1965), pp. 496–501.

Lambrecht, J., 'Paul's Second Letter to the Corinthians': *BiTod* 37 (1999), pp. 132–38.

Landmesser, C., *Wahrheit als Grundbegriff neutestamentlicher Wissenschaft* (Tübingen: 1999) (WUNT 113).

Lang, B., 'Homiletische Bibelkommentare der Kirchenväter': Assmann, J./B. Gladigow (eds.), *Text und Kommentar. Archäologie der literarischen Kommunikation IV* (Munich: 1995), pp. 199–218.

Lategan, B.C., 'Revisiting Text and Reality': *Neotest.* 28 (1994), Special edn., pp. 121–35.

Lefèvre, E., 'Die römische Literatur zwischen Mündlichkeit und Schriftlichkeit': *Strukturen der Mündlichkeit in der römischen Literatur* (ed. Vogt-Spira, G.; Tübingen: 1990) (Script Oralia 19), pp. 9–15.

Lehmann, J., *Bekennen – Erzählen – Berichten. Studien zu Theorie und Geschichte der Autobiographie* (Tübingen: 1988).

Lesky, A., *Geschichte der griechischen Literatur* (Bern/Munich³: 1971).

Levens, R.G.C./P.G. Fowler/D.P. Fowler, 'Letters, Latin': *OCD*³ (1996), pp. 847–48.

Levinson, S.C., *Pragmatik* (Tübingen²: 1994) (Konzepte der Sprach- und Literaturwissenschaft 39).

Lewandowski, T., *Linguistisches Wörterbuch 1–3* (Heidelberg/Wiesbaden⁶: 1994) (UTB 1518).

Lindemann, A., 'Antwort auf die "Thesen zur Echtheit und Datierung der sieben Briefe des Ignatius von Antiochien"': *ZAC* 1 (1997), pp. 185–94.

—'Apostolische Väter': *RGG*⁴ 1 (1998), pp. 652–53.

—'Der Apostel Paulus im 2. Jahrhundert': *The New Testament in Early Christianity. La réception des écrits néotestamentaires dans le christianisme primitif* (ed. Sevrin, J.-M.; Leuven: 1989) (BEThL 86), pp. 39–67. (repr.: Lindemann, A., *Paulus, Apostel und Lehrer der Kirche. Studien zu Paulus und zum frühen Paulusverständnis* (Tübingen: 1999), pp. 294–322.

—'Die Logienquelle Q. Fragen an eine gut begründete Hypothese': *The Sayings Source Q and the Historical Jesus* (ed. Lindemann, A.; Leuven: 2001) (BEThL 158), pp. 3–26.

—'Hilfe für die Armen. Zur ethischen Argumentation des Paulus in den Kollektenbriefen II Kor 8 und II Kor 9': *Exegese vor Ort* (Festschrift P. Welten; eds. Maier, C. *et al.*; Leipzig: 2001), pp. 199–216.

—'Introduction': *The Sayings Source Q and the Historical Jesus* (ed. Lindemann, A.; Leuven: 2001) (BEThL 158), pp. XIII–XXII.

—'Paulinische Theologie im Brief an Diognet': *Paulus, Apostel und Lehrer der Kirche. Studien zu Paulus und zum frühen Paulusverständnis* (Tübingen: 1999), pp. 280–93.

—*Paulus im ältesten Christentum. Das Bild des Apostels und die Rezeption der paulinischen Theologie in der frühchristlichen Literatur bis Marcion* (Tübingen: 1979) (BHTh 58).

—'Paulus in den Schriften der Apostolischen Väter:' *Paulus, Apostel und Lehrer der Kirche. Studien zu Paulus und zum frühen Paulusverständnis* (Tübingen: 1999), pp. 252–79.

Lindemann, A. (ed.), *The Sayings Source Q and the Historical Jesus* (Leuven: 2001) (BEThL 158).

Llewelyn, S.R./R.A. Kearsley, *New Documents Illustrating Early Christianity*, Vol. 7: *A Review of the Greek Inscriptions and Papyri published in 1982–83*, NDIEC (1993).

Löhr, W.A., 'Kanonsgeschichtliche Beobachtungen zum Verhältnis von mündlicher und schriftlicher Tradition im zweiten Jahrhundert': ZNW 85 (1994), pp. 234–58.

Looks, C., *Das Anvertraute bewahren. Die Rezeption der Pastoralbriefe im 2. Jahrhundert* (Munich: 1999).

Loubser, J.A., 'Orality and Literacy in the Pauline Epistles. Some New Hermeneutical Implications': *Neotest.* 29 (1995), pp. 61–74.

Ludwig, H., *Der Verfasser des Kolosserbriefes. Ein Schüler des Paulus*, Dissertation (Göttingen: 1974).

Ludwig, O., 'Geschichte des Schreibens': *Schrift und Schriftlichkeit. Writing and Its Use. Ein interdisziplinäres Handbuch internationaler Forschung. An Interdisciplinary Handbook of International Research* (Vol. 1; eds. Günther, H./O. Ludwig; Berlin/New York: 1994), pp. 48–65.

Lührmann, D., *Auslegung des Neuen Testaments* (Zurich: 1984).

Lyons, G., *Pauline Autobiography. Toward a New Understanding* (Atlanta, Georgia: 1985) (SBL 73).

Maartens, P.J., 'The Relevance of "Context" and "Interpretation" to the Semiotic Relations of Romans 5,1–11': *Neotest.* 29 (1995), pp. 75–108.

MacRae, G.W./W.R. Murdock/D.M. Parrott, 'The Apocalypse of Paul (V,2)': Robinson, J.M. (ed.); *The Nag Hammadi Library in English* (Leiden, etc.: 1996), pp. 256–59.

Maehler, H., 'Books, Greek and Roman': OCD^3 (1996), pp. 249–52.

Maier, J., *Zwischen den Testamenten. Geschichte und Religion in der Zeit des Zweiten Tempels* (Würzburg: 1990) (NEB Ergbd. 3).

Malina, B.J./J.H. Neyrey, *Portraits of Paul. An Archaeology of Ancient Personality* (Louisville: 1996).

Markschies, C., 'Origenes und die Kommentierung des paulinischen Römerbriefs – einige Bemerkungen zur Rezeption von antiken Kommentartechniken im Christentum des dritten Jahrhunderts und ihrer Vorgeschichte': *Commentaries-Kommentare* (ed. Most, G.W.; Göttingen: 1999) (Aporemata 4), pp. 66–94.

Marshall, P., *Enmity in Corinth. Social Conventions in Paul's Relations with the Corinthians* (Tübingen: 1987) (WUNT 2.23).

Mason, S., *Flavius Josephus und das Neue Testament* (Tübingen/Basel: 2000) (UTB 2130).

Mazal, O., *Geschichte der Buchkultur* Vol. 1: *Griechisch-römische Antike* (Graz: 1999).

McDonnell, M., 'Writing, Copying, and Autograph Manuscripts in Ancient Rome': *CQ* 46 (1996), pp. 469–91.

McKay, K.L., 'Observations on the Epistolary Aorist in 2 Corinthians': *NT* 37 (1995), pp. 154–58.

—'On the Perfect and Other Aspects in New Testament Greek': *NT* 23 (1981), pp. 289–329.

McKnight, E.V., 'Der hermeneutische Gewinn der neuen literarischen Zugänge in der neutestamentlichen Bibelinterpretation': *BZ* 41 (1997), pp. 161–73.

Mees, M., *Die Zitate aus dem Neuen Testament bei Clemens von Alexandrien* (Rome: 1970) (QVetChr 2).

Meiser, M./U. Kühneweg *et al.*, *Proseminar II. Neues Testament – Kirchengeschichte. Ein Arbeitsbuch* (Stuttgart, etc: 2000).

Merk, O., 'Literarkritik II': *TRE* 21 (1991), pp. 222–33.

—'Redaktionsgeschichte/Redaktionskritik II. Neues Testament': *TRE* 28 (1997), pp. 378–84.

Merklein, H., 'Die Einheitlichkeit des ersten Korintherbriefes': *Studien zu Jesus und Paulus* (Tübingen: 1987) (WUNT 43), pp. 345–75.

Mews, C.J., *The Lost Love Letters of Heloise and Abelard. Perceptions of Dialogue in Twelfth-Century France* (Hampshire: 2001).

Michel, O., 'οἶκος κτλ.': *ThWNT* 5 (1954), pp. 122–61.

—'Freude': *RAC* 8 (1972), pp. 348–418.

Millard, A.R., *Pergament und Papyrus, Tafeln und Ton. Lesen und Schreiben zur Zeit Jesu* (Gießen/Basel: 2000) (Biblische Archäologie und Zeitgeschichte 3).

Misch, G., *Geschichte der Autobiographie* Vol. 1: *Das Altertum. Zweite Hälfte* (Frankfurt/ M.⁴: 1974).

Mitchell, M.M., 'Concerning ΠΕΡΙ ΔΕ in 1 Corinthians': *NT* 31 (1989), pp. 229–56.

—'Korintherbriefe': *RGG*⁴ 4 (2001), pp. 1688–94.

—*Paul and the Rhetoric of Reconciliation. An Exegetical Investigation of the Language and Composition of 1 Corinthians* (Tübingen: 1991) (HUTh 28).

—'The Corinthian Correspondence and the Birth of Pauline Hermeneutics': Burke, T.J./J. K. Elliott (eds.); *Paul and the Corinthians. Essays in Honour of M. Thrall* (Leiden/Boston: 2003), pp. 17–53.

Momigliano, A., *The Development of Greek Biography* (Cambridge, Massachusetts/London²: 1993).

Montanari, F./M.-A. Söllner, 'Artemon': *DNP* 2 (1997), pp. 60–61.

Most, G.W., 'Hermeneutik': *DNP* 5 (1998), pp. 423–26.

Most, G.W. (ed.), *Editing Texts. Texte edieren* (Göttingen: 1998) (Aporemata 2).

Motsch, W. (ed.), *Ebenen der Textstruktur. Sprachliche und kommunikative Prinzipien* (Tübingen: 1996) (RGL 164).

Mratschek, S., *Der Briefwechsel des Paulinus von Nola. Kommunikation und soziale Kontakte zwischen christlichen Intellektuellen* (Münster: 1999).

Mühlenberg, E., 'Griechische Patristik. II. Bibelauslegung': *Theol Rund* 61 (1996), pp. 275–310.

—'Katenen': *TRE* 18 (1989), pp. 14–21.

—'Schriftauslegung III. Kirchengeschichtlich': *TRE* 30 (1999), pp. 472–88.

Müller, M., 'Der sogenannte "schriftstellerische Plural" – neu betrachtet. Zur Frage der Mitarbeiter als Mitverfasser der Paulusbriefe': *BZ* 42 (1998), pp. 181–201.

Müller, P., *Anfänge der Paulusschule. Dargestellt am zweiten Thessalonicherbrief und am Kolosserbrief* (Zurich: 1988) (AthANT 74).

Müller, U.B., *Prophetie und Predigt im Neuen Testament. Formgeschichtliche Untersuchungen zur urchristlichen Prophetie* (Gütersloh: 1975).

Müller, W.G., 'Brief': *Historisches Wörterbuch der Rhetorik* 2 (1994), pp. 60–76.

—'Der Brief als Spiegel der Seele. Zur Geschichte eines Topos der Epistolartheorie von der Antike bis zu Samuel Richardson': *Antike und Abendland* 26 (1980), pp. 138–57.

Mullins, T.Y., 'Disclosure. A Literary Form in the New Testament': *NT* 7 (1964/65), pp. 44–50.

Murphy-O'Connor, J., 'Co-Authorship in the Corinthian Correspondence': *RevBib* 100 (1993), pp. 562–79.

—*Paul the Letter-Writer. His World, His Options, His Skills* (Collegeville, Minnesota: 1995) (GNS 41).

Nagel, T., *Die Rezeption des Johannesevangeliums im 2. Jahrhundert. Studien zur vorirenäischen Aneignung und Auslegung des vierten Evangeliums in christlicher und christlich-gnostischer Literatur* (Leipzig: 2000) (Arbeiten zur Bibel und ihrer Geschichte 2).

Neuschäfer, B., 'Katene': *Lexikon der antiken christlichen Literatur* (1998), pp. 374–75.

—'Katene': *Lexikon der antiken christlichen Literatur* (2002)³, pp. 424–25.

—*Origenes als Philologe* (Basel: 1987) (SBA 18/1).

Nickel, R., *Lexikon der antiken Literatur* (Darmstadt: 1999).

Nickisch, R.M.G., *Brief* (Stuttgart: 1991) (Sammlung Metzler 260).

—'Brief': *Fischer Lexikon Literatur* (Vol. 1; ed. Ricklefs, U.; Frankfurt/M.: 1996), pp. 321–35.

Niggl, G. (ed.), *Die Autobiographie. Zu Form und Geschichte einer literarischen Gattung* (Darmstadt: 1989) (WdF 565).

Noke, K., 'Rezension M. Scherner, "Sprache als Text" ': *Zeitschrift für Germanistik* 8 (1987), pp. 113–15.

Noormann, R., *Irenäus als Paulusinterpret. Zur Rezeption und Wirkung der paulinischen und deuteropaulinischen Briefe im Werk des Irenäus von Lyon* (Tübingen: 1994) (WUNT 2.66).

Norden, E., *Die antike Kunstprosa* (Vols. 1 and 2; Darmstadt⁵: 1958).

Noret, J., 'Un fragment exégétique de Chrysostome trouvé dans une reliure': *AnBoll* 93 (1975), p. 182.

Oegema, G.S., *Apokalypsen. Supplementa*: eds. Lichtenberger, H./G.S. Oegema, *Einführung zu den Jüdischen Schriften aus hellenistisch-römischer Zeit* (Gütersloh: 2001) (JSHRZ VI/1,5).

Oeming, M./A.-R. Pregla, 'New Literary Criticism': *ThR* 66 (2001), pp. 1–23.

Olbricht, T.H., 'Exegesis in the Second Century': *Handbook to Exegesis of the New Testament*, (ed. Porter, S.E.; (Leiden: 1997) (NTTS 25), pp. 407–23.

De Oliveira, A., ' "Ihr seid ein Brief Christi" (2 Kor 3,3). Ein paulinischer Beitrag zur Ekklesiologie des Wortes Gottes': *Ekklesiologie des Neuen Testaments* (Festschrifte K. Kertelge; eds. Kampling, R./T. Söding; Freiburg, etc.: 1996), pp. 356–77.

Ollrogg, W.-H., *Paulus und seine Mitarbeiter. Untersuchungen zu Theorie und Praxis der paulinischen Mission* (Neukirchen-Vluyn: 1979) (WMANT 50).

Ong, W.J., *Oralität und Literalität. Die Technologisierung des Wortes* (Opladen: 1987).

Pardee, D., *Handbook of Ancient Hebrew Letters* (Chico: 1982) (SBibSt 15).

Pasco, A.H., *Allusion. A Literary Graft* (Toronto: 1994).

Pearson, B.W.R., 'New Testament Literary Criticism': *Handbook to Exegesis of the New Testament* (ed. Porter, S.E.; Leiden, etc.: 1997), pp. 241–66.

Pépin, J./K. Hoheisel, 'Hermeneutik': *RAC* 14 (1988), pp. 722–71.

Perrin, N., *What is Redaction Criticism?* (London: 1970).

Peter, H., *Der Brief in der römischen Litteratur. Litterargeschichtliche Untersuchungen und Zusammenfassungen* (Leipzig: 1901).

Pöhlmann, E., *Einführung in die Überlieferungsgeschichte und in die Textkritik der antiken Literatur* Vol. 1 *Altertum* (Darmstadt: 1994).

Porter, S.E., Καταλάσσω *in Ancient Greek Literature, with Reference to the Pauline Writings* (Cordoba: 1994) (Estudios de Filologia Neotestamentaria 5).

—'Linguistics and Rhetorical Criticism': *Linguistics and the New Testament. Critical Junctures* (eds. Porter, S.E./D. A. Carson; Sheffield: 1999) (JSNT.S 168), pp. 63–92.

—'Paul of Tarsus and His Letters': *Handbook of Classical Rhetoric in the Hellenistic Period 330 B.C.—A.D. 400* (ed. Porter, S.E.; Leiden, etc.: 1997), pp. 533–85.

—*Verbal Aspect in the Greek of the New Testament, with Reference to Tense and Mood* (New York: 1989) (Studies in Biblical Greek 1).

Porter, S.E./D.A. Carson (eds.), *Biblical Greek Language and Linguistics. Open Questions in Current Research* (Sheffield: 1993) (JSNT.S 80).

Porter, S.E./D.L. Stamps (eds.), *Rhetorical Criticism and the Bible* (Sheffield: 2002) (JSNT.S 195).

Pöttner, M., *Realität als Kommunikation. Ansätze zur Beschreibung der Grammatik des paulinischen Sprechens in 1 Kor 1,4–4,21 im Blick auf literarische Problematik und Situationsbezug des 1. Korintherbriefes* (Münster: 1995) (Theologie Vol. 2).

—'Sprachwissenschaft und neutestamentliche Exegese': *ThLZ* 123 (1998), pp. 929–42.

Powery, E.B., *Jesus Reads Scripture. The Function of Jesus' Use of Scripture in the Synoptic Gospels* (Leiden: 2003) (Biblical Interpretation Series 63).

Preisker, H., 'μισθός κτλ.': *ThWNT* 4 (1942), pp. 699–710, 718–36.

Preuschen, E., *Antilegomena. Die Reste der außerkanonischen Evangelien und urchristlichen Überlieferungen* (Giessen²: 1905).

Probst, H., *Paulus und der Brief. Die Rhetorik des antiken Briefes als Form der paulinischen Korintherkorrespondenz (1 Kor 8–10)* (Tübingen: 1991) (WUNT 2.45).

Prümm, K., *Diakonia pneumatos. Der zweite Korintherbrief als Zugang zur apostolischen Botschaft. Auslegung und Theologie*, Vol. 2: *Theologie des zweiten Korintherbriefes*, Teil 1: *Apostolat und christliche Wirklichkeit* (1960), Teil 2: *Das christliche Werk. Die apostolische Macht* (1962) (Rome, etc.: 1960–62).

Pürer, H., *Einführung in die Publizistikwissenschaft. Systematik, Fragestellungen, Theorieansätze, Forschungstechniken* (Munich⁵: 1993) (Uni-Papers 1).

Raible, W., 'Orality and Literacy': *Schrift und Schriftlichkeit. Writing and Its Use. Ein interdisziplinäres Handbuch internationaler Forschung. An Interdisciplinary Handbook of International Research* (Vol. 1; eds. Günther, H./O. Ludwig; Berlin/New York: 1994), pp. 1–17.

Rathke, H., *Ignatius von Antiochien und die Paulusbriefe* (Berlin: 1967) (TU 99).

Reck, R., *Kommunikation und Gemeindeaufbau. Eine Studie zu Entstehung, Leben und Wachstum paulinischer Gemeinden in den Kommunikationsstrukturen der Antike* (Stuttgart: 1991) (SBB 22).

Reed, J.T., 'The Epistle': *Handbook of Classical Rhetoric in the Hellenistic Period 330 B.C.–A.D. 400* (ed. Porter, S.E; Leiden, etc.: 1997), pp. 171–93.

Reicke, B., *Re-examining Paul's Letters. The History of the Pauline Correspondence* (eds. Moessner, D.P./I. Reicke; Harrisburg: 2001).

Reiff, A., *Interpretatio, imitatio, aemulatio. Begriff und Vorstellung literarischer Abhängigkeit bei den Römern*, Dissertation (Cologne: 1958).

Reiser, M., *Sprache und literarische Formen des Neuen Testaments. Eine Einführung* (Paderborn: 2001) (UTB 2197).

Rengstorf, K.H., 'ἀπόστολος': *ThWNT* 1 (1933), pp. 397–446.

—'ἐπιστέλλω, ἐπιστολή': *ThWNT* 7 (1964), pp. 593–95.

—'ψευδαπόστολος': *ThWNT* 1 (1933), pp. 446–47.

Reynolds, L.D./N.G. Wilson, *Scribes and Scholars. A Guide to the Transmission of Greek and Latin Literature* (Oxford[3]: 1991).

Richards, E.R., 'The Codex and the Early Collection of Paul's Letters': *BullBibRes* 8 (1998), pp. 151–66.

—*The Secretary in the Letters of Paul* (Tübingen: 1991) (WUNT 2.42).

Richter, W., *Exegese als Literaturwissenschaft. Entwurf einer alttestamentlichen Literaturtheorie und Methodologie* (Göttingen: 1971).

Rigaux, B., *Paulus und seine Briefe. Der Stand der Forschung* (Munich: 1964) (BiH II).

Rinser, L., 'Der Brief des Schriftstellers': *Deutsche Akademie für Dichtung und Sprache. Jahrbuch 1975* (Darmstadt: 1976), pp. 107–12.

Rissi, M., *Studien zum 2 Korintherbrief. Der alte Bund – Der Prediger – Der Tod* (Zurich: 1969) (AThANT 56).

Roberts, C.H., *Manuscript, Society and Belief in Early Christian Egypt* (London: 1979).

Roberts, C.H./T.C. Skeat, *The Birth of the Codex* (London[3]: 1989).

Roller, O., *Das Formular der paulinischen Briefe. Ein Beitrag zur Lehre vom antiken Briefe* (Stuttgart: 1933).

Roloff, J., 'Apostel/Apostolat/Apostolizität I': *TRE* 3 (1978), pp. 430–45.

Rösler, W., 'Schriftkultur und Fiktionalität. Zum Funktionswandel der griechischen Literatur von Homer bis Aristoteles': Assmann, A. and J./C. Hardmeier (eds.) *Schrift und Gedächtnis. Archäologie der literarischen Kommunikation I* (Munich[3]: 1998), pp. 109–22.

Russell, D.A./F.M., 'Literary Criticism in Antiquity': *OCD*[3] (1996), pp. 869–71.

Russell, D.A./M. Winterbottom, *Classical Literary Criticism* (Oxford: 1989).

Rusterholz, P., 'Verfahren der Textanalyse. 1. Formen "textimmanenter Analyse"': *Grundzüge der Literaturwissenschaft* (eds. Arnold, H.L./H. Detering; Munich: 1996), pp. 365–85.

Sallmann, K., 'P. Aelius Hadrianus' and 'L. Septimius Severus': *Die Literatur des Umbruchs. Von der römischen zur christlichen Literatur 117 bis 284 n. Chr. Handbuch der lateinischen Literatur der Antike* (Vol. 4; ed. Sallmann, K.; Munich: 1997) (HAW VIII,4), pp. 57–66.

Sand, A., *Kanon. Von den Anfängen bis zum Fragmentum Muratorianum* (Freiburg, etc.: 1974) (HDG 1, Faszikel 3a (1)).

—'Überlieferung und Sammlung der Paulusbriefe': Kertelge, K. (ed.), *Paulus in den neutestamentlichen Spätschriften. Zur Paulusrezeption im Neuen Testament* (Freiburg, etc.: 1981) (QD 89).

Schäublin, C., *Untersuchungen zu Methode und Herkunft der antiochenischen Exegese* (Cologne/Bonn: 1974).

Schelkle, K.H., 'Patrist. Exegese': *LThK* 3 (1959), pp. 1278–80.

Schenk, W., 'κατακρίνω κτλ.': *EWNT* 2 (1981), pp. 639–42.

—'Rezension C.W. Davis, "Oral Biblical Criticism"': *ThLZ* 125 (2000), pp. 400–401.

Schenke, H.-M., 'Das Ägypter Evangelium aus Nag-Hammadi-Codex III': *NTS* 16 (1969–70), pp. 196–208.

Schenke, H.-M./K.M. Fischer, 'Einleitung in die Schriften des Neuen Testaments. I': *Die Schriften des Paulus und die Schriften des Paulinismus* (Gütersloh: 1978).

Schenkeveld, D.M., 'Unity and Variety in Ancient Criticism. Some Observations on a Recent Study': *Mn* 45 (1992), pp. 1–8.

Schepers, H., 'Kohäsion, Kohärenz': *HWPh* 4 (1976), pp. 878–79.

Scherner, M., 'Der "Horizont" – ein sprachliches Kenntnissystem? Ein kritischer Vergleich zweier texttheoretischer Begriffsbildungen vor dem Hintergrund neuerer Entwicklungen in der Kognitionswissenschaft': *Die deutsche Sprache – Gestalt und Leistung* (ed. Harweg, R. *et al.*; Münster: 1991), pp. 229–51.

—'Nichttextualisierte Verstehensvoraussetzungen als sprachwissenschaftliches Problem': *Integrale Linguistik* (Festschrift H. Gripper; ed. Bülow, E./P. Schmitter; Amsterdam 1979), pp. 319–57.

—*Sprache als Text. Ansätze zu einer sprachwissenschaftlich begründeten Theorie des Textverstehens. Forschungsgeschichte – Problemstellung – Beschreibung* (Tübingen: 1984) (RGL 48).

—'Text': *HWPh* 10 (1998), pp. 1038–44.

Scherr, A., 'Kommunikation': Schäfers, B. (ed.), *Grundbegriffe der Soziologie* (Opladen:[6] 2000) (UTB 1416), pp. 176–82.

Schlaffer, H., *Die kurze Geschichte der deutschen Literatur* (Munich/Vienna: 2002).

—'Einleitung': *Entstehung und Folgen der Schriftkultur* (Frankfurt/M.[3]: 1997), pp. 7–23.

Schlieben-Lange, B., 'Geschichte der Reflexion über Schrift und Schriftlichkeit': *Schrift und Schriftlichkeit. Writing and Its Use. Ein interdisziplinäres Handbuch internationaler Forschung. An Interdisciplinary Handbook of International Research* (Vol. 1; eds.; Günther, H./O. Ludwig; Berlin/New York: 1994), pp. 102–21.

—'Schriftlichkeit und Mündlichkeit in der französischen Revolution': Assmann, A. and J./C. Hardmeier (eds.), *Schrift und Gedächtnis. Archäologie der literarischen Kommunikation I* (Munich[3]: 1998), pp. 194–211.

Schlier, H., 'ἀνέχω κτλ.': *ThWNT* 1 (1933), pp. 360f.

—'ἰδιώτης': *ThWNT* 3 (1938), pp. 215–17.

Schmid, U., *Marcion und sein Apostolos. Rekonstruktion und historische Einordnung der marcionitischen Paulusbriefausgabe* (Berlin/New York: 1995) (ANTT 25).

Schmidt, E.A., 'Lateinische Philologie als hermeneutische Textwissenschaft': *Die Wissenschaften vom Altertum am Ende des 2. Jahrtausends n. Chr.* (ed. Schwinge, E.-R.; Stuttgart/Leipzig: 1995), pp. 90–117.

Schmidt, P.L., 'Cicero und die Republikanische Kunstprosa': *Römische Literatur* (ed. Fuhrmann, M; Frankfurt/M.: 1974) (NHL 3), pp. 147–79.

—'Einleitung': *Die Literatur des Umbruchs. Von der römischen zur christlichen Literatur 117 bis 284 n. Chr. Handbuch der lateinischen Literatur der Antike* (Vol. 4; ed. Sallmann, K.; Munich: 1997) (HAW VIII,4), pp. 67–68.

—'Epistolographie': *KlP* 2 (1979), pp. 324–27.

Schmithals, W., *Die Briefe des Paulus in ihrer ursprünglichen Form* (Zurich: 1984).

—*Die Gnosis in Korinth. Eine Untersuchung zu den Korintherbriefen* (Göttingen[3]: 1969).

—'Die Korintherbriefe als Briefsammlung': *ZNW* 64 (1973), pp. 263–88.

—'Methodische Erwägungen zur Literarkritik der Paulusbriefe': *ZNW* 87 (1996), pp. 51–82.

—'Zur Abfassung und ältesten Sammlung der paulinischen Hauptbriefe': *Paulus und die Gnostiker. Untersuchungen zu den kleinen Paulusbriefen* (Hamburg: 1965) (ThF 35), pp. 175–200.

Schneemelcher, W., 'Paulus in der griechischen Kirche des zweiten Jahrhunderts': *ZKG* 75 (1964), pp. 1–20.

Schneider, J., 'Brief': *RAC* 2 (1954), pp. 564–85.

Schneider, N., *Die rhetorische Eigenart der paulinischen Antithese* (Tübingen: 1970) (HUTh 11).

Schnelle, U., 'Bibel III. Neues Testament': *RGG*[4] 1 (1998), pp. 1417–24.

—*Einführung in die neutestamentliche Exegese* (Göttingen[5]: 2000) (UTB 1253).

—*Einleitung in das Neue Testament* (Göttingen[3]: 1999) (UTB 1830).

—*Einleitung in das Neue Testament* (Göttingen[4]: 2002) (UTB 1830).

—*Neutestamentliche Anthropologie. Jesus – Paulus – Johannes* (Neukirchen-Vluyn: 1991) (BThSt 18).

Schnider, F./W. Stenger, *Studien zum neutestamentlichen Briefformular* (Leiden, etc.: 1987) (New Testament Tools and Studies 11).

Schnotz, W., 'Lesen als Textverarbeitung': *Schrift und Schriftlichkeit. Writing and Its Use. Ein interdisziplinäres Handbuch internationaler Forschung. An Interdisciplinary Handbook of International Research* (Vol. 2; eds. Günther, H./O. Ludwig; Berlin/ New York: 1996), pp. 972–82.

Schöllgen, G., 'Die Ignatianen als pseudepigraphisches Briefcorpus. Anmerkungen zu den Thesen von Reinhard M. Hübner': *ZAC* 2 (1998), pp. 16–25.

—'Diognetbrief': *RGG*[4] 2 (1999), p. 858.

Scholtissek, K., '"Ihr seid ein Brief Christi" (2 Kor 3,3). Zu einer ekklesiologischen Metapher bei Paulus': *BZ* 44 (2000), pp. 183–205.

Schreckenberg, H./G. Mayer/W.E. Gerber, 'Exegese': *RAC* 6 (1966), pp. 1174–229.

Schrenk, G., 'γράφω κτλ.': *ThWNT* 1 (1933), pp. 742–73.

Schröter, J., *Der versöhnte Versöhner. Paulus als unentbehrlicher Mittler im Heilsvorgang zwischen Gott und Gemeinde nach 2 Kor 2,14–7,4* (Tübingen/Basel: 1993) (TANZ 10).

—'Schriftauslegung und Hermeneutik in 2 Korinther 3. Ein Beitrag zur Frage der Schriftbenutzung des Paulus': *NT* 40 (1998), pp. 231–75.

Schunack, G., 'Neuere literaturkritische Interpretationsverfahren in der anglo-amerikanischen Exegese': *VF* 41 (1996), pp. 28–55.

Searle, J.R., 'A Taxonomy of Illocutionary Acts': *Expression and Meaning. Studies in the Theory of Speech Acts* (Cambridge, etc.: 1979), pp. 1–29.

—*Speech Acts. An Essay in the Philosophy of Language* (Cambridge: 1970).

Seeley, D., *Deconstructing the New Testament* (Leiden, etc.: 1994) (Biblical interpretation series 5).

Sellin, G., 'Das lebendige Wort und der tote Buchstabe. Aspekte von Mündlichkeit und Schriftlichkeit in christlicher und jüdischer Theologie': *Logos und Buchstabe. Mündlichkeit und Schriftlichkeit im Judentum und Christentum der Antike* (eds. Sellin, G./F. Vouga; Tübingen/Basel: 1997) (TANZ 20), pp. 11–31.

—*Der Streit um die Auferstehung der Toten. Eine religionsgeschichtliche und exegetische Untersuchung zu 1. Korinther 15* (Göttingen: 1986) (FRLANT 138).

—'Hauptprobleme des Ersten Korintherbriefes': *ANRW* II.25.4 (1987), pp. 2940–3044.

Sellin, G./F. Vouga, *Logos und Buchstabe. Mündlichkeit und Schriftlichkeit im Judentum und Christentum der Antike* (Tübingen/Basel: 1997) (TANZ 20).

Sharpe, J.L., 'The Dakleh Tablets and Some Codicological Considerations': *Bibliologia* 12 (1992), pp. 127–48.

Sherwin-White, A.N., *The Letters of Pliny. A Historical and Social Commentary* (Oxford: 1966).

Sieben, H.J., *Exegesis Patrum. Saggio bibliografico sull' esegesi biblica dei Padri della Chiesa* (Rome: 1983).

—*Kirchenväterhomilien zum NT* (Den Haag: 1991), pp. 185–201.

Siebenborn, E., *Die Lehre von der Sprachrichtigkeit und ihren Kriterien. Studien zur antiken normativen Grammatik* (Amsterdam: 1976) (SAPh 5).

Siegert, F., *Argumentation bei Paulus gezeigt an Röm 9–11* (Tübingen: 1985) (WUNT 34).

Simon, J., *Sprachphilosophie* (Munich: 1981) (HPh).

Simonetti, M. (trans. J. A. Hughes), *Biblical Interpretation in the Early Church. An Historical Introduction to Patristic Exegesis* (Edinburgh: 1994).

Sirat, C., 'Le livre hébreu dans les premiers siècles de notre ère. Le témoignage des textes': *Bibliologia* 9 (1989), pp. 115–24.

—'Les tablettes à écrire dans le monde juif': *Bibliologia* 12 (1992), pp. 53–59.

Skeat, T.C., 'The Origin of the Christian Codex': *ZPE* 102 (1994), pp. 263–68.

—'Was papyrus regarded as "cheap" or "expensive" in the ancient world?': *Aeg.* 75 1–2 (1995), pp. 75–93.

Sloan, R.B., '2 Corinthians 2:14–4:6 and "New Covenant Hermeneutics" – A Response to Richard Hays': *Bulletin of Biblical Research* 5 (1995), pp. 129–54.

Söding, T., *Die Trias Glaube, Hoffnung, Liebe bei Paulus. Eine exegetische Studie* (Stuttgart: 1992) (SBS 150).

—*Wege der Schriftauslegung. Methodenbuch zum Neuen Testament* (Freiburg, etc.: 1998).

Speyer, W., 'Baruch. Christlich': *JbAC* 17 (1974), pp. 185–90.

—*Die literarische Fälschung im heidnischen und im christlichen Altertum. Ein Versuch ihrer Deutung* (Munich: 1971) (HAW I.2).

Stagg, F., 'The Abused Aorist': *JBL* 91 (1972), pp. 222–31.

Stamps, D.L., 'Rhetorical and Narratological Criticism': *Handbook to Exegesis of the New Testament* (ed. Porter, S.E.; Leiden, etc.: 1997), pp. 219–39.

—'The Theological Rhetoric of the Pauline Epistles. Prolegomenon': *The Rhetorical Interpretation of Scripture. Essays from the 1996 Malibu Conference* (eds. Porter, S.E./D.L. Stamps; Sheffield: 1999) (JSNT.S 180), pp. 249–59.

Standhartinger, A., *Studien zur Entstehungsgeschichte und Intention des Kolosserbriefs* (Leiden: 1999) (NT.S 94).

Stanford, W.B., *The Sound of Greek. Studies in the Greek Theory and Practice of Euphony* (Berkeley/Los Angeles: 1967).

Steinmann, M., 'Römisches Schriftwesen': *Einleitung in die lateinische Philologie* (ed. Graf, F.; Stuttgart/Leipzig: 1997), pp. 74–91.

Stewart-Sykes, A., 'Ancient Editors and Copyists and Modern Partition Theories. The Case of the Corinthian Correspondence': *JSNT* 61 (1996), pp. 53–64.

Stillers, R., 'Adaptation': *DNP* 13 (1999), pp. 7–16.

Stirewalt, M.L., *Studies in Ancient Greek Epistolography* (Atlanta: 1993) (SBL 27).

Stocker, P., *Theorie der intertextuellen Lektüre. Modelle und Fallstudien* (Paderborn, etc.: 1998).

Stowers, S.K., *Letter Writing in Greco-Roman Antiquity* (Philadelphia: 1986) (LEC 5).

—'Peri men gar and the Integrity of 2 Cor. 8 and 9': *NT* 32 (1990), pp. 340–48.

Strauss, G., *Schriftgebrauch, Schriftauslegung und Schriftbeweis bei Augustin* (Tübingen: 1959) (BGBH 1).

Strecker, G., 'Die Legitimität des paulinischen Apostolates nach 2 Korinther 10–13': *NTS* 38 (1992), pp. 566–86.

—*Literaturgeschichte des Neuen Testaments* (Göttingen: 1992) (UTB 1682).

Stroumsa, G.G., 'Early Christianity – A Religion of the Book?': Finkelberg, M./G.G. Stroumsa, *Homer, the Bible, and Beyond. Literary and Religious Canons in the Ancient*

World (Leiden/Boston: 2003) (Jerusalem Studies in Religion and Culture 2), pp. 153–73.

Stuhlhofer, F., *Der Gebrauch der Bibel von Jesus bis Euseb. Eine statistische Untersuchung zur Kanonsgeschichte* (Wuppertal: 1988).

Suhl, A., *Paulus und seine Briefe. Ein Beitrag zur paulinischen Chronologie* (Gütersloh: 1975).

Sumney, J.L., *Identifying Paul's Opponents. The Question of Method in 2 Corinthians* (Sheffield: 1990) (JSNT.S 40).

Sundermann, H.-G., *Der schwache Apostel und die Kraft der Rede. Eine rhetorische Analyse von 2 Kor 10–13* (Frankfurt: 1996) (EHS.T 575).

Sykutris, J., 'Epistolographie': *RE.S* 5 (1931), pp. 185–220.

Taatz, I., *Frühjüdische Briefe. Die paulinischen Briefe im Rahmen der offiziellen religiösen Briefe des Frühjudentums* (Freiburg/Göttingen: 1991) (NTOA 16).

Taylor, N.H., 'The Composition and Chronology of Second Corinthians': *JSNT* 44 (1991), pp. 67–87.

Terry, R.B., *A Discourse Analysis of First Corinthians* (Dallas: 1995) (Summer Institute of Linguistics and the University of Texas at Arlington Publications in Linguistics, Publication 120).

Theißen, G., 'Legitimation und Lebensunterhalt. Ein Beitrag zur Soziologie urchristlicher Missionare': *NTS* 21 (1975), pp. 192–221.

Thomas, J.D., 'The Latin Writing-Tablets from Vindolanda in North Britain': *Bibliologia* 12 (1992), pp. 203–209.

Thomas, R., *Literacy and Orality in Ancient Greece* (Cambridge: 1992).

Thorley, J., 'Aktionsart in New Testament Greek. Infinitive and Imperative': *NT* 31 (1989), pp. 290–315.

Thraede, K., *Einheit, Gegenwart, Gespräch. Zur Christianisierung antiker Brieftopoi*, Dissertation (Bonn: 1967).

—*Grundzüge griechisch-römischer Brieftopik* (Munich: 1970) (Zet. 48).

Torrance, T.F., *Divine Meaning. Studies in Patristic Hermeneutics* (Edinburgh: 1995).

Trapp, M.B., 'Letters, Greek': *OCD*[3] (1996), pp. 846–47.

Trobisch, D., *Die Endredaktion des Neuen Testaments. Eine Untersuchung zur Entstehung der christlichen Bibel* (Göttingen: 1996) (NTOA 31).

—*Die Entstehung der Paulusbriefsammlung. Studien zu den Anfängen christlicher Publizistik* (Göttingen: 1989) (NTOA 10).

—*Die Paulusbriefe und die Anfänge der christlichen Publizistik* (Gütersloh: 1994).

Turner, E.G., *Greek Manuscripts of the Ancient World* (Princeton: 1971).

Vallance, J.T., 'Galen, Proclus and the Non-submissive Commentary': *Commentaries-Kommentare* (ed. Most, G.W.; Göttingen: 1999) (Aporemata 4), pp. 223–44.

Vater, H., *Einführung in die Textlinguistik. Struktur, Thema und Referenz in Texten* (Munich[2]: 1994) (UTB 1660).

Verhoef, E., 'Numerus, Sekretär und Authentizität der paulinischen Briefe': *Protokolle zur Bibel* 4 (1995), pp. 48–58.

—'The Senders of the Letters to the Corinthians and the Use of "I" and "We"': *The Corinthian Correspondence* (ed. Bieringer, R.; Leuven: 1996) (BEThL 125), pp. 417–25.

Vielhauer, P., *Geschichte der urchristlichen Literatur. Einleitung in das Neue Testament, die Apokryphen und die Apostolischen Väter* (Berlin/New York: 1975).

Voelz, J.W., 'Present and Aorist Verbal Aspect. A New Proposal': *Neotest.* 27.1 (1993), pp. 153–64.

Vogt, H.J., 'Bemerkungen zur Echtheit der Ignatiusbriefe': *ZAC* 3 (1999), pp. 50–63.

Vogt-Spira, G. (ed.), *Strukturen der Mündlichkeit in der römischen Literatur* (Tübingen: 1990) (Script Oralia 19).

Volz, P., *Jüdische Eschatologie von Daniel bis Akiba* (Tübingen/Leipzig: 1903).

Vössing, K., 'Archiv': *DNP* 1 (1996), pp. 1021–25.

—'Bibliothek II. Bibliothekswesen B. Griechenland, Rom, Christliche Bibliotheken': *DNP* 2 (1997), pp. 640–47.

Vouga, F., 'Apostolische Briefe als "scriptura". Die Rezeption des Paulus in den katholischen Briefen': *Sola scriptura. Das reformatorische Schriftprinzip in der säkularen Welt* (eds. Schmid, H.H./J. Mehlhausen; Gütersloh: 1991), pp. 194–211.

—'Der Brief als Form der apostolischen Autorität': Berger, K. *et al.* (eds.), *Studien und Texte zur Formgeschichte* (Tübingen: 1992) (TANZ 7), pp. 7–58.

—'Mündliche Tradition, soziale Kontrolle und Literatur als theologischer Protest. Die Wahrheit des Evangeliums nach Paulus und Markus': *Logos und Buchstabe. Mündlichkeit und Schriftlichkeit im Judentum und Christentum in der Antike* (eds. Sellin, G./F. Vouga; Tübingen: 1997) (TANZ 20), pp. 195–209.

Walter, N., 'Hellenistische Eschatologie bei Paulus': *ThQ* 176 (1996), pp. 53–64.

Watson, D.F., 'The Contributions and Limitations of Greco-Roman Rhetorical Theory for Constructing the Rhetorical and Historical Situations of a Pauline Epistle': *The Rhetorical Interpretation of Scripture. Essays from the 1996 Malibu Conference* (eds. Porter, S.E./D.L. Stamps; Sheffield: 1999) (JSNT.S 180), pp. 125–51.

Watzlawick, P./J.H. Beavin/D.D. Jackson, *Menschliche Kommunikation. Formen, Störungen, Paradoxien* (Bern[10], etc.: 2000).

Webb, W.J., *Returning Home. New Covenant and Second Exodus as the Context for 2 Corinthians 6.14–7.1* (Sheffield: 1993) (JSNT.S 85).

Wehrli, F., 'Literaturkritik': *LAW* (1965), pp. 1751–52.

Weimar, K., *Enzyklopädie der Literaturwissenschaft* (Tübingen/Basel[2]: 1993) (UTB 1034).

Weiß, J., *Das Urchristentum. Nach dem Tode des Verfassers* (ed. Knopf, R.; Göttingen: 1917).

Weiß, K., 'στόμα': *ThWNT* 7 (1964), pp. 692–701.

Welborn, L.L., 'Like Broken Pieces of a Ring. 2 Cor 1,1–2,13; 7,5–16 and Ancient Theories of Literary Unity': *NTS* 42 (1996), pp. 559–83.

—'The Dangerous Double Affirmation. Character and Truth in 2 Cor 1, 17': *ZNW* 86 (1995), pp. 34–52.

—'The Identification of 2 Corinthians 10–13 with the "Letter of Tears" ': *NT* 37 (1995), pp. 138–53.

Wenger, L., *Die Quellen des römischen Rechts* (Vienna: 1953).

Wengst, K., 'Diognetbrief': *Lexikon der antiken christlichen Literatur* (2002)[3], pp. 200–201.

Wentzel, G., 'Artemon': *RE* 2 (1896), pp. 1446–47.

Werner, J., *Der Paulinismus des Irenäus. Untersuchungen über das Verhältnis des Irenaeus zur paulinischen Briefsammlung und Theologie* (Marburg: 1889) (TU 6,2).

White, J.L., *Light from Ancient Letters* (Philadelphia: 1986).

—'New Testament Epistolary Literature in the Framework of Ancient Epistolography': *ANRW* II.25.2 (1984), pp. 1730–56.

—*The Form and Function of the Body of the Greek Letter. A Study of the Letter-Body in the Non-Literary Papyri and in Paul the Apostle* (Missoula, Montana: 1972) (SBL.DS 2).

Wickert, U., 'Die Persönlichkeit des Paulus in den Paulus-Kommentaren Theodors von Mopsuestia': *ZNW* 53 (1962), pp. 51–66.

—'Einheit und Eintracht der Kirche im Präskript des ersten Korintherbriefes': *ZNW* 50 (1959), pp. 73–82.

Wilk, F., *Die Bedeutung des Jesajabuches für Paulus* (Göttingen: 1998) (FRLANT 179).

Wilpert, G.v., *Sachwörterbuch der Literatur* (Stuttgart⁷: 1989) (KTA 231).

Wilson, N.G., 'Griechische Philologie im Altertum': *Einleitung in die griechische Philologie* (ed. Nesselrath, H.-G.; Stuttgart/Leipzig: 1997), pp. 87–103.

Wilss, W., *Anspielungen. Zur Manifestation von Kreativität und Routine in der Sprachverwendung* (Tübingen: 1989).

Wimmer, R., 'Kohärent/Kohärenz': *EPhW* 2 (1984), pp. 417–18.

Wirth, U. (ed.), *Performanz. Zwischen Sprachphilosophie und Kulturwissenschaften* (Frankfurt/M.: 2002).

Wischmeyer, O., *Der höchste Weg. Das 13. Kapitel des 1. Korintherbriefes* (Gütersloh: 1981) (StNT 13).

—*Die Kultur des Buches Jesus Sirach* (Berlin/New York: 1995) (BZNW 77).

—'Staat und Christen nach Röm 13,1–7. Ein hermeneutischer Zugang': *Kirche und Volk Gottes* (Festschrift J. Roloff; eds. Karrer, M. *et al.*; Neukirchen-Vluyn: 2000), pp. 149–62.

—'Thesen zum Verstehen des Neuen Testaments. Die Bedeutung der neutestamentlichen Hermeneutik für die Theologie': *Daß Gott eine große Barmherzigkeit habe. Konkrete Theologie in der Verschränkung von Glauben und Leben* (Festschrift G. Schneider-Flume; eds. Hiller, D./C. Kress; Leipzig: 2001), pp. 57–76.

—'2. Korinther 12,1–10. Ein autobiographisch-theologischer Text des Paulus': *Was ist ein Text?* (eds. Wischmeyer, O./E.-M. Becker; Tübingen/Basel: 2001) (NET 1), pp. 29–41.

Wischmeyer, W., 'Cyprian von Karthago': *RGG*⁴ 2 (1999), pp. 508–509.

—'Hoc usque in pridie muneris egi. Autobiographien als kirchengeschichtliche Quellen': *Wiener Jahrbuch für Theologie* 2 (1998), pp. 143–56.

Wisse, J., 'Affektenlehre. I. Antike': *Historisches Wörterbuch der Rhetorik* 1 (1992), pp. 218–24.

Wolf, P., 'Referenz': *Metzler Lexikon Literatur- und Kulturtheorie. Ansätze – Personen – Grundbegriffe* (ed. Nünning, A.; Stuttgart/Weimar²: 2001), pp. 542–43.

Wolf, W., 'Metafiktion': *Metzler Lexikon Literatur- und Kulturtheorie. Ansätze – Personen – Grundbegriffe* (ed. Nünning, A.; Stuttgart/Weimar²: 2001), pp. 429–30.

—'Metatext und Metatextualität': *Metzler Lexikon Literatur- und Kulturtheorie. Ansätze – Personen – Grundbegriffe* (ed. Nünning, A.; Stuttgart/Weimar²: 2001), pp. 435–36.

Wolff, H.W., *Anthropologie des Alten Testaments* (Munich: 1973).

Wolter, M., *Die Pastoralbriefe als Paulustradition* (Göttingen: 1988) (FRLANT 146).

Wrobel, A., 'Phasen und Verfahren der Produktion schriftlicher Texte': *Text- und Gesprächslinguistik. Linguistics of Text and Conversation. Ein internationales Handbuch zeitgenössischer Forschung. An International Handbook of Contemporary Research* (Vol. 1; eds. Brinker, K. *et al.*; Berlin/New York: 2000), pp. 458–72.

—*Schreiben als Handlung. Überlegungen und Untersuchungen zur Theorie der Textproduktion* (Tübingen: 1995) (RGL 158).

Wünsch, H.-M., *Der paulinische Brief 2 Kor 1–9 als kommunikative Handlung. Eine rhetorisch-literaturwissenschaftliche Untersuchung* (Münster: 1995) (Theologie 4).

Wuthenow, R.-R., 'Autobiographie und autobiographische Gattungen': *Fischer Lexikon Literatur* (Vol. 1; ed. Ricklefs, U.; Frankfurt/M.: 1996), pp. 169–89.

Young, F.M./D.F. Ford, *Meaning and Truth in 2 Corinthians* (Grand Rapids/Michigan: 1987).

Zanker, P., *Die Maske des Sokrates. Das Bild des Intellektuellen in der antiken Kunst* (Munich: 1995).

Zelzer, M., 'Buch und Text von Augustus zu Karl dem Großen': *MIÖG* 109 (2001), pp. 291–314.

—'Der Brief in der Spätantike. Überlegungen zu einem literarischen Genus am Beispiel der Briefsammlung des Sidonius Apollinaris': *WSt* 107/108 (1994/95), pp. 541–51.

—'Die Briefliteratur. Kommunikation durch Briefe: Ein Gespräch mit Abwesenden': *NHL* 4 (1997), pp. 321–53.

—'Die Umschrift lateinischer Texte von Rollen auf Codices und ihre Bedeutung für die Textkritik': *Bibliologia* 9 (1989), pp. 157–67.

—'Epistel. G. Literarische Briefe und H. Briefsammlungen': *DNP* 3 (1997), pp. 1164–66.

—'Si Pergamenis Digna Canimus Paginis. Die "Wege" des Pergamentcodex vom Taschenbuch zur Luxusform': *Steine und Wege* (Festschrift D. Knibbe; eds. Scherrer, P. *et al.*; Vienna: 1999) (Österreichisches Archäologisches Institut Sonderschriften Vol. 32), pp. 419–23.

Zmijewski, J., *Der Stil der paulinischen 'Narrenrede'. Analyse der Sprachgestaltung in 2 Kor 11, 1–12, 10 als Beitrag zur Methodik von Stiluntersuchungen neutestamentlicher Texte* (Cologne/Bonn: 1978) (BBB 52).

—'καυχάομαι κτλ.': *EWNT* 2 (1981), pp. 680–90.

Zuntz, G., *The Text of the Epistles. A Disquisition Upon the Corpus Paulinum* (London: 1953).

Zwierlein, O., *Antike Revisionen des Vergil und Ovid* (Wiesbaden: 2000) (Nordrhein-Westfälische Akademie der Wissenschaften Vorträge G 368).

INDEXES

INDEX OF REFERENCES

Index of Authors